CHANG AND ENG RECONNECTED

Cynthia Wu

Chang and Eng Reconnected

The Original Siamese Twins in American Culture

Temple University Press
Philadelphia

TEMPLE UNIVERSITY PRESS
Philadelphia, Pennsylvania 19122
www.temple.edu/tempress

Published 2012

Library of Congress Cataloging-in-Publication Data

Wu, Cynthia, 1973–
Chang and Eng reconnected : the original Siamese twins in American culture / Cynthia Wu.
p. cm.
Includes bibliographical references and index.
ISBN 978-1-4399-0868-6 (hardback : alk. paper) — ISBN 978-1-4399-0869-3 (paper : alk. paper) — ISBN 978-1-4399-0870-9 (e-book) 1. Conjoined twins in literature. 2. American literature—19th century—History and criticism. 3. American literature—20th century—History and criticism. 4. Bunker, Chang, 1811-1874—In literature. 5. Bunker, Eng, 1811-1874—In literature. 6. Literature and society—United States. 7. Popular culture—United States. 8. Asian Americans in literature. I. Title.
PS217.C63W8 2012
810.9′351—dc23

2012008892

Printed in the United States of America

080613-P

As social conditions become more equal, the number of persons increases who, although they are neither rich nor powerful enough to exercise any great influence over their fellows, have nevertheless acquired or retained sufficient education and fortune to satisfy their own wants. They owe nothing to any man, they expect nothing from any man; they acquire the habit of always considering themselves as standing alone, and they are apt to imagine that their whole destiny is in their own hands.

—Alexis de Tocqueville, *Democracy in America*

For, before we proceed further, it must be said that the monkey-rope was fast at both ends; fast to Queequeg's broad canvas belt, and fast to my narrow leather one. So that for better or for worse, we two, for the time, were wedded; and should poor Queequeg sink to rise no more, then both usage and honor demanded, that instead of cutting the cord, it should drag me down in its wake.

—Herman Melville, *Moby-Dick*

The problem is not simply the "selfhood" of the nation as opposed to the otherness of other nations. We are confronted with the nation split within itself, articulating the heterogeneity of its population.

—Homi K. Bhabha, "DissemiNation: Time, Narrative, and the Margins of the Modern Nation"

Contents

List of Figures

Acknowledgments

Chang and Eng Reconnected began as a dissertation in the American Culture program at the University of Michigan. The attentive and sustained guidance provided by my committee members—Martin Pernick, Tobin Siebers, Sidonie Smith, and Patricia Yaeger—helped shape this project from its earliest stages. Although Stephen Sumida left the university before I was at the dissertation stage, his influence is clearly visible in these pages. The following sources of financial support allowed me to finish my degree in a timely manner: a Rackham Merit Fellowship and a Dean's Candidacy Fellowship, both from the University of Michigan, and an external fellowship from the Consortium for Faculty Diversity funded by the Andrew W. Mellon Foundation at Macalester College.

Offsetting the cost of travel to archives were the following funding sources: a professional development grant from Agnes Scott College, the Archie K. Davis Grant from the North Caroliniana Society, and the State University of New York at Buffalo (University at Buffalo) Faculty Start-up Program. A Humanities Institute faculty research fellowship and a junior sabbatical, both completed in connection with the University at Buffalo, provided teaching releases during which the manuscript for *Chang and Eng Reconnected* was revised. The Julian Park Fund offset the cost of permissions and reproduction of images for the book.

This work grew from conversations with audiences at the Modern Language Association, the Future of Minority Studies Research Project, the Berkshire Conference on the History of Women, the University of Minnesota Disabled Student Cultural Center, the University at Buffalo New Faculty Seminar Series, the University at Buffalo Humanities Institute Fellows Lecture Series, and symposia at the University of California, Berkeley, and Pomona College in Claremont, California. For the opportunity to present at these events, I thank Rachel Lee, Ernesto Martinez, Emily Smith Beitiks, Carrie Bramen, Tim Dean, Shannon Jackson, Susan Schweik, Leslie Bow, Jenell Johnson, Ellen Samuels, and

Kyla Tompkins. Alice Dreger introduced me to the Bunker family. Invitations to speak at reunions for the descendants of Chang and Eng generated insightful feedback from my toughest audience yet. Special thanks go to Tanya Jones and the Surry Arts Council for travel funding.

The following colleagues read and commented on various drafts of the manuscript either in whole or part: Charlotte Artese, Carrie Bramen, Yoonmee Chang, Christian Flaugh, Eunjung Kim, Robin Li, Tamiko Nimura, Jun Okada, Ellen Samuels, Bill Solomon, and Ramón Soto-Crespo. The final version of the book is stronger because of their advice. Along the way, interchanges with the following people further contributed to the development of this work: Leslie Bow, Russ Castronovo, Sally Chivers, James Cook, Jessica Cooley, Cindy Current, Amber Dermont, Martha Fineman, Ann Fox, Rosemarie Garland-Thomson, Sander Gilman, Jennifer James, Bruce Henderson, Lynn Hudson, Paul Lai, Neil Lerner, Nhi Lieu, Anita Mannur, Nicole Markotić, Robert McRuer, Julie Minich, Scott Morgensen, Susan Moynihan, Denise Nepveux, Wilas Nirunsuksiri, Margaret Price, Benjamin Reiss, Jane Rhoads, Carrie Sandahl, Cathy Schlund-Vials, Min Song, John Kuo Wei Tchen, and Chris Vials. Parts of *Chang and Eng Reconnected* were completed at self-styled writing boot camps with Lisa Hall.

The University at Buffalo has been a great place to have a career. Sincere thanks are in order to my department chair, Keith Griffler, whose tireless leadership is extraordinary. I am lucky to be part of a collective of junior faculty whose weekly check-ins keep me on track. Carole Emberton, Theresa McCarthy, Theresa Runstedtler, and LaKisha Simmons make me account for my time but also tell me to relax when I need to. For advice on future research, I acknowledge Susan Cahn, Tim Dean, David Gerber, Bruce Jackson, Arabella Lyon, and Cristanne Miller.

My editor, Janet Francendese, made the entire process of putting my work into print as smooth as possible. She along with her assistant Amanda Steele and the rest of her staff at Temple University Press are amazing. I am indebted to two readers whose careful and detailed review of the manuscript pushed it further. Parts of the introduction and an earlier version of Chapter 4 were published as "The Siamese Twins in Late-Nineteenth-Century Narratives of Conflict and Reconciliation," *American Literature* 80, no. 1 (2008): 29–55. I thank Duke University Press for permission to reprint the article.

Staff at the following collections were helpful with navigating materials: the National Library of Medicine, the North Carolina State Archives, the Mütter Museum of the College of Physicians of Philadelphia, and the Southern Historical Collection at the University of North Carolina at Chapel Hill. I owe a debt of gratitude in particular to the late Gretchen Worden.

I am thankful for my family, biological and otherwise. I would not be where I am today if not for my parents, Shu-Fang and Jung-Yi Wu. Connie Wu and Ernie Garcia are an inspiration for their view of the bigger picture. Many thanks are due to the Bunker family for welcoming me into their fold and entrusting me with this project. I am humbled to be an honorary Bunker. Special recognition goes to those in Atlanta, Buffalo, and several other places who know and accept me by a different first name. Although they will never read these words, it needs to be said that their company has sustained me in immeasurable ways.

Finally, this book is dedicated to my students, past and present. My students have kept me writing all along, especially at times when the going was most difficult. There will be times—as I remind them—when it is difficult, but the final product is always a labor of love.

Introduction

No one watching from the dock knew what Abel Coffin hid under the sheet that covered a shapeless but ambulatory form disembarking with him from the USS *Sachem* in Boston Harbor on August 16, 1829. Coffin, a mariner who specialized in overseas trade, led the rumpled mass down the gangplank and into an enclosed carriage, whereupon he and the swaddled creature were whisked away. An article that appeared in the *Patriot* the next day aroused even more curiosity about the strange cargo. The reporter announced that "two Siamese youths, males, eighteen years of age, their bodies connected from their birth" had arrived in the city and that "they will probably be exhibited to the public when proper arrangements have been made."[1] After an examination by a prominent anatomist at the Harvard Medical School, whose observations were publicized to generate more interest in the upcoming spectacle, the two young men went onstage for the first time as the Siamese Double Boys.[2] Ultimately, their stage name became the Original Siamese Twins.

Thus began the American lives of Chang and Eng. They were discovered in a Thai village by a Scottish merchant named Robert Hunter who collaborated with Coffin to bring them to the United States. Early on, Chang and Eng toured under contract with Coffin and his business associate, James Webster Hale, but as soon as they fulfilled the agreement's terms, they went into business for themselves. Even though P. T. Barnum is often falsely credited with making the careers of the Original Siamese Twins, Chang and Eng had only a brief contract with the famous showman. The sideshow industry in the United States and abroad serendipitously peaked at the same time as Chang and Eng's career. The twins toured extensively throughout North America, Europe, and parts of Latin America, and it is speculated that more people worldwide saw them than any other entertainer in the nineteenth century. One could say that these early transnational circuits of popular culture grew up alongside Chang and Eng. They were so well known as public figures and so ubiquitous as conjoined twins that the term "Siamese twins" eventually came to describe all such twins even, anachronistically, those who had lived before they did. Their ancestry was more Chinese than Thai, but their origins in Siam, a nation that existed in the minds of Westerners as a mystical, isolated, and impenetrable space, was foregrounded in their stage name. Their adoption of the Anglo surname "Bunker," however, places them in more familiar territory for many Americans.

Cultural Legacies of the Siamese Twins

Chang and Eng Reconnected uses a cultural studies approach to explore how the Original Siamese Twins captivated the American imagination. Not only did the real-life Chang and Eng Bunker attract a tremendous following in the fan cultures of the entertainment industry; a series of fictionalized twins emerged, too. This preoccupation with a pair of famous entertainers persisted long after the twins' natural life span. Writers, visual artists, medical professionals, film directors, and others continued to pursue the multiple—potentially endless—meanings behind them. Over and again, we see that the Bunker twins display countless possibilities for signification across time, space, and culture, showing that fascination with their extraordinary body is widespread. Moreover, the ways in which this figure of racialized conjoinment has been summoned are not static but contingent on shifting ideas about medicine, nation, race, gender, sexuality, and class. These conjoined twins from Asia, either as material presence or as metaphor, present a template for a wide range of cultural producers who engage in debates about the challenges of U.S. nation-building at moments in history when the imagined unity of the nation appears most threatened. From Reconstruction, to the standardization of medical authority, to the labor rebellions, to the Japanese American internment, to the Anglo-American women's movements, and beyond, these conjoined twins—separate individuals who inhabit one body—offer a way to think about how difference is expressed, managed, maintained, suppressed, or resolved in modernity's nationalist narrative of progress.

This book is not a biography of Chang and Eng Bunker. Already, two book-length biographies and countless shorter essay-length accounts of their lives have been published.[3] Nor is this book an interpretive history of their touring careers, tracking their appearances and theorizing spectacle and performance in nineteenth-century popular entertainment. A considerable amount of scholarship already addresses the politics of the sideshow in Jacksonian and industrial age America.[4] Rather, *Chang and Eng Reconnected* aims to reveal how dimensions of power operate within American cultures by providing a transhistorical analysis of materials from the nineteenth, twentieth, and early twenty-first centuries that feature the Bunkers as fictional characters, literary or visual metaphor, medical specimen, museum artifact, or venerated ancestors. Of these sources, I ask the following questions: What does the persistence of unusual anatomy mean for a society that is becoming increasingly standardized? How do the Asian diaspora's multiple points of contact in the United States force a reconsideration of race? How are kinship and kin-like forms of sociality implicated in larger discussions about the nation? What is at stake in challenging unitary concepts of national membership?

The epigraphs to *Chang and Eng Reconnected* offer three contrasting visions of nation that exemplify the paradox inherent in its modern formation. The first, from Alexis de Tocqueville's *Democracy in America*, portrays the United States as an egalitarian enclave of self-sufficient individuals. Having defined themselves against the feudalism and nepotism of Europe, these citizens in the early republic fashioned an ethics of republican governance based on the exercise of free will and independence. The second epigraph, from Herman Melville's *Moby-Dick*, turns Toqueville's observation about U.S. society on its head. Rather than an ethics of autonomy and noninterference, Melville imagines a dangerous, yet strangely pleasurable, space of cross-racial fraternizing that demands an absolute pact for its insular homosociality to function. These two opposing models give way to Homi Bhabha's vision of endless fracture and multiplicity in the third epigraph. Rather than a singular nation imagining itself dialectically in relation to other nations, the nation in late modernity is crosscut with its own heterogeneity. Difference comes from within more so than from without. The texts I examine in the chapters that follow tend to struggle with the frictions these different models present. The conjoined physical body, which wavers between unity and plurality, becomes a gold standard of sorts among literary and visual metaphors when debating the particulars of an idealized national community.

In this book, I reference Chang and Eng Bunker in the plural form to reflect how they almost always functioned in civic life as separate individuals. When I discuss their combined "body," however, I use the singular to express their shared somatic existence and their deliberate comanagement of embodiment. This dislocation between personhood and corporeality sometimes produces jarring shifts from the plural to the singular subject in my prose, and I retain this tension because it performatively displays the paradoxes that *Chang and Eng Reconnected* is about.

Chang and Eng Bunker in the Nineteenth-Century United States

Born in a Siamese fishing village on the banks of the Meklong River in 1811, Chang and Eng were the fifth and sixth of nine children, and their mother reported no more difficulty with their birth than with those of her other children. As young boys, they were accustomed to contributing to their family's income by selling duck eggs at the local market where their unusual anatomy drew attention that helped with business. News of the unusual twins eventually traveled to King Rama III who feared that they were a bad omen and ordered their death. However, when Chang and Eng arrived at the royal palace in Bangkok, the king had an unexpected change of heart and lifted the order of execution. The twins continued to live inconspicuously until Captain Robert Hunter, a Scottish merchant, saw them swimming in the Meklong while he was on a shipping assignment. He was so taken by the strange creature with two heads, four arms, and four legs moving in perfect coordination that he waited on the riverbank for Chang and Eng to emerge so that he could introduce himself and request a meeting with their family. After a series of negotiations with the family and King Rama, Hunter received permission to take the twins on a five-year tour. Their father had died from cholera several years earlier, and their mother reasoned that this offer would relieve some of the family's financial burden and provide other means of support. However, the twins never returned to Siam.

While employed by Robert Hunter, Chang and Eng proved to be ambitious and determined to take charge of their linked lives. They learned to read and write in English from one of their attending physicians. After their five-year contract expired, the twins became the owners of their own act, hiring managers and other support staff rather than working for supervisors. Their agreement with Hunter amounted to indentured servitude, and only after breaking from their former employer did they begin to gain a measure of financial affluence. The twins' rise in class status gave way to other forms of transformation as well. They became naturalized as U.S. citizens, inexplicably, at a time when naturalization was available only to free white persons, and they took the name "Bunker" at the ceremony when the judge declared the necessity for a Christian surname.[5] While passing through North Carolina on one of their tours, Chang and Eng decided to settle in the small town of Mount Airy.

They integrated themselves into the local tobacco farming community as seamlessly as they could and won the hands in marriage of two white women, sisters Adelaide and Sarah, of the Yates family. It is unclear how two Asian men with extraordinarily unusual anatomy could have been accepted into one of the antebellum South's more prominent plantation families. There are stories that their in-laws' home was vandalized on the night before their double wedding to Adelaide and Sarah, but accounts of hostility from neighbors end there. As a wedding gift, David Yates—their father-in-law—presented them with an enslaved woman who worked as a house servant. Between the two couples, twenty-two children were born, and some of these children would eventually accompany their fathers onstage during their shows. The Bunkers maintained a modest touring schedule as they built their family, deciding to devote their energies to their plantation. During the Civil War, two of their sons fought for the Confederate Army. After they lost their slaves in the downfall of the Confederacy, they returned to show business full time and began traveling extensively once again. They died at the age of sixty-two, making them—at this writing—the longest-lived conjoined twins in history.[6]

Over the Bunkers' life span, some pivotal social changes occurred in their adopted homeland. The end of the U.S.-Mexico War in 1848 extended the border of the United States to the Pacific Ocean. The acquisition of this new territory sparked a large-scale recruitment of inexpensive labor from China. These workers continued to fill labor demands not only along the California coast but also in the interior of the continent until 1882, when the Chinese Exclusion Act all but halted immigration. The Civil War reunited the former Union and former Confederacy, and the emancipation of enslaved people compelled new ways of conceptualizing labor. The industrial revolution taking place in urban northeastern and midwestern locales further complicated the nexus of race and class as large numbers of European immigrants arrived. A quieter but no less significant revolution took place in the consolidation of academic medicine and the professionalization of physicians at the end of the nineteenth century.

Thus, Chang and Eng Bunker existed in tension with their environment in quite a few ways. They entered the United States two decades before the first major wave of migration from Asia. As slaveholding members of the Confederacy, they occupied a position of class privilege relative to other Asian workers. As successful entertainers in an industry that attracted a working-class audience base, they experienced constant contact with European immigrants. However, as physically anomalous beings, they were subjected to scrutiny by medical professionals who had honed their skills on the social underclasses. The Bunkers eluded categorization, but this indeterminacy was emblematic of the contradictions of American life during this period.

The Conjoinment of Disability Studies and Asian American Studies

Chang and Eng Reconnected bridges two fields that have tremendous potential to inform each other in refreshing ways. The respective historiographies of disability studies and Asian American studies have taken different paths, but their intellectual and political commitments have been strangely parallel. I do not simply use an analytic from one field to invigorate the other but attempt to show how these two strands of academic thought can and do function in tandem because of the ways that multiple valences of difference interlock in the operation of power. In fact, I show that a critical interrogation of ableism—that is, a system that produces and privileges physical, sensory, and neural normativity—invoked racial difference from the onset.

In 1969, literary critic Leonard Kriegel published an essay titled "Uncle Tom and Tiny Tim: Some Reflections of the Cripple as Negro." Writing during the civil rights and decolonization movements both in and outside of the United States, Kriegel displays an unveiled envy for the cultural capital these claims to liberation have attained while the visibility of disability rights has remained low:

> [In] virtually every corner of the globe those who have been invisible to themselves and to those they once conceived of as masters now stridently demand the right to define meaning and behavior in their own terms, [but] the cripple is still asked to accept definitions of what he is, and of what he should be, imposed on him from outside his experience. In the United States alone, spokesmen for the Negro, the Puerto Rican, the Mexican, the Indian have embarked upon an encounter with a society that they believe has enriched itself at their expense. . . . Late-night television interviewers vie with one another in the effort to titillate their viewers with "militant" after "militant" who rhetorically massages whatever guilt resides in the collective consciousness of white America.[7]

Reading this in the present, one sees a reliance on facile conflations between race and ability status. Throughout his essay, Kriegel makes frequent reference to "the black man" in ways that suggest he references not an actual person. Rather, he uses a figural device that conjures questionable images of black rage, further sedimented by media coverage of the then-recent Watts riots, in the collective white mind.

Almost a decade later, Leslie Fiedler takes up the question of physical difference and replicates a similar invocation of racial difference. Writing in 1978, Fiedler—like Kriegel—addresses the tricky issue of terminology when referencing people with disabilities. While Kriegel shepherds the political edginess of the term "cripple," Fiedler prefers "freak." As he dismisses one label after another before defending a historically pejorative slur, Fiedler explains:

> For me . . . such euphemisms lack the resonance necessary to represent the sense of quasi-religious awe with which we experience first and most strongly as children: face to face with fellow humans more marginal than the poorest sharecroppers or black convicts on a Mississippi chain gang.[8]

Race rears its head again in an argument about the significance of physical anomaly. Fiedler references not only blackness but also economic exploitation in order to provide a predictable example for his white middle-class readership to grasp. As his logic goes, those who are physically extraordinary (and within this logic, they are presumed to be racially unmarked) are even more marginalized, more denigrated than these commonly recognized figures of marginalization.

As would be expected in a field whose seminal article references two ubiquitous fictional personages—Uncle Tom and Tiny Tim—the earliest incarnations of disability studies focused on the significance of disabled characters in literature. By "disabled" I do not necessarily mean impaired in function.

Rather, I use that term in the way that aligns with how scholars and activists have defined it, as a means through which to describe friction between modes of embodiment and the social and material environment in which that embodiment occurs. The early scholarship in disability studies has shown that disabled literary characters are almost always imagined as metaphoric and rarely are granted the status of protagonist. They tend to be objects of scorn, fear, or disgust. They are strategically crafted to invite a negative identification on the part of the intended reader. Instead of functioning as multidimensional characters, they are tropes and devices meant only to advance a plot that favors a normatively constituted protagonist. So-called positive portrayals of disability do not significantly differ as they, too, lack complexity in their development. Cast as childlike and innocent, this incarnation of the disabled character is a redemptive figure for an otherwise corrupt world. As an object of pity, he or she elicits sympathy, which is yet another type of negative identification. This purportedly favorable portrayal of disability, one having a corresponding flatness to its characterization, also alienates the reader. In sum, it was a focus on "representation" through which disability studies in the arts and humanities gained an institutional foothold.[9] This methodology became so commonplace and mundane that by the mid-1990s, certain sectors inferred its demise and distanced themselves from it.[10]

A turn from the portrayal of disability per se to a wholesale interrogation of nondisabled normativity has been one of disability studies' most significant paradigm shifts. As the field matured, it legitimated itself in larger academic conversations by speaking to its relevancy beyond select identitarian groupings. This recent scholarship emphasizes the relevance of an analysis that focuses on ability status more broadly. By calling out the discursive production of privileged and subjugated subject positions alike—and the slipperiness of those categories—this newer wave inaugurates a hermeneutic practice that moves the field beyond simply being "about" disabled people and toward an analysis of how socially significant valences of difference generate the material and cultural conditions of everyday life.[11]

To be sure, this demarcation between disability studies then and now is an oversimplification. *Chang and Eng Reconnected* exists in the space between these two poles: (1) earlier literary-critical models that examine metaphors of physical anomaly and (2) what Lennard J. Davis has recently called the "dismodern" incarnations of the field, which commit to problematizing and accommodating all forms of physical, sensory, and neural constitution.[12] My treatment of literary metaphor in these pages would seem to echo the work performed by scholars from previous generations. However, my purpose is not so much to expose the ableist politics behind these invocations of Chang and Eng Bunker as it is to unravel how a host of seemingly unremarkable and quotidian concerns coalesced around this figure of racial and anatomical difference. Ultimately, this project works within an interpretive framework that defamiliarizes and denaturalizes the constructions of normativity that are all too often taken for granted.

I have shown how references to race in the seminal thinking on disability have tended to rely on an assumption of unmarked middle-class whiteness. It is telling that racial difference—more specifically, blackness—served as an all-too-available trope through which early scholars have articulated an otherwise important argument about physical variation. Correspondingly, one can easily imagine that discourses of race may also have been inflected with a concern about disability. The question of "fitness" has historically attended discussions about racial difference in many ways, and in the field of Asian American studies, this has been most evident in the trajectory of immigration law.

In 1882, the United States passed the Chinese Exclusion Act after more than three decades of actively recruiting migrants from China to fill labor needs in the expanding West. It is sometimes confused with the Immigration Act of 1882, which actually barred the entry of prospective immigrants based on disease, disability, or other broadly defined conditions that would make the individual likely to become a public charge. The simultaneous appearance of these two restrictions suggests, however, that they may not have been distinct in their purposes at that historical moment. At a time when the United States was rapidly industrializing, the temporal conflation of Chinese origin and disability through the machinery of immigration law spoke to the desirability of certain citizen-workers. Additionally, the somewhat opposing implications of these two laws suggest that the federal government was ambivalent about maintaining a commitment to capitalist progress at all costs. If the unruly subjects targeted by the Immigration Act of 1882 endangered the nationalist promise of growth by their purported incapacity for work, the workers singled out by the Chinese Exclusion Act were perceived as threatening precisely because of their willingness to perform work refused by whites and their undercutting of white wages.[13] The first group failed at labor while the second group devalued it.

Another way to think about the convergence between the Immigration Act of 1882 and the Chinese Exclusion Act is to see their overlapping concerns about the physical body's integrity. Although it is true that the Chinese were considered unfair labor competition, or "hyper-able," compared to working- and lower-class whites who made more demands of their employers, it was also widely believed that they were prone to harbor and spread disease. The port city of San Francisco, where many Chinese immigrants landed, was subjected to constant scrutiny by public heath officials because of nativist fears about various forms of contagion issuing from Chinese people. Smallpox, leprosy, and bubonic plague were among the diseases that were thought to concentrate within Chinese populations.[14] Chinese women, prostitutes in particular, were regarded as carriers of syphilis who would perniciously infect white men and boys.[15] Perceptions of the racially marked body—as already impaired, already compromised, and already diseased—took on an ableist cast from the very beginnings of racialist discourse in the eighteenth century. As Tobin Siebers points out, disability is the one valence of difference through which all other forms of difference have been articulated.[16]

Chang and Eng Bunker were inarguably the nineteenth century's best known Asian figures, enjoying a level of class and geographical mobility that was unprecedented for others who were similarly racially situated. Any attempt to bring them under the purview of Asian American studies, a field with Marxian origins, generates much productive frustration. The life of the Bunkers seems to defy legibility within Asian American studies because of the time and circumstances of their migration to the United States, their economic success, their settlement in the American South, and other factors. As immigrants from Asia who preceded the first wave of migration in 1849, as Asians who were able to circumvent the Naturalization Act of 1790, and as members of the slaveholding Confederacy, the Bunkers impel the field to find other lenses through which to examine the Asian diaspora in the United States. Although I am not proposing that we jettison Asian American studies' earlier materialist lens that examined histories of labor, immigration restriction, and civil rights,[17] the Bunkers provide a convincing case as to why these models may need to be problematized and why the field's master narratives may need to be rethought. Far from being exceptions that prove the rule, these unusual historical figures beg a reconsideration of easy divisions between privilege and oppression that accompany the global circulation of Asian bodies.

Conjoined Methods

Disability studies and Asian American studies have, from their very beginnings, conceived of themselves as fields that traverse traditional disciplinary and methodological boundaries. I could not have conceived this book using a framework from a single institutional discipline or a single method of inquiry. My title, *Chang and Eng Reconnected*, is not only a pun on Chang and Eng Bunker's anatomy; it is also a call to find linkages between different intellectual tools. As such, this book is as much about the pleasures and challenges of doing mixed-methods research as it is about the quest for meaning behind a pleasurably challenging historical figure. Part I, "Locating Material Traces in the Archives," consists of three chapters that have been hewed from qualitative social science methods. The most traditionally literary-critical portion of the work comprises Part II, "Reading Literature and Visual Cultures," which also contains three chapters. Part III, "Observing and Participating," consists of a single chapter employing ethnographic techniques.

Chapter 1, "Labor and Ownership in the American South," continues establishing the conceptual lens for a reading of these sources on Chang and Eng Bunker. It addresses the interplay of black, white, and Asian in the nineteenth century. By linking the racialization of possessive individualism to the twins' embodiment within Enlightenment logic, this section lays out the paradoxes that inform the analyses in the chapters that follow. Chapter 2, "The Mystery of their Union," places the Bunkers' autopsy report within the history of postmortem examination and foregrounds its significance in nineteenth-century medical perception, the standardization of medical training, and the development of anatomy as a discipline. Although the physicians who conducted Chang and Eng's autopsy may have felt triumphant about being entrusted with it, the ambiguities of their findings leave more questions open than they answer and frustrate medical science's expectations about exclusive access to specialized knowledge. Chapter 3, "Strange Incursions into Medical Science at the Mütter Museum," covers the Bunker artifacts at the College of Physicians of Philadelphia Mütter Museum. These and other items on display in the gallery spaces at the Mütter blur the distinctions among scientific education, art, and popular entertainment.

Part II brings a series of literary and visual texts together to discuss the metaphorical possibilities of the conjoined twin. The first of these, in Chapter 4, "Late-Nineteenth-Century Visions of Conflict and Consensus," addresses texts by white Americans at a pivotal moment in U.S. history, the end of the Civil War and the labor rebellions during that timeframe. Here, the Bunker twins are co-opted into polemical tracts about national progress, unity, and disunity. Chapter 5, "Asian Americans Bare/Bear the Hyphen," examines authors who write from a place of racial alterity and are more skeptical of the egalitarian and inclusive promise of national belonging than the authors covered in Chapter 4. Whether these texts reference the Bunkers explicitly or only implicitly, they call to mind the contradictory perceptions of the Asian diaspora in the United States. The texts in Chapter 6, "Disciplining and Normalizing the Woman Subject in Contemporary Literature and Film," are about shifts in U.S. society in the wake of the Anglo-American women's movement. Prominently featuring conjoined twins, these texts situate themselves within late-twentieth-century and early-twenty-first-century contestations of nonreproductive sex, the conjugal family, and compulsory heterosexuality.

Part III, which is made up of Chapter 7, "Our Esteemed Ancestors," addresses the kinship-building activities of Chang and Eng Bunkers' descendants, focusing in particular on the role of the annual family reunion. By conducting participant observation and interviews, I analyze this event as both intimate family ritual and international media spectacle. These reunions are yet another source of knowledge production about these famous twins, and the narratives their descendants generate convey complex ideas about disability, celebrity, Asian ancestry, and Southern identities. Although the Bunker family cherishes the sanctity of hereditary ties that are conceived as premodern and based on face-to-face contact, this community's actualization depends in part on the record-keeping apparatus of the state, an emblem of modernity. Even as it values traditionally imagined lines of kinship, the community adopts a loose approach to membership through which nonconsanguineous individuals may enter.

Metaphors and Materiality

Much of *Chang and Eng Reconnected* focuses on the collecting, assembling, and parsing of portrayals of the twins in various genres of cultural production, showing how their representational aftereffects perform important cultural work. Thus, what I present here is very much about the *discursive* Bunkers—that is, the set of significatory possibilities generated through a collective working through of debates about the body and the nation. At the same time, I seek to avoid the pitfall of relegating the Bunkers strictly to the realm of metaphor. As mentioned previously, the repeated use of the anomalous body solely as figurative device in much of Anglo-European arts and culture is a problem. For this reason, I do not want to ignore what exists in the material record about them as real people. I hope that my attention to the substance of the twins' presence in actual time and space as well as the existence of these representations—whether in literature, art, or film—in actual time and space treats the subject of my analysis fairly and respectfully.

Although one can read metaphors of the prodigious body in ways that are politically recuperative, I am suspicious of interpretive strategies akin to that of Mikhail Bakhtin's in his elucidation of the grotesque. According to Bakhtin, the prodigious body has the potential to undermine and explode oppressive social orders because it collapses easy binaries between self/other, interior/exterior, and so on.[18] He celebrates the grotesque uncritically and erases any materialist awareness that there are actual people inhabiting actual environments for whom having this type of body is what justifies their subordination. This interpretive maneuver is yet another way of erasing the subjectivity of people embodied in socially troubling ways by positing them only as rhetorical tools. The very glamorization of Bakhtin's grotesque ironically depends on the ongoing unglamorous denial of full cultural citizenship for disabled people.

However, we need to see Chang and Eng Bunker with heightened levels of nuance because any claims to their victimization by nineteenth-century cultural forces are specious given the privilege they assumed as a result of their non-normativity. Their unusual anatomy, one that today would be subjected to correction and/or containment and would cause an abridgement of their civil rights, is what allowed them to become agents of capital in the historical moment they occupied. The affluence resulting from their celebrity allowed them to take part in the containment, enslavement, and abridgement of freedom of others. By looking at these contradictions, I do not want to portray these famous twins uncomplicatedly as those who were burdened by the social constraints of their anatomy and race. Nor do I want to give the impression that their realization of a version of the American Dream was noiseless and smooth. As they worked and participated in the spaces that opened up to them, Chang and Eng Bunker both transformed and replicated oppressive orders. Neither wholly guilty nor wholly innocent, they made a mark on this world that continues to fascinate many long after their passing.

Part I

Locating Material Traces in the Archives

1

Labor and Ownership in the American South

A complex history looms behind the exhibition of unusual bodies for monetary profit. Susan Schweik's account of unsightly beggar ordinances in the United States, colloquially known as "ugly laws," shows how disability and class disadvantage have repeatedly converged from the late nineteenth century onwards. People with sensory impairments, amputations, and other disabilities have had to negotiate legislative measures taken against them to prevent their appearance in public spaces. These actions on the part of state authorities both reflected and informed popular opinions about the nature of work and self-sufficiency. Although the sphere of ritualized performance seemed to legitimate the labor of entertainers employed by sideshows, carnivals, and circuses, the organic and spontaneous appearance of beggars on public streets called into question all forms of conspicuously brandished anatomy. Whether these incidents took place in show business or on the sidewalk, "both were reduced to examples of disgusting bodily display."[1]

The already porous line between the agency of the working body and appeals to charity on the part of the "nonworking" poor is blurred even more when transposing Schweik's class-based analysis onto existing scholarship about the history of the sideshow. Schweik goes on to clarify that "unsightly begging *was* work."[2] The class advantage that Chang and Eng Bunker amassed during their career, then, is tinged with these troublings of laboring selfhood and property ownership. These Enlightenment-era ideals, in turn, are every bit as much about race as they are about class when it comes to the logic of material gain in the display of socially troubling bodies.

In 1835, a young man named Phineas Taylor Barnum purchased an elderly enslaved woman from her previous owner who had been exhibiting her with declining success. Despite his predecessor's difficulties, the emerging business tycoon was able to turn this human curiosity around through shrewd and aggressive marketing.[3] The woman, Joice Heth—rumored to be 161 years old and a former nursemaid to George Washington—was blind, almost completely deaf, and had very little physical mobility. As she toured all across the antebellum Northern and Southern states, she was reported to have chatted amiably with spectators about Washington, recounting the events of his birth and her nursing and raising of him. After she died, the joke was ultimately on those who believed in her performance, a contingent in which Barnum claims to include himself because her autopsy revealed her to be no older than 80. What seemed like a transparent, acquiescent display of "the black mammy" held up for the epistemological ownership of Barnum's customers was merely an act.

Benjamin Reiss makes an important claim about the speciousness of Barnum's insistence that he, too, was duped by Heth. Similar to how Saidiya Hartman troubles the forced performances of enslaved people on the auction block, Reiss is not so quick to let Barnum off the hook and indulge the possibility of Heth's agency. He implicates the famous showman in systems of chattel slavery despite Barnum's copious efforts to cover his tracks.[4] This chapter in P. T. Barnum's professional trajectory initiated an important milestone in American social history, for it was this radically uneven economic relationship between a disabled black woman and a class-privileged white man that marked the beginnings of mass entertainment in the United States.

The coerced compliance in Heth's dealings with her handler-owner gave way to a very different relationship later in Barnum's career with a pair of already famous sideshow entertainers. In 1860, Chang and Eng Bunker signed a three-week contract with Barnum to appear in his American Museum in New York, and eight years later, they entered into another brief agreement with him on a tour of England.[5] Contrary to popular belief about the stardom of the Original Siamese Twins, the making of the Bunkers' reputation had very little to do with Barnum. At the time of their association with the showman, they were already well-established celebrities who had toured extensively over the world. Even though the Bunkers endured a stint in indentured servitude when they first arrived in the United States, they were able to wrangle themselves out of their contract with Abel Coffin, whereupon they began a career as self-made managers of their own act.

Like Barnum, who owned Heth, the Bunkers were also slaveholders, and their tobacco plantation in North Carolina provided income. By the time they found themselves haggling with Barnum over the particulars of their contract, they were already seasoned and savvy about financial matters. According to biographers, the Bunkers found Barnum to be "tight-fisted and exploitative," while Barnum thought of them as "too independent-minded."[6] The fact remains that they were rivals in a highly lucrative entertainment market, and there was resentment between Barnum and the brothers over their business acumen. Moreover, the Bunkers had appeared on numerous occasions at Peale's Museum, which was owned by naturalist Charles Willson Peale, yet another Barnum competitor. As these circumstances attest, the Bunker brothers would have regarded Barnum and he them with a measure of respectful caution. Unlike Heth, the Bunkers were able to leverage their dealings with Barnum so that the three men could draft a mutually beneficial arrangement.

I present these two acts Barnum managed at either end of his career to contrast the differing levels of control Heth and the Bunkers possessed in their involvement with the sideshow industry. As racially and anatomically marked subjects who were involved with a burgeoning form of popular culture, the elderly enslaved woman and the conjoined twin slaveholders existed in proximity to one another in the nineteenth-century cultural landscape. However, it would be a mistake to conflate these historical figures simply on the basis of their alterity and means of earning a living. The two parties had vastly differing amounts of leverage, economically and in their representation to the public. Heth's unprompted and unscripted interactions with Barnum's customers could be seen as the exercising of the small bit of agency someone in her position might have had. As an experienced bonded servant, she would have been well aware of the consequences of failing to comply with her owner's expectations.[7] The Bunkers, as proprietors of their own act, left behind an accumulation of communication with business associates—letters, contracts, receipts, and so on—as well as a meticulously maintained account book. These personal effects reveal the extent to which they were able to command the respect of others in the industry and practice the rules of good commerce.[8] Not unexpectedly, the premium they placed on careful balance keeping in their entertainment business seeped into the management of their plantation. Their property items, human and inanimate, were carefully documented, as were their losses and gains and sales and purchases.

These two examples of anomalous bodies engaged in work call attention to the fissures in what political philosopher C. B. Macpherson first called possessive individualism. Emerging from Enlightenment-era epistemologies of the body, largely those of Thomas Hobbes and John Locke, the possessive individual is defined by a system of property rights that are now today considered the hallmarks of modernity. According to this logic, if a subject owns his body, he asserts ownership of the labor generated by his body and, consequently, the products of that labor. These propertied subjects[9] are conceived as atomized entities who are able to create, transform, exchange, and dispose of their property willfully, rationally, and independently. The sovereign control of one's body as a requirement for entering into a set of social relations informed by labor, accumulation, competition, and consumption was central to the emergence of an ethos of individualism accorded to white men. Together, these components of ownership mark the onset of the liberal democratic state that replaced an older monarchic system. Thus, the egalitarian fantasy of possessive individualism lay in connecting somatic sovereignty to a market-based sociality.[10]

The political tracts that comprise the primary sources in Macpherson's analysis come out of seventeenth-century England. However, the spatial and temporal movements of these pervasive philosophies reveal the extent to which they were exported and circulated transnationally, particularly to settlements in North America. Here, these liberal humanist ideals revised themselves to accommodate, contain, and erase the paradox that slavery presented in the New World. In an oft-cited article, Barbara Jeanne Fields claims that the ideology of race emerged with the Atlantic slave trade to reconcile the value Europeans placed on abstracted ideas of freedom with the materiality of bonded African labor in the Americas. The Anglo-American populace, "whose terrain was founded on radical doctrines of liberty and natural rights,"[11] needed to exclude unfree populations from these principles of self-owning agency and obscure the fact that it was the very existence of unfree labor that made possible the freedom of others. The ideology of race—that is, the belief in an inextricable and irreconcilable difference on the part of African-descended slaves—allowed the fantasy of possessive individualism to continue for these white settler subjects because it excluded enslaved Africans, by dint of this new form of classification, from republican notions of rational self-control.

Not unexpectedly, the concept of possessive individualism—which, as Fields argues, worked initially in tandem with racist theories of polygenesis—later became the vehicle through which white abolitionists in the nineteenth century couched their arguments against the slave trade. Amy Dru Stanley's analysis of antislavery tracts reveals the gendered dimensions of liberal humanism's self-owning subject in references to black women. The enslaved woman, the subjugated figure par excellence, became the public face of abolitionist thought. Her sexually charged physical abuse was strategically deployed to trigger the greatest amount of horror and sympathy: "Dishonored, stripped bare, the bondswoman literally embodied the denial of property in the self. . . . [She was] the symbol of the dispossessed self, someone without any rights, the paradigmatic chattel."[12] The different ways in which these concepts of property could be invoked—either to support or challenge racialist ideologies—attests to their malleability and flexibility.

Becoming "Their Own Men"

If the basis for participation in social relations organized around principles of freedom and equality is the ability to own property, beginning with property in the self, the example of the Asian conjoined twin slaveholders both troubles and confirms these foundations of personhood. When Chang and Eng first arrived in the United States, they were indentured to Abel Coffin, a business associate of Robert Hunter, the mariner who met them during his travels in Siam. The terms of the contract that Coffin drew up were exploitative, and this became increasingly clear to the twins as they acquired more experience in the industry. For the period in which the twins were bonded to this agreement, their day-to-day affairs were actually handled by Coffin's wife, Susan, and a series of managers hired to accompany them on tour. Abel Coffin himself usually tended to other interests abroad. When the contract expired after three years, the twins severed their association with the Coffins by letter and set out as self-employed workers.[13]

The entrepreneurial spirit of self-fashioning issuing from this event is evident in their biographers' emphasis on the link between full personhood and financial self-determination. In their book, *The Two*, Irving Wallace and Amy Wallace call the chapter that describes the Bunkers' emancipation from this abusive contract "Their Own Men," and the Wallaces write of the twins' decision to break with Coffin with a sense of exhilaration and relief that such a change might have elicited:

> They ended it because they felt that the Coffins treated them as second-class beings, and because they believed that they had been unfeelingly and ruthlessly overworked. They ended it because they resented being in bondage, ordered about, controlled and driven by fellow humans. They ended it because they believed they had a legal right to do so, that their verbal contract expired on their twenty-first birthday. They ended it because they wanted to be independent and to reap the profits from their exhibits themselves, while it was still possible.[14]

The language in this account about the beginnings of Chang and Eng Bunker's propertied relationship to themselves shows how the interlocked concepts of citizenship, fair treatment, contractual agreement, and economic self-determination inform modernity's constitution of rational, sovereign personhood. "Second-class" status necessarily leads to the state of being "overworked," which is, of course, associated with "bondage," a condition that involves being "controlled . . . by fellow humans." Buttressed by the state (which, in Locke's view, emerged precisely to protect the property of individuals), the Bunkers understood that "they had a legal right" to change the terms on which they worked so that they could be "independent" and enjoy their "profits . . . themselves." Putting their agency to the test, the twins then set off on their next tour, in Europe, this time as free agents. Further asserting their ability to function in the world of propertied sociality, they hired help in this new venture. One of their employees was actually a manager who had previously functioned as their overseer during their period of indenture to Coffin.

The case of the possessively individuated conjoined twins sounds like an oxymoron. If exercising sovereign control of one's body is the first step in actualizing a subjectivity based on property rights, it seems as if the Bunkers should have been disqualified from the start. As two sentient beings who share one body, dual-consciousness conjoined twins trouble the very foundations of social relations in the liberal democratic state. The import Anglo-European modernity accords to the properly individuated subject is so great that it is no surprise that conjoined twins tend not to see themselves as exceptions to these ideals. Instead, it appears that they confront the imperative to individuate by doing so in their own way. Anecdotal evidence about the Bunkers indicates that Eng was the quiet introvert while Chang was spirited and gregarious; Eng's low-key style contrasted with Chang's quick-fire temper. Modern-day conjoined twins Lori and Reba Schappell brandish their individuated selves, almost in campy fashion, in the documentary *Face to Face*. At one point, Reba chides a curious passerby who aims a camera at them. She then tells him that she will grant him permission to take her picture but—gesturing towards Lori, who is more reserved—not hers, to the man's confusion. In another scene, the Schappells are at their hair salon, where Reba has her hair dyed red while Lori prefers to keep hers naturally brown. The line dividing the two colors in the craniopagus twins' shared head of hair is striking and beautiful. In this documentary of the Schappells' lives, medical ethicist Alice Dreger stresses that conjoined twins are not forced to abandon individuality and privacy; they simply adapt and accommodate themselves to these prized concepts.[15]

For J. David Smith, conjoined twins are the ultimate wrench thrown into the misguided nature-versus-nurture debates. As identical twins, they are genetically alike, and as conjoined twins, they have spent the entirety of their lives in the same environment. However, a pattern among conjoined twins shows that the two siblings in such a dyad take on diametrically opposing dispositions. Smith hypothesizes that the tendency for conjoined twins to develop in this way stems from the need to individuate as distinctly as possible from the other sibling in order to assert a measure of independent selfhood under unusual conditions.[16] Additionally, one can say that it is through their extremely rare embodiment that some conjoined twins develop economic self-reliance and individuality in a society that values such attributes. For instance, Allison Pingree finds that the famous Hilton sisters, Violet and Daisy, became a symbol for an early-twentieth-century self-propertied femininity. As two white women entertainers who flaunted their autonomy from men, their unusual physical constitution was what allowed them to forego the institution of marriage, which then was coming under scrutiny by Anglo-American feminists for how it curtailed the independence of women.[17] These and other examples reveal a false dichotomy between possessively individuated independence and anatomical conjoinment. In fact, they can and do constitute each other.

The Asian Diaspora in the American South

Chang and Eng Bunker occupied a curious time and space in the trajectory and terrain of U.S. racial politics. Barbara Jeanne Fields might agree that the ideology of race that excluded African slaves from the doctrines of self-possession led to the exploitation of Joice Heth and others like her in the entertainment industry. However, there was also a contemporaneous, if not equivalent, discourse and structural system surrounding labor on the part of Mongols during the nineteenth century that relegated Asian workers to a non- or minimally participatory status in a society informed by Lockean ideals. Ronald Takaki claims that debates about the favorability of courting Chinese immigration to the United States pivoted on questions pertaining to bonded versus free labor. Black and Chinese workers alike "were stereotyped as enemies to republican and free-labor society."[18] Najia Aarim-Heriot's analysis of journalistic and government tracts similarly shows that anti-Chinese sentiment during the nineteenth century articulated itself by calling attention to the proximity of the Chinese to blacks. "Like black labor, Chinese labor was allegedly liable to supplant white labor, not because of its superiority but because of its inferiority."[19] Disrupting the egalitarian myth of fair competition, both blacks (free and unfree) and Asians were considered threats to white self-possession and property rights.

The legislation to balance the capitalist interests of recruiting labor from China with the fear that this workforce would endanger white property hindered the migrants' capacity to participate as self-owning subjects and indexed their perceived inherent inability to do so. The Foreign Miner's Tax of 1850 targeted Chinese miners specifically. The Sidewalk Ordinance of 1870 prohibited the transporting of bundles on sticks on sidewalks; laundrymen commonly carried their loads that way. The Cubic Air Ordinance of 1870 assigned a 500-cubic-foot minimum per resident in each household, responding to how crowded Chinese living quarters, borne out of economic necessity, offended Anglo-American sensibilities. The pathologized hyper-sociality of Chinese residents that the Cubic Air Ordinance regulated seemed to indicate the presence of Anglo-American fears that the Chinese were inadequately individualized.[20] Moreover, the private sphere of their homes was considered inadequately demarcated from the public spheres of their commerce. According to cultural critic Chris Vials, sensationalistic accounts of domestic spaces behind Chinese laundries and other establishments were cast as "mysterious and sinister place[s] into which young, innocent white girls were often lured and brought to ruin through opium addiction and slavery."[21] The Alien Land Law of 1913 barred aliens ineligible for citizenship from owning land or leasing it long term—thus making an explicit connection between property ownership and civic participation in a democratic society.

While the conflation of Chinese and black populations mobilized anti-immigrant policies, Chinese immigrants existed at a structural distance from African Americans that placed them in a peculiar position within the United States' black-white racial system. Transnational Asia actually gained a foothold in the American South before Chinese migrants began arriving in California in 1849. Protestant Christian missionaries in the United States, particularly in South Carolina, launched evangelizing missions to China starting in 1829. On a regular basis, converts would be transported to the United States and displayed to their constituencies to rally more support for evangelical efforts abroad. Many of these visitors returned to China, but some remained in the United

States.[22] As early as the 1850s, Chinese men were living and working all along the eastern seaboard, particularly in urban port areas, such as Boston, New York, Baltimore, Charleston, and New Orleans. Further inland, Chinese workers in 1854 were hired at an iron factory in Louisville, Kentucky. Some of these workers came directly from China, others were secondary migrants who did a stint first on Cuban sugar plantations, and still others had landed in California before relocating elsewhere.[23]

The master narratives of Asian American history locate the seeds of the Chinese Exclusion Act in a predictable set of overdetermined West Coast concerns: white working-class resistance to Chinese workers' undercutting of wages, public health tracts that cast Chinese laborers as dirty and diseased, and other related factors. However, Moon-Ho Jung finds a strong connection between post–Civil War discourses of emancipation in the American South and "the Chinese problem" on the opposite site of the continent. Having abandoned a system of chattel slavery, antislavery republicans couched propositions to restrict Chinese immigration in the language of emancipation, warning that failure to change the course of bonded and indentured labor into the United States would threaten the status of free labor.[24] The Chinese population in the Southern regions of the United States increased after the end of the Civil War when capitalist interests identified Chinese immigrants—along with European immigrants—as good surrogates for black labor.[25] Many of these workers were hired as contract laborers, and the Southern economy saw them as key to keeping recently freed slaves in positions of social and economic disempowerment.[26] The presence of a Chinese workforce, indentured or not, continued to undermine the efforts of enterprising African Americans when Chinese contract laborers fulfilled their initial obligations to their employers and went into business for themselves. Laundry services run by African American women clashed frequently with those set up by Chinese men, and local launderers on one occasion shut down a Chinese laundry in Galveston, Texas, and drove its operators out of the city.[27]

Classificatory practices that accounted for biracial black-Chinese children called attention to the inadequacies of the state's efforts to draw distinctions based on race. These individuals tended to be identified as "mulatto,"[28] suggesting a likeness with biracial black-white children even if it did not necessarily equate "Chinese" with "white." Antimiscegenation laws, in language, largely prohibited intermarriage across any racial category but functioned to protect white men's exclusive access to white women. Thus, they were unevenly enforced in intermarriages between nonwhites. Insofar as the institution of marriage enabled some social and financial stability, Chinese men regarded partnerships with African American women highly because they tended to fly under the radar of regulatory regimes that prohibited other interracial configurations. Moreover, Chinese shopkeepers often welcomed the customer base from the black community that would issue from these marriages.[29] Later, the rising social and economic status of the Chinese diaspora in the United States changed the perceptions Chinese Americans had about their prior association with African Americans. As more Chinese Americans became acculturated into white society, the less positively social, kinship, and economic ties with blacks were perceived. For instance, before 1940, 20 percent of Chinese men in Mississippi were married to black women, but this number dropped sharply so that by the 1980s, it was less than 5 percent.[30]

Leslie Bow presents an insightful study of how Asian populations in the South were repeatedly invoked in debates about Jim Crow. The "interstitial" category of "Asian," as Bow argues, functioned for both black and white Southerners as a way to lay claim either to preserving or to questioning the existing social order under segregation. While white Southerners who opposed immigration did so by appealing to nativist fears of Asians' purported blackness, African Americans gained traction in their challenges to the separate-but-equal logic by calling attention to the near-whiteness of the Chinese in this system. Among the examples of how a nonwhite/nonblack rhetorical presence flexibly accommodated these disparate stances was the 1927 Supreme Court *Gong Lum v. Rice* ruling, which tracked students of Asian descent into "colored" public schools. The irony, however, was that this decision "affirmed the constitutionality of *Plessy v. Ferguson* . . . [even] as the dissenting opinion to Plessy [in 1896] invoked Chinese privileges under segregation."[31]

From Exotic Spectacle to Genteel Respectability

Nothing explains how Chang and Eng Bunker were able to circumvent federal policies that would have barred them from obtaining U.S. citizenship during their lifetimes. The 1790 Naturalization Act that limited the privileges of naturalized citizenship to "free white persons" was not repealed until 1952, almost a century after their deaths. Meanwhile, African Americans gained citizenship with the passage of the Fifteenth Amendment, and indigenous people were declared citizens following the Snyder Act of 1924. However, the twins were noiselessly naturalized at a time when this option was not open to Asians. A 1839 document issued by the Wilkes County courthouse authorizing Chang and Eng Bunker's petition for citizenship clearly indicates that "they are natives of the Kingdom of Siam in Asia" without qualifying that statement with an explanation of how their naturalization could be performed in a case otherwise forbidden by federal law. Following boilerplate legal language, the declaration of naturalization goes on to state that "they have behaved as men of good moral character, that they are attached to the principles of the constitution of the United States" before mentioning their nation of origin once again in the agreement to "renounce his [*sic*] allegiance to the King of Siam."[32]

Likewise, the dearth of juridical noise on the part of their marriages to white women long before North Carolina repealed its antimiscegenation law (after *Loving v. Virginia* in 1967) is conspicuous by its absence. An unidentified news clipping from the late 1930s or early 1940s reports that "NYA and WPA workers . . . were working as usual one day when without any warning, one of them came across the original marriage bonds issued when the original Siamese Twins, Chang and Eng married the Yates sisters."[33] The article goes on to describe the documents, "faded, yellow papers," that list their date of application as April 13, 1843, and show that Jesse Yates, the father of the brides-to-be, posted the fee of $1,000 for each marriage. There is no mention of any feature about the wedding licenses that would indicate anything unusual about the marriages. Even though anecdotal narratives from the twins' descendants—and reiterated in their biographers' account—point toward disapprobation on the part of local residents in the days leading up to their weddings, there is no trace of any legal faltering associated with this union. Interestingly, it is reported that the Bunkers' racial difference was more of a problem than their anatomy when neighbors initially expressed their displeasure,[34] but this is quickly underplayed with claims of the twins' quick assimilation into rural North Carolina life and their rise in status as respected planters.

The Bunkers' marriage to Adelaide and Sarah Yates marked their entrance into the Southern slaveholding elite. The wedding gift their father-in-law presented them was a woman, called Aunt Grace, who eventually served as nursemaid to their children. Following Barbara Jeanne Fields's assertion that denying freedom to some was crucial to what enabled the freedom of others, we see that the Bunkers' management between themselves of their human property, in telling ways, further possessively individuated them in antebellum social and juridical processes. A bill of sale dated November 20, 1855, records the transfer of ten slaves, ages six to sixty, for the amount of one dollar from Chang to Eng.[35] Although the drafting of this legal document is part of the rote conventions of ownership in this time and place, what makes it notable is that it clearly demarcates the boundaries between one brother and the other through the state-generated codes of property rights. It recognizes Eng, the buyer of the slaves, and Chang, the seller, as separate parties in this exchange. However, the amount for which these slaves were sold—it being clear that one dollar was not the market value—indicates that this was not a transaction made with the logic of profit against costs in mind, at least not directly. Already accustomed to the practices of dual ownership in their joint show-business venture, the Bunkers effected this transfer to better comanage the ownership of their shared human property *against* the reach of the state. Slaves were taxed at the highest rate among all property items by the Confederate government, and this selling maneuver most likely distributed the Bunkers' holdings more evenly to minimize Chang's tax liability since it appears he owned more than Eng.[36] In this exchange, the Bunkers used the channels of the state to produce themselves as individuated property owners and maximize the extent to which their legal individuation supported their economic interdependence.[37]

Possessive individualism can be articulated through a set of visual codes. Early in the Bunkers' career, artists' renditions of them tended to stress their "exotic" origins (see Figure 1.1). An image of the young Chang and Eng presents

Figure 1.1 The young Chang and Eng in an orientalist setting. Lithograph, circa 1830. *(Courtesy of the Wellcome Library.)*

them clad in pantaloons and tunics with ornate brocade. Their complexions are swarthy, even dark, and their slanted eyes and bulbous foreheads make them appear inextricably foreign. They stand barefoot against a backdrop that suggests a comfortable coexistence with what is presumed their natural habitat. Lush tropical vegetation graces the foreground. Behind them are palm trees and huts. Farther in the distance is domed architecture evocative of North Africa and West Asia, collapsing multiple Orients into one another. Even when the twins were depicted within their usual stage setting, one that resembled a Victorian parlor, and dressed accordingly, their features remained distinctively racialized (see Figure 1.2). Despite their Western-style suits and props, such as Chippendale furniture, a checkerboard, and corded drapes, the image of Chang and Eng—still slant-eyed—within the space of Anglo-American domesticity is one of dissonance rather than harmony.[38] British renditions of Chang and Eng at this time were no different (see Figure 1.3). In one lithograph, Chang and Eng appear in a panorama of scenes where they hit a shuttlecock with badminton racquets, shake hands with another sideshow performer (probably

Figure 1.2 Chang and Eng as young men in a sitting room. Lithograph, 1839. *(Courtesy of the Southern Historical Collection, Louis Round Wilson Special Collections Library, University of North Carolina, Chapel Hill.)*

Figure 1.3 Chang and Eng as represented during their first tour of England. Lithograph, circa 1830. *(Courtesy of the History of Medicine Division at the National Library of Medicine.)*

Charles Stratton, the entertainer of short stature with the stage name of General Tom Thumb), and play checkers with a patron. Although they were eighteen years old at the time of their first European tour and, thus, fully grown, the pen-and-ink illustration portrays them as young children. In real life, Eng stood at five feet two inches and Chang at five feet one inch, so if this illustration were drawn to scale, the two men in the center would stand about seven feet tall and everyone else (save for General Tom Thumb) at least six feet.

The overtly racialized and infantilized depictions of Chang and Eng Bunker at the beginning of their careers transformed into a different set of images later in life, after their class advancement and their marriage to Adelaide and Sarah Yates. Taking their cue from an iconic photograph of the twins reproduced on *cartes de visite*, souvenir cards sold at celebrity appearances (see Figure 1.4), the artists from this period depict the twins with an air of striking, but not exaggerated, dignity. An unsigned drawing shows the Bunkers seated for a family photograph in a living room decorated according to upper-middle-class tastes (see Figure 1.5). Chang and Eng are in the center, flanked by Adelaide and Sarah on either side. The twins in this picture are drawn with features so that they look almost as if they are white. Sarah cradles an infant in her arms while Adelaide poses demurely with downcast eyes. Altogether, eleven children from the two couples appear in front of them, their round faces and eyes conveying

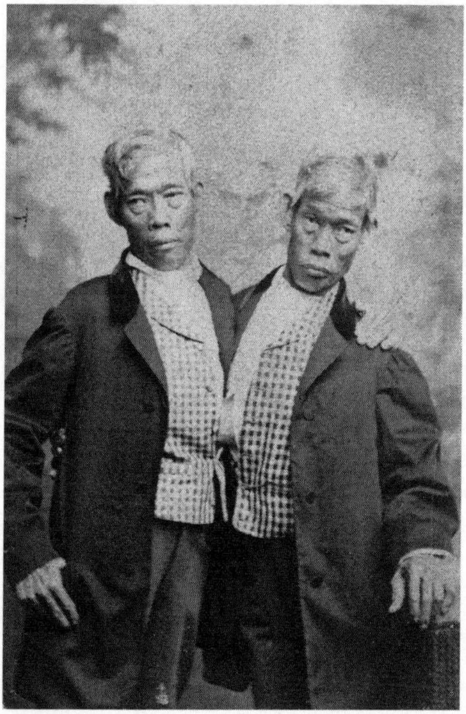

Figure 1.4 *Cartes de visite* photograph of Chang and Eng in midlife. Circa 1860. *(Courtesy of the Southern Historical Collection, Louis Round Wilson Special Collections Library, University of North Carolina, Chapel Hill.)*

Figure 1.5 Unsigned drawing of Chang and Eng with their wives and children. Date unknown. *(Courtesy of the North Carolina State Archives.)*

a domesticated cuteness that is qualitatively different from the childlike manner in which Chang and Eng are portrayed in the earlier images. In a Nathaniel Currier and James Merritt Ives lithograph (see Figure 1.6), a head-to-toe portrait of Chang and Eng attired similarly as in their *carte de visite* photograph occupies the center while smaller images of their wives and children and of the twins themselves frame it. In the style associated with Currier and Ives, Chang and Eng are shown engaging in activities associated with Victorian-era American sentimentalism: plowing a field, chopping wood, fishing, hunting, riding in a horse-drawn buggy, rowing a boat, and playing music. The visual rhetoric of these later images conveys the twins' class-based ascension into sanctioned forms of property ownership, kinship, and domesticity, a transformation that the phenotypic whiteness of their portrayal seals.

However, to read the Bunkers' entrance and absorption into white America as an example of the immigrant success story risks anachronizing this narrative—which did not appear until the emergence of European immigrant literature in the early twentieth century—and overlooking the fact that they themselves probably did not regard their personal histories in this manner. When the twins left Siam with Robert Hunter and Abel Coffin, the expectation was that they would return after five years. The contract they signed clearly

Figure 1.6 Chang and Eng as they were imagined by Nathaniel Currier and James Merritt Ives. Lithograph, 1860. *(Courtesy of the History of Medicine Division at the National Library of Medicine.)*

stipulated these terms.[39] However, following their break from Coffin, it appears that the entertainers plunged themselves into their careers even more vigorously so that the original plan of returning to their homeland faded into the background. They never did so—even for a visit.

Despite what resulted in the Bunkers' permanent departure from Siam, one letter they wrote to a mariner named Captain Davison indicated a pressing wish:

> Dear Sir,
>
> A gentleman called at Peale's Museum a few days ago and left your card, mentioning at the same time that you intended to sail for Siam very soon. We now write to ask you to inform us when you will leave Boston, to what place you are bound, and whether you go to Siam directly, also what the passage money would be if we should go out with you.
>
> Please write immediately.
>
> Truly yours,
> Chang-Eng[40]

The word "immediately" is underlined three times, communicating the urgency of the request. The letter is dated April 16, 1838; by then, the twins had been away from Siam for eight years—which was three beyond what was originally expected. Given that this was before they purchased their home in North Carolina and met their wives, it is difficult to discern whether they were considering a return to Siam permanently or if they wanted to see family briefly before resuming their show-business careers. No evidence is available as to whether there was further correspondence between the twins and Captain Davison. It is unknown whether Davison was unable to offer passage, whether the terms he set were not favorable to the Bunkers, whether his own plans shifted, whether the Bunkers changed their minds, or whether any other factors intervened to prevent this arrangement from taking place. In any case, this letter raises the possibility that the twins could have intended to resettle in Siam after traveling throughout the United States and other parts of the world.

This longing for home would return more than twenty years later but in a different fashion. As middle-aged fathers, the Bunkers traveled and performed occasionally with their children, who accompanied them onstage. In a December 10, 1860, letter to the Bunker family from Eng and an unidentified child, the child's salutation, "My dear Brothers and Sisters," is followed by excited reports of the sights on this tour to San Francisco, which they reached by first sailing to Panama, crossing the Panamanian isthmus by train, and then sailing north along the western coast of the continent. Among the diversions this child encountered were "whales" and "flying fish."[41] However, at a time when the port city of San Francisco was home to a bustling Chinese diaspora, there was no mention of those who, like the child's father, sat conspicuously outside the opposing racial poles of black and white. The absence of any account of Chinese people seems to suggest that the Bunkers' position in the United States was no longer proximal to those working-class laborers, even though the twins arrived in the country under a contract that carried similar stipulations. Additionally, the way Asia was viewed in the 1860s had shifted from that of only a generation earlier. Before the end of the U.S.-Mexico War, China connoted opulence and wealth, given that its main exports globally were luxury items, such as silk, tea, and spices. With the first major wave of Chinese immigration to the United States in 1849, another export started arriving on American shores—cheap labor. The class-based connotations of Asia had changed. As landed gentlemen planters, the Bunkers' distance from these newer immigrants was accentuated by their economic ascension. "Home" to these propertied subjects, possessively but not anatomically individuated, was now their North Carolina plantation.

The Propertied Subject after Emancipation

The economic affluence attained by the Bunkers corresponded with their increasing whiteness in the collective imagination, but it was this very privilege that permitted them to abridge the freedom of others. With the advent of emancipation, however, the Bunker families found themselves rethinking and renegotiating their relationships with those they owned in their former capacity as slaveholders. In a letter dated February 13, 1866, Christopher Wren Bunker, eldest son of Chang, wrote to update his father on the business of the house while he and Eng were away on tour: "We are getting along splendid with our out door's work. De has hired Jord to fix up the fences. He has done it quicker and better than when he belonged to us."[42] In an epistle reporting the mundane news of the Bunker home and various and sundry neighborhood gossip, this bit of information about the new relationship between the family and a man who less than one year previously had been their chattel property begs further attention. Christopher's observation of Jord's work habits could be an expression of wry exasperation for the man's purposeful withholding during his enslavement, a moment that confirms what slaveholders suspected all along about the need for constant surveillance of their purportedly shiftless slaves.

However, there appears to be some acceptance of the conditions that have inaugurated a market economy dictated not by the violent lash of subjugation and punishment but by the invisible hand of supply and demand. Jord's "quicker" and "better" services rendered to the Bunkers, who became his clients when they were previously his owners, reflected his new status as a participatory *subject*—however circumscribed by racial and class disadvantage—in this market economy, which contrasted with his former status as an *object* of exchange in a slave economy.[43] The unit of exchange went from being Jord's body to his labor. Perhaps Christopher did not resent what the increased productivity and quality of Jord's work implied about his previous stint in enslavement but was suggesting that the new economic order was an improved one even for those who benefited from the slave system. Free labor, according to Christopher—who was himself a Confederate Civil War veteran—seemed to be a "quicker" and "better" option overall.

There is a tone of respectful approbation that shows Christopher's admiration of how people like Jord managed their initiation into the realm of propertied selfhood. Christopher's account of this transformation indicates a willingness to accept the Bunker family's changed relationship with this man in ways that might possibly project onto him the postbellum South's determination to overcome the economic downturn after its loss in the Civil War. By interacting with someone who used to be one of the Bunkers' property items on terms that recognize his rebirth as an equivalent—though not equal—subject in liberal humanism's social contract, the Bunker family serves as a synecdoche for the vanquished Confederacy's own optimism for rebirth. Just as the former enslaved man remakes himself into a participatory economic citizen, the New South remakes its economy to announce its arrival into modernity's fold.

The departure of an older social order in the former Confederacy turned this abjected region into an object of visual amusement for outsiders, as Chang and Eng Bunker were for their customers. Five years after the end of the Civil War, someone who was probably an antiques dealer based in New York sent this letter:

> To Messrs Chang-Eng Esqs.
> Sirs
> I noticed an advertisement . . . in the Sun that you had a lot of Confederate money for sale. If you have please send me a statement of how you sell it as I would like to purchase some. I have a great many curiosities and I would like to add some of each denominations of Confederate money to my curiosities.
>
> Yours Trully,
> J. C. Shields . . .
>
> p.s. If satisfactory my friends will purchase a lot.[44]

This letter shows that the infamous worthlessness of Confederate dollars in the wake of the Civil War was recuperated by a specific sector in the North that saw the currency as a prized collectible. These bills, abstracted units of exchange in a federal jurisdiction that no longer existed, later turned into *objects* to be bought and sold in another economy. As they ceased functioning as intangible markers of a propertied *subject's* purchasing power, they became tangible commodities in and of themselves. That the letter writer calls Confederate money "curiosities" on two accounts would not have been lost on the Bunkers. The term was commonly used in the sideshow industry to refer to human performers, animal menageries, and inanimate attractions alike, all of which were hawked as warranting attention because of their rarity. Moreover, the obsolescence of these "curious" bills in the postbellum age removed them from their former abstraction. They became hyper-material in collectable form—the paper, ink, and overall condition needing to be "satisfactory" in antiques dealers' appraisal for them to function in this new incarnation.

This letter, which cast Confederate dollars as commodities and objects of visual consumption, resembled an earlier one the Bunkers received from a P. A. Browne, who had a peculiar hobby. Browne announced to the twins that he had "been engaged for several years examining under the microscope the hair of the head of the people of all countries and feel a great desire to examine yours." No information exists as to whether his request for "a small lock of each, with two or three hairs drawn (not cut)" was ever met.[45] Despite the whitening of the twins' public image once they settled into their Southern landholding, self-possessed lives, moments such as these occasionally and randomly erupted to remind them of their difference.

Connected and Apart

The framework this chapter constructs through its close reading of selected period documents informs my analyses in the subsequent chapters. Influenced by comparative ethnic approaches in the field of Asian American studies, *Chang and Eng Reconnected* examines the stories that surround the Bunkers within the context of their slippery location in the U.S. racial order. The prior scholarship in this area of inquiry suggests that nonblack/nonwhite categories are not outlying anomalies but necessary and integral buffer zones that allow the ongoing bifurcation and delineation between black and white to take place.

The role that Asian American studies has played in conceptualizing race in the United States has experienced many turns since its inception during the civil rights and antiwar movements in the late 1960s and 1970s. It was then that the field's founding intellectuals, along with those in Latino studies, linked arms with the already-burgeoning collective of scholar-activists teaching in African American studies. The 1960s and 1970s were a time when building coalitional links and finding common ground between Asian Americans and African Americans made pressing sense both in and outside of the academy. Domestic resistance to the war in Southeast Asia was part of a larger sensibility that marked decolonization globally, and this milieu gave rise to a Third World coalitional identity among people of color in the United States.[46] However, the post–World War II economic prosperity enjoyed by formerly working-class Chinese and Japanese Americans, along with the 1965 Immigration and Nationality Act that lifted national quotas for immigrants, created new ways of playing Asian Americans and African Americans against each other. Seen as paragons of upward mobility in the face of racism, these affluent Asian Americans and recent Asian immigrants found themselves cast as model minorities who overcame social barriers through a Franklinian ethos of hard work and self-sufficiency in contrast to African Americans, who were commonly portrayed by mainstream media sources as unruly.[47]

The volume of work in Asian American studies that adopts a comparative ethnic studies framework is too great to reference in its entirety. The production of knowledge about the Asian diaspora in the United States established itself in the academy in its earlier years by locating Asian American populations in relation to other racialized groups and indigenous Americans.[48] This work surged after the 1992 Rodney King verdict. The acquittal of four police officers in the African American motorist's beating, coming on the heels of the light sentence handed Soon Ja Du for the shooting death of Latasha Harlins, incited six days of rioting in South Central Los Angeles where Korean-owned businesses were set aflame by African American and Latino residents. In the wake of sensationalized media accounts of black-Korean conflict, Asian American intellectuals, both organic and academic, laid claim to solidarity with African Americans, stressing the shared history of activism and stating that "insofar as Asians and Africans share a subordinate position to the master class, yellow is a shade of black, and black, a shade of yellow."[49]

Although nobody who produced this work in the wake of the Los Angeles riots naively took an ahistorical position for solidarity between Asian Americans and African Americans—being careful to note the different patterns of discrimination these two groups have experienced—it was not until somewhat later that scholars would use this pivotal event to acknowledge the structural circumstances that have, on occasion, aligned Asian Americans with whites. In particular, Claire Jean Kim, Min Hyoung Song, and Nadia Kim all focalize their nuanced critiques of Asian American nonblack privilege through the long shadow of black-Korean discord that shaped understandings of U.S. racial divides in the 1990s.[50] The aforementioned scholars were joined by others who, while not referencing the circumstances of the King verdict directly, nevertheless interrogated the relative material privilege Asian Americans have historically experienced above African Americans.[51]

I hope that, by operating with these comparative frameworks forged in Asian American studies, my treatment of the cultural residue that trails Chang and Eng Bunker is mindful of how these actual people existed in time and space even as my analyses of the primary sources about them, from the nineteenth century to the present, show how their concomitant figurations shift. As Asian-raced subjects, the Bunkers were inevitably connected to larger currents informing the United States' growing transnational claims to Asia in the nineteenth century. However, as exceptional cases, they stood apart from many others who were similarly racialized. They entered and remained in the United States under conditions different from most other Asian immigrants, and they circumvented many of the restrictions, de jure and de facto, that other Asians confronted. As nonwhites in a republic founded on European-descended ideals of propertied selfhood, their racial alterity placed them, at times, in proximity to other nonwhites in the United States. As landed antebellum slaveholders, the ways in which their property rights were upheld by the state confirmed their possessive individuality, setting them apart from those marked by what Orlando Patterson calls "the social death" of slavery.[52] These tensions between connectedness and partition, on multiple levels, constitute the numerous contradictions the Bunkers present to the complicated landscape of American culture.

2

The Mystery of Their Union

Ruminating on the gazes at play in both the sideshow and medical laboratory, Susan Stewart observes that "it does not matter whether the freak is alive or dead."[1] Anomalous bodies in whatever state have long been prized by entertainment purveyors and scientists alike. When Chang and Eng Bunker embarked on their first European tour, among the items traveling with them onboard the transatlantic steamer were embalming fluids. Their manager, Abel Coffin, was not going to allow an inconvenient circumstance like the death of the twins at sea stop him from circulating their body.[2] The connection Stewart finds between the freak show and scientific medicine is clearly evident in the Bunkers' autopsy. The discursive and material results of the postmortem interventions performed on the twins reveal that—like the institution of the freak show—science, rather than definitively fixing and categorizing physical difference, produces multiple ways of viewing the extraordinary body, provides arenas for open-ended debate, and often generates more questions than it is prepared to answer.

This chapter provides historically contextual and close readings of the medico-scientific literature on the autopsy examination of Chang and Eng Bunker, focusing on four artifacts. First, I explore the phonographic report of the lecture presented by William Pancoast and Harrison Allen, the two physicians who conducted the autopsy, for a group of select medical professionals in Philadelphia on February 18, 1874. This text was printed in the *Philadelphia Medical Times* one day after the event. Second, I look at the *Philadelphia Medical Times* editorial accompanying this phonographic report. Third, I present the full autopsy report delivered by Harrison Allen on April 1, 1874, and published in the *Transactions of the College of Physicians of Philadelphia* in

1875. Finally, I explore a follow-up report delivered on May 5, 1875, by William Pancoast that addressed the feasibility of surgically separating the Bunkers during their lifetime. Together, these documents show a failure and/or reluctance on the part of several prominent medical men to achieve unquestioned control over meaning within the realm of anatomical examination. Despite efforts on the part of physicians to distance their study of unusual anatomy from the ways popular culture portrayed unusual bodies, these professionals often found little escape from prevailing concepts of normativity maintained by the lay public. Nor could they avoid dealing with this lay contingent on terms that they did not themselves set. As the Bunker twins' strange afterlives in the medical sphere show, the anatomical theater and the carnival stage shared more similarities than those who worked within the former would have readily claimed.

Early Practice of Postmortem Examination

The first recorded autopsy by white men in the Americas was, incidentally, performed on a pair of conjoined twins. In 1533, on the island of Hispaniola (now divided into the nations Haiti and the Dominican Republic), Melchiora and Juan Lopez Ballestero became parents to conjoined sisters they named Johanna and Melchiora. The priest performing the baptism puzzled over how best to conduct it—whether there should be one ritual or two—given the confusion as to whether the girls were believed to have one soul or two. Eventually, he chose to apply water to the heads of both infants. The twins died eight days later, and this uneasiness over the status of the girls' souls prompted the parents to have an autopsy performed, whereby physicians Hernando de Sepulveda and Rodrigo Navarro noted that there was a full set of internal organs in both halves of the conjoined body. The twins were then pronounced two separate souls by the medical authorities in what two medical historians have claimed was quite possibly "the only post-mortem examination ever conducted to study the soul of the deceased."[3]

A. Peña Chavarria and P. G. Shipley, writing in 1924, found this story in the travel narrative of Fernandez de Oviedo y Valdez, a Spanish-born member of the class elite in Hispaniola. *Historia General y Natural de las Indias*, published in 1535, is Oviedo's account of his migration from Spain and settlement in the colony. Fidelio A. Jimenez, another historian writing much later than Chavarria and Shipley, points out that Oviedo may have regarded the autopsy as unnecessary. Quoting from Oviedo, Jimenez writes:

> When [the doctors] asked if the creatures while alive showed any differences in feeding habits or other activities, the father answered that sometimes one cried while the other was silent. This I observed the first time I saw them and so did the other witnesses. He added that at times one was asleep while the other was awake, and that while one defecated

> or urinated the other did none of the above. However, occasionally they will do these functions simultaneously, at times one would anticipate the other. This will prove, even without having them cut open, that they were two separate persons and two souls.[4]

If this deduction came from the father's observation that the two girls often performed bodily functions separately, it seems to render superfluous the postmortem examination the physicians had conducted. Sepulveda and Navarro garnered evidence for their claim by incising the body and scrutinizing the internal organs, but the twins' father came to the same conclusion simply by noting their behavior, a considerably less invasive process. This incident demonstrates how the cultural and intellectual capital of specialized professionals can be dismantled when creating usable knowledge about the nature of dead bodies, especially those considered socially troubling. Whether the truths that issue from professional training were problematized on account of their redundancy, as in the case of the Ballestero twins, or their indeterminacy, as in the case of the Bunker twins, we see that clinical medicine often stumbles in the face of nonprofessionals regardless of whether these laypersons have consciously intended to take it to task.

More than three centuries after the autopsy of the Ballestero twins, Chang and Eng Bunker die in the home that Eng shared with his wife, Sarah, and their children. This time, medical science did not conduct an autopsy for religious purposes, but the secular imperative behind this operation unearthed similar tensions between the knowledge-producing processes of lay family members and academically trained physicians. The twins, who were survived by two wives and numerous children, found themselves in death at the center of events that pitted the interests of kin with those of medical science. Even when the Bunker widows, Sarah and Adelaide, granted permission to the physicians to dissect their husbands, the internal examination left the medical professionals with fewer definitive answers than the finality of a postmortem would purport to provide. These tensions between credentialed physicians and laypersons and among physicians themselves revealed the extent to which the medicalization of difference, far from stabilizing the meanings the extraordinary body holds, produced yet another set of contradictions that were every bit as puzzling as those that accompanied any exhibit on the carnival fairgrounds.

Nineteenth-century physicians played a large part in the sideshow industry. Within two years of Chang and Eng's departure from Siam, a large number of the most prominent physicians in the United States and Britain seized the opportunity to examine them. John Collins Warren, renowned anatomist at the Harvard Medical School, was one of the first doctors to attend to the twins following their arrival in Boston. Samuel Latham Mitchell and William Anderson of Rutgers Medical College soon followed suit. During the twins' first British tour, which took place several months after their arrival in the United States, all of London's most well-respected medical experts—among them Leigh Thomas, Astley Paston Cooper, and George Buckley Bolton—examined them. Bolton eventually became the twins' attending physician during their fifteen-month tour of England. Not only did physicians accompany many sideshow performers on the road; they were commonly integrated into the performance and involved in their publicity. After John Collins Warren conducted some tests on the Bunkers, Abel Coffin circulated the findings in the Boston press, and the media attention fueled the twins' rising celebrity. There was considerable discussion about the authenticity of their connecting band, and a large part of their allure, as with many other sideshow attractions, stemmed from the possibility they could be gaffed spectacles. Warren's testimony in the press legitimatizing their conjoinment, far from being a bizarre incident, was common practice in mid-nineteenth-century popular entertainment advertising. Publicity materials about sideshow performers often included testimony from physicians and other scientists.[5] Moreover, it was not uncommon for these experts to appear onstage alongside the performers, and sometimes their entrance was planned as they emerged from the audience as a seemingly disinterested third party. In sum, the medical gaze was part of the act.[6]

Despite the role physicians played in popular entertainment throughout the nineteenth century, social historian Robert Bogdan reports that scientific medicine contributed to the sideshow's decline in the early twentieth century.[7] Whereas physicians had once been involved very visibly in an industry that brought certain types of physical difference into public view, they later—as a result of the standardization of medical training in the United States—restricted the viewing and examination of unusual anatomy to the gaze of credentialed professionals. The increasing prestige gained by physicians in the late nineteenth century created a paradigm shift that affected how they understood their role. From participating in a form of mass entertainment to becoming a member of a new elite with specialized training, physicians had gone from generating wonder and open-ended discussion among laypeople to assigning diagnoses and clinicalizing people with disabilities.

However, I question how totalizing medical discourses may have been and how powerless nonprofessionals subjected to medical purview really were. As this chapter shows, the deceased body of the Bunkers did, in fact, create the conditions for multiple and competing interpretations that pitted differing contingents against each other: those among medical men themselves and those between the Bunker family and physicians. As an object of medical study, the Bunkers generated possibilities for signification that shifted according to where the value of the deceased lay for each stakeholder in these interchanges. In turn, these multiple meanings required a considered negotiation among all parties. Each was required to acknowledge that the investment the others had in this body varied, although not insurmountably, according to how they were positioned.

Final Moments

On Monday, January 12, 1874, William Hollingsworth, the Bunker family physician, advised the twins to remain indoors and stay warm because of a bout of bronchitis Chang was suffering. In response to growing tension between the two men in later years, Chang and Eng arranged for each to have his own residence for his wife and children, spending a series of three alternating days at each house. The houses were about a mile apart, and while at the home of one brother, the other would remain silent and yielding to the other's wishes until the time to switch arrived. Thursday, January 15, was the appointed day to return to Eng's household, but seeing as Chang had not fully recovered, both Eng and Adelaide—Chang's wife—reasoned it would be best to remain at Chang's house until his health improved. Always the more stubborn of the two, Chang stood adamantly against this change in plan and resolved to make the trip despite pleas from Eng and Adelaide. After much argument, the twins bundled up to face the cold weather and departed in their horse-drawn carriage.

Thursday night progressed without much incident as Chang appeared to recover, but on Friday night, he once again complained of chest pains and difficulty breathing. When the twins retired to bed, Chang was unable to breathe lying down and insisted on lighting the fireplace and sitting in front of it. Although Eng was perfectly healthy, he was wearied from spending a week with an increasingly irritable and debilitated Chang and wanted to stay in bed. They argued for some time before Eng agreed to leave their bed, and the twins got into their chair in front of the fire. Eng drifted in and out of sleep for a few hours before asking Chang to get into bed again, and this time Chang relented. In the early hours of Sunday morning, January 17, one of Eng's sons checked on the two men. Eng stirred from sleep and asked the boy how his uncle was doing. "Uncle Chang is dead," the boy responded. Knowing then that he would die, too, Eng exclaimed, "Then I am going!" Immediately, Dr. Hollingsworth was summoned to attempt to separate the twins, but he arrived too late. Eng's last words were "May God have mercy on my soul."

The Bunkers' death takes place a few decades before the time period in which Robert Bogdan locates the shift in medical involvement with the sideshow industry. Although the death of the Bunkers effectively retired them as performers, it did not retire them from public life altogether. It simply opened up new possibilities for display—this time in the medical sphere. The public afterlives of these famous twins began when a front-page story about their deaths in the *New York Herald* inspired William Pancoast, a professor of anatomy at Jefferson Medical College in Philadelphia, to wage a plea to the Bunker widows for the opportunity to examine the body. Seeking assistance, Pancoast wrote a telegram signed on his behalf by the mayor of Philadelphia to the mayor of Greensboro, North Carolina, the closest city to Mount Airy. He was provided with the names of William Hollingsworth and his brother Joseph, who was also a physician. Joseph Hollingsworth went to Philadelphia to meet with Pancoast and the well-known surgeon Samuel Gross. This meeting of the three physicians was followed by another meeting that included doctors John Neill, Joseph Leidy, and William Ruschenberger, thus forming the Commission on the Siamese Twins. At this meeting, the commission entrusted Pancoast and colleague Harrison Allen to travel to Mount Airy. Before departing Philadelphia, Pancoast and Allen enlisted another physician, Thomas H. Andrews, to accompany them.[8]

The physicians who visited the Bunker family were members of the College of Physicians of Philadelphia, an elite professional association. At this time, the city of Philadelphia was the epicenter of medical progress in the United States, and the association's membership included every high-profile physician who was part of this scientific and clinical vanguard that imagined itself a competitor to more established medical societies in Europe. About this trip to the Bunker widows, the *Philadelphia Medical Times* reported: "It will be seen at once that the College of Physicians was in no wise responsible for the acts of the Commission, although its name was freely used by the prominent Fellows engaged in the transaction. Indeed, these gentlemen, recognizing this, were prepared to meet the expenses of the trip had the College failed to endorse their action."[9] This name-dropping on the part of these medical professionals, even before the College of Physicians extended its support, may have indicated apprehension and uncertainty over their ability to legitimize permission for the autopsy on their own. The physicians understood from the beginning that they had to appease the widows' skepticism and resistance by invoking the cultural capital of an association that held considerable weight in nineteenth-century medical cultures.

The team of physicians arrived at the house shared by Eng and Sarah on February 1. Upon exhuming the body from the shallow grave in the cellar, they were pleased to find that it had little decay, despite the twins' having been dead for more than two weeks.[10] Apparently, the winter cold had sufficiently preserved the corpse. Since the conditions in Sarah's house were not conducive to an extensive examination, the physicians arranged to have the body shipped by express train to the College of Physicians, where the autopsy was completed. At a meeting of a select group of Philadelphia medical men on February 18, Pancoast and Allen presented the body in the College of Physicians lecture hall and delivered a talk that included preliminary findings of the postmortem still in progress. A transcript of the presentation was published in the *Philadelphia Medical Times* the next day. Allen compiled a final, more extensive report, and it subsequently appeared in *Transactions of the College of Physicians of Philadelphia*.

The coaxing of Sarah and Adelaide Bunker into offering their husbands' body for autopsy examination was a tricky matter. Rumors abounded that Pancoast and the other physicians offered to buy it from the widows for large sums of money, but these anecdotes were never substantiated. A report that Pancoast published after the autopsy was completed revealed that he and the other physicians most likely used tactics of coercion that called into questions the widows' obligation to medical science.

> It was held to be a duty to science and humanity, that the family of the deceased should permit an autopsy. The twins had availed themselves most freely of the services of our profession in both hemispheres, and it was considered by many but as a proper and necessary return, that at their death this *quoestio vexata* (the possibility of a successful section of the band) should be settled by an examination of its anatomical structure. Conversing upon this subject with several of my medical friends, I became impressed with its importance, and felt that it was the duty of the medical profession of this country to make an effort to elucidate the point at issue.[11]

Pancoast may have been conveying embarrassment over scientific medicine's prior involvement in the sideshow as this reference to the twins' travel in "both hemispheres" suggests. Furthermore, the declaration of his rights to the body hints of entitlement on the part of medical science to access unusual anatomy. This entitlement, by extension, frames itself as a physician's duty to a higher calling.[12] Pancoast's statement shows that the greater medical good to which the Bunker widows were exhorted to contribute was cast as coterminous with "humanity," assuming a boundless universality. However, Pancoast then references the duty of the medical profession of "this country," which delimits the boundaries of this humanity somewhat. Despite his nod to the Bunkers having benefited from the "services" of physicians in Europe and North America, this particular opportunity for autopsy examination that he and his colleagues sought was ultimately cast as a U.S.-based endeavor. Given the competitive eye with which American physicians regarded Europe (in particular, France), this high-profile procedure would have more firmly placed them on equal footing with their transatlantic counterparts.

The year before the deaths of Chang and Eng Bunker, physician A. J. Thomas stated in an autopsy manual that "the physician should feel it a duty which he owes to himself and the profession at large, to seek permission to make a post-mortem examination" upon a person's death.[13] Chances are that Pancoast, a key researcher in the field of anatomy, read Thomas's book, but even if he had not, he was part of a larger professional culture informed by the sentiments of access informing medical practice. Pancoast echoed these beliefs about a physician's obligations in the February 18 lecture to the fellows of the College of Physicians, stating that "one of the main reasons why the Commission [on the Siamese Twins] made such exertions to obtain this post-mortem, was that the American profession might not be charged with having neglected an effort to obtain an autopsy, which would solve the mystery of their union."[14] In reifying and pursuing the answer to this "mystery," he makes several verbal slippages: Pancoast, the physician, conflates himself and his colleagues with the field of scientific medicine in general. The labeling of medico-scientific institutions in the United States as a nation-specific movement—"the American profession"—suggests that Pancoast was defining himself apart from his European predecessors. More important, Pancoast avers that a lack of access to the Bunkers' body would have indicated "neglect" for which he and the American medical establishment may be "charged" with or accused of. Like A. J. Thomas's autopsy manual, Pancoast's lecture merges entitlement and duty in the practice of postmortem dissection and examination.

The *Philadelphia Medical Times* reported that the widows "received the Commission hospitably," thereby acknowledging the sensitive nature of this encounter in the paper's very mitigation of assumptions about the level of tension involved. However, it also stated that Sarah and Adelaide enlisted the services of a lawyer, who was present at the time Pancoast, Allen, and Andrews arrived at their home.[15] The paper's reporting of this detail reveals that the Bunker widows did not acquiesce meekly to the request Pancoast and his colleagues posed but exercised measures to ensure a fair and informed negotiation with the medical men. The care with which the Bunker family set the terms for its interactions with the physicians is significant in light of the fact that autopsy examination during this historical time frame was informed by its political valences. There was much at stake for the Bunker widows and children when they agreed to cooperate with the anatomists.[16]

Knowledge Production, Autopsy, and Social Identity

During the nineteenth century, postmortem dissection caught itself in a bind because the medical vanguard valued and prized this method of research while denigrating and debasing the people who supplied their bodies for this procedure. The rise of anatomy as a scientific discipline began with the emergence of clinical medicine in eighteenth-century France, where the growth of the hospital industry permitted systemic and widespread autopsy examination. According to Lester King and Marjorie Meehan:

> "Hospital medicine" was the road to progress, achieved through large numbers of patients, carefully observed while alive, and carefully autopsied when dead. The same clinician who observed them during life performed the autopsy. The correlation of clinical data and autopsy findings, carried out on a large scale, yielded magnificent progress.[17]

The emergence of clinical medicine, a social change initiated by the French Revolution, correlated with paradigm shifts in medico-scientific thought. For the first time, physicians could track and study patients on an aggregative level in ways that were previously not possible.

King and Meehan cite the writings of one French physician who weighed clinical observation and postmortem dissection equally when it came to their relative importance in acquiring knowledge about the body. Michel Foucault's account of the theory and practice of the autopsy in eighteenth-century France differs from King and Meehan's findings. Foucault claims that autopsy examination superseded other avenues of knowledge production about the human body when the medical gaze shifted from one that was external to internal. However, contemporaneous French medical thought created its own explanation about the autopsy's then-recent institutionalization. According to this logic, the beliefs and values of the Enlightenment rested on the era's urge to reject an irrational past that frowned on the dissection of dead bodies on religious or superstitious grounds. It was believed that this past animism had prevented physicians from examining the interiors of cadavers with a sensibility and rationality that relied on empirical knowledge.

Foucault claims that this explanation about the institutionalization of the autopsy is false. Certainly, the rising emphasis on empiricism in medical and other forms of science during the Enlightenment changed those fields considerably, but to complicate this cause-and-effect model about the increasing social acceptance of autopsy examination, he points out that autopsies had been widely performed in ages long before.[18] Autopsies became common during the Enlightenment not because there had been a prohibition against them in the years preceding the rise of clinical medicine but because a key change in medical perception—from one that examined anatomical structures in two dimensions to one that considered all three dimensions in space—had occurred at this historical juncture.[19]

The rise of anatomy as a discipline in the United States effected an institutionalized system of power relations whereby professional white middle-class men consorted and competed with one another to appropriate the bodies of disenfranchised social minorities for scientific advancement. As the autopsy became the gold standard for determining the legitimacy of medical research and training, the interest in obtaining cadavers increased while anxieties held by the lay public about postmortem dissection were exacerbated. The social underclasses had particular reason to be worried because of their disproportionate representation in this arena. In many areas of the United States and Britain, legislation passed that allowed medical schools to acquire the cadavers of indigent people and condemned criminals, and these bodies became commodities that could be bought and bartered among medical professionals.[20] In the case of executed criminals, dissection was often part of the sentence. The procedure was often feared by the condemned as even more harrowing than the execution because many Christians believed dismemberment of the body would prevent its resurrection.

In addition to these state-sanctioned methods of providing cadavers for medical schools, extralegal measures abounded. Medical schools hired grave-robbing "resurrectionists," and medical students themselves also took part in this practice. Grave robbing was regarded as an unofficial initiation into the profession.[21] Although the middle and upper classes could afford to inter their dead in vaults that were guarded by sentries, the poor had no such security measures and were vulnerable to body snatching. Medical schools in the U.S. South regularly plundered slave cemeteries, and at least one school enlisted the assistance of an enslaved person to furnish their supply of fresh cadavers from the burial sites of his brethren.[22]

If the practice of dissection was regularly meted out to the poor, the indigent, the condemned, and the enslaved, it is no surprise that sideshow performers with socially problematic bodies were regularly autopsied upon death. The procedure was often a public event that extended their exhibition beyond their natural life spans. When Sara Baartman, known as the "Hottentot Venus," was autopsied in 1815, the public dissection of her body replicated the racialized sexual dynamics that were present in her exhibition while she was alive. Her genitals and other remains were owned by and displayed at the Musée de l'Homme in Paris until 2002, when they were repatriated to South Africa after an international protest.[23] In 1836, Joice Heth, the performer who played the part of a 161-year-old slave, was publicly autopsied after she died. A ticket-paying audience of fifteen hundred gathered for the spectacle orchestrated by her keeper, P. T. Barnum and conducted by two physicians. In the end, Heth was determined to have been no more than eighty years old.[24]

In sum, postmortem dissection during the nineteenth century depended on and reinforced social hierarchies along lines of race, class, gender, ability status, and colonial subject status. Because the autopsy was associated with racialized difference and/or class disadvantage, the Bunker family's reservations about turning the body of its loved ones over to physicians was no small matter. When the widows finally acquiesced, it was not before they established strict guidelines with regard to storage, treatment, and examination. Under the terms of the agreement Sarah and Adelaide set, the body needed to be kept in a guarded, fire-proof building; no incisions were to be made on the heads or faces of the twins; and the front of their connecting ligament was not to be cut. A small incision was permitted on the back of the band as long as it was not severed.

These restrictions were telling, particularly those pertaining to the ligament, as they suggested that the ligament's significance to the identities of the twins was on a level with their faces. It is perhaps too obvious a point that the ligament was linked to the Bunkers' public and private identities in ways that facial features are linked with the personhood of the bearer of one's face. Even though many people, including Chang and Eng themselves, may have had ambivalent feelings about the band that held them together, the widows' guidelines to the anatomists showed that within the intimate spaces of the family, this anatomical feature was not an unwanted appendage to be severed but a distinctive and valued part of their body. The widows' placement of the ligament on a level with their faces reclaimed it from the discourses of anatomical pathology and the sideshow. However, given that the widows had allowed an incision to be made on its back surface, they showed that they were not entirely opposed to working cooperatively with medical science while maintaining themselves as keepers of the gate.

What Front? Which Back? *Whose* Side?

The limits the widows imposed came with certain impediments. There were several references in the lecture by Pancoast and Allen and in the final autopsy report as to how these guidelines affected the process of examination. The restriction about which surface of the connecting band could be cut was more complicated than the one against cutting the faces for two reasons: first, because the ligament was a location of intense interest for these medical professionals and, second, because it was not immediately obvious which surface was the back surface. The beginning of the autopsy report noted that while it was a fairly straightforward undertaking to determine which parts were the upper and lower surfaces, the labeling of the front and the back could not be done by appealing to the fetal positioning of the twins but by considering the acquired position they had developed and maintained throughout their life spans. Although their fetal orientation was one that placed them face to face, the twins eventually acquired the convention of positioning themselves side by side, with Chang standing to the left of Eng. In interpreting the widows' stipulation that the front of the band not be cut, Allen wrote:

> Viewing the band as a separate form—as it was spoken of during the life of the twins—we will see that the terms front ("anterior") and back ("posterior"), as given to the lateral surfaces were derived from studying the acquired position. Thus we were bound not to cut the "front" of the band, but allowed to make an incision on the "back." Now this position of selection was destroyed, and its terms deprived of what meaning they may have had, by the reproduction of the congenital relations of the bodies.[25]

The first part of this excerpt from the autopsy report makes the curious maneuver of secluding the Bunkers' connecting band from the rest of each brother's body. The physicians' chagrin seems evident in their rather defensive declaration that their decision to regard the band as a "separate form" was not an idea that originated from themselves but that others had similarly done so while the men were still alive. Nevertheless, the anatomists' conceptual isolation of this body part had some interesting consequences. The passive tense in references to the band—"as it was spoken of during the life of the twins"—omitted the central question of who did the speaking or, in other words, exactly who had regarded this anatomical feature thusly. It seems improbable that the twins or surviving kin did so. This passage in the autopsy report provides a stark contrast to how the Bunker family members, as shown in their wishes to preserve the front surface, regarded their deceased loved ones' unusual body. The language of the report suggests that the medical professionals saw the band not as an inseparable part of the twins or an integral part of their identities but as a conceptually detached entity that had to be regarded as such for the physicians to continue with their examination.

However, the physicians could not ignore a sense of agency on the part of the twins in interpreting the stipulation the widows placed on not cutting the "front" but allowing for an incision on the "back." The twins were birthed face to face, with each one having his head between the legs of the other. Their mother did not report having had any more difficulty with their delivery than she did with her other children, and it was discovered that the babies were conjoined only when the midwife attending their birth went to untangle and bathe them. Given that there had not been any "front" or "back" to the band in utero and that their death had erased any agential positioning on their part, the physicians had to rely on their knowledge of an "acquired position" or "position of selection," whereby Chang stood to the left of Eng. The physicians were very clear and definitive, even wordy, in their designation of the ligament's sides, which take into account the twins' acquired position. One wonders if the tortuous description was produced not only to maintain the integrity of scientific record keeping but also to protect themselves—given that they had entered into a civil contract—in the legal arena. About the band, Allen further wrote:

> There is no doubt that in infancy and early childhood there was no acquired position, and, therefore, neither "front" nor "back" to the band. And later, when, as we have reason to believe, the position of selection was gradually adopted, the terms "front" and "back" were reversible—the "front" meaning that which corresponded to the surface of least thoracic approximation. Thus when the adult condition was fixed, and the "front" answered to the widely separated right side of Eng's chest and left side of Chang's chest, the "back" was in relation with the closely approximated left side of Eng's chest and right side of Chang's.
>
> To avoid awkward repetition of phrases expressing the facts of the last sentence, the following characters will be employed in describing the "lateral" surfaces of the band.
>
> E. R., C. L. (Eng's right, Chang's left) will designate the "anterior" surface of the acquired position. C. R., E. L. (Chang's right, Eng's left) will designate the "posterior" surface. Since the right side of Chang's half of the band merged into the left on Eng's half, while the right side of Eng's half, after it passed the middle line, became the left half of Chang's, we propose using the characters E. L., E. R and C. R., C. L., which will be understood as signifying left side Eng, right side Eng, etc.[26]

The convoluted way in which "front," "back," and "side" were defined in the report reveals the tensions between the fetal and the acquired positions, showing that the physicians were forced to recognize the primacy of the latter in order to record their examinations.

Perhaps these very semantic gymnastics undergone by the physicians expressed covertly their dismay over what they perceived to be the arbitrariness of the widows' restrictions. The sides of the band that were designated the "front" and the "back" probably did not seem, in the eyes of the physicians, to be anatomically significant in and of themselves. This is implied in Allen's statement that "front" and "back" had been nonexistent in the womb and "reversible" early in childhood. The physicians' labored interpretive maneuver calls attention to the widows' guidelines in a way that acknowledges a gulf between the interests of the family and those of medical science. The widows' insistence on maintaining the "face"—so to speak—of the band ran counter to that of the physicians in anticipation of dissection and internal examination. Furthermore, the convoluted language used indexes a fundamental inability of language itself to accommodate the embodied experiences of conjoinment. The band went from being viewed as a separate body part, extraneous to either twin, to being a part of the twins' anatomy, divided in two, each half designated as belonging to either Eng or Chang. However, this separating into two "halves" and the drawing of a line partitioning the twins' from each other disregarded the possibility that the Bunkers—and other conjoined twins—may have considered their body a shared one in whole rather than two connected forms that could be divided.[27]

The View of the Inside

By autopsying the Bunkers, what did the Commission on the Siamese Twins think it would find? What was, in William Pancoast's words, "the mystery of their union" the commission was so eager to solve? What queries did it want answered, and what conclusions did it draw? At the time, medical institutions, medical professionals, and the general lay public recognized anatomical evaluation as the method by which the medico-scientific vanguard measured itself. Medical training, thus, was synonymous with anatomical training.[28] When Chang and Eng died, autopsy examination was considered the method through which physicians, trained to read and generate knowledge anatomically, gained esoteric insight about the body. Thus, while postmortem dissection depended on the existence of a hierarchical society in order to sustain itself and further diminished the underclasses in the process of medical inspection, the act of performing an autopsy—an activity initiated by clinically educated middle-class white men—elevated the wielders of the scalpel even more.[29] However, while this method of internal examination revealed some insights about the twins' body, it also revealed more intriguing insights about autopsy itself. Essentially, it was an autopsy about autopsy practice.

According to Michel Foucault, pathological anatomy as a scientific field has always been wracked with its own shortcomings:

> Disease is the passive, confused object to which [analysis] must be applied only insofar as it is already, of itself, the active subject that exercises

> it pitilessly upon the organism. If the disease is to be analysed, it is because it is itself analysis; and ideological decomposition can be only the repetition in the doctor's consciousness of the decomposition raging in the patient's body. . . . Anatomy could become pathological only insofar as the pathological spontaneously anatomizes. Disease is an autopsy in the darkness of the body, dissection alive.[30]

The impetus behind dissection rested on two key assumptions: the first being that pathology manifests itself in ways observable in internal tissues and the second being that unusual anatomy is itself a disruption (hence, "analysis") of normal bodily surfaces. In the language Foucault uses, disease is given greater agency than the physician, it having preceded the physician in the dissection of the body. The knowledge that allows the anatomist to dissect and interpret a cadaver can arrive only in a second place finish, losing to disease. Dissection always comes after death.

The primacy of visuality is obvious in Foucault's framework. He stresses that when physicians observe internal surfaces, they do so overwhelmingly through the realm of the optical, but he also concedes that medical science during this era employed an increasing use of other senses. The invention of the stethoscope brought an auditory element to medical observation. The palpation of organs for tumors and other irregularities involved touch. Despite the cooperation of these multiple sensory elements, however, Foucault maintains that sight persisted as the most significant sensory faculty and that hearing and touch merely reinstated the sovereignty of sight: "[The] ear and hand are merely temporary, substitute organs until such time as death brings to truth the luminous presence of the visible."[31]

If autopsy examination relied on the visible, and if the visible relied on an unquestioned presumption behind its superior reliability, lapses in visuality's potential during the autopsy of Chang and Eng Bunker reveal cracks in the relationship between sight and knowledge. After the physicians made the permitted incisions, they observed that the interior of the connecting ligament consisted mostly of connective tissue and was entirely devoid of fat. A portion of the ensiform cartilage from each twin protruded into the upper portion of the ligament. During the preliminary examination, the physicians noted that parts of Eng's liver and parts of Chang's liver extended into the connection as did the peritoneal cavities of each twin, but they determined that the internal cavities of both twins were closed off from each other. Small veins ran from one twin to the other, particularly between the two livers, and the liver tissue was continuous between one and the other, creating a conjoined liver. The twins shared an umbilical vein, but this had been inferred even before the dissection because they had one navel between the two of them located in the center of the band.

Although the sense of sight did not drop out of the picture in these encounters with Chang and Eng's internal structures, the sense of touch played a starring role in a key portion of the autopsy. Harrison Allen described the role of touch in the lecture he delivered with William Pancoast to an audience of College of Physicians fellows assembled over the cadaver:

> My finger is now in the umbilical pouch of Chang. . . . The motion is noticeable in the under surface of the band. On the side of Eng no such motion will be observed. I can very clearly see my finger passing between the two folds of the suspensory ligament. . . . When the finger is passed from Chang into Eng, it is received between the folds of the suspensory ligament of Eng. . . . When the finger is introduced behind the [peritoneal] pouch, it is observed to terminate blindly, showing, we think, that it is adventitious, due to the presence of that suspensory ligament.[32]

Even in a procedure that Foucault claims exalted the visual, the sense of sight was not only corroborated but substituted by one other sense. Through feeling the interior surfaces and observing the movement of his finger, Allen was able to deduce how far the body cavities extended into the connection. This union of touching and seeing seems logical. As experts in anatomy, Pancoast and Allen would have had access to Francis Delafield's 1872 publication, *A Handbook of Post-Mortem Examinations and of Morbid Anatomy*, a manual for autopsy examination that was filled with exacting references to the placement of the hands of the attending physician during a procedure (Delafield assumed a right-handed orientation) and what to feel for inside various organs.[33] Even so, the rhetoric of sight entered into these observations garnered by the hand. Allen spoke of the peritoneal pouch "terminat[ing] blindly," his words calling attention to the failure of sight, when his finger pushed up against the end of it. Ultimately, the movement of his fingers through the skin of the band was confirmed by what he saw from the exterior.

In his portion of the lecture, Pancoast provided more thought-provoking description of the significance of touch in conducting the autopsy:

> By placing my hand in the peritoneal cavity of Eng and my colleague [Allen] placing his hand in the peritoneal cavity of Chang, we pushed before us processes of peritoneum, which ran on to the median line of the band; and we could feel our fingers in the lower portion of the band, behind the median line, with a distinct layer of peritoneum between them, demonstrating at once the prolongation of the peritoneum into the band, and the complete separation of one peritoneal cavity from the other at this median line. Above that we felt some traces of vascular connection, apparently running from one liver to the other.[34]

Although Foucault's model of sensory triangulation, that of hearing and touch with sight, assumed that listening and feeling while examining a live body surrogated for the more favored action of seeing when that body eventually expired, the report from the presentation Pancoast and Allen delivered raised questions about the limitations of sight even when the body being examined was dead. When the physicians used the sense of touch in their autopsy, it suggested that even when examining a deceased individual, sight alone was not sufficient.

Additionally, it is interesting to note what the sense of touch registered for these two physicians. Pancoast and Allen each felt from inside the connecting band their fingers pressing up against the fingers of the other man through the twins' soft tissue. Observations about the range and the separation of the cavities of each twin came about from one physician feeling the other inside the cavity through a layer of cadaver tissue. The assessment of the depth of the two peritoneal cavities relied on each man's touch, and while it may have been possible for either Pancoast or Allen to come to the same conclusion alone using a single examiner's left and right hands in each incision, the kinesthetic awkwardness of leaning and bending over an examination table in this manner suggests that this maneuver was more reasonable as a joint venture.[35]

What do we make of this strange caress? As these two medical men buried themselves up to their wrists and stroked each other inside this body, what kinds of pleasures and frustrations may they have been enacting for their audience of like-minded peers? While I am tempted to flippantly read this as an act of theatrical double-penetration fisting within the context of a homoerotic triangle (or quadrangle?) so that I can dismiss the silliness of that interpretation, I do not think my initial reaction is far-fetched. Historian Michael Sappol observes that as the cadavers of social minorities were appropriated in a process that reproduced power relations between the underclasses and professionally trained white men, this same dynamic of domination created complex intimacies among the men themselves. The shared illicit thrill of body snatching was as much a part of medical training, albeit a de facto one, as dissection itself. Accordingly, the conquest from a grave of a cadaver, which tended to be gendered female, had sexual overtones that cemented homosocial and homoerotic attachments between men. This traffic in gendered and racialized bodies that were passive yet hard to get "served to bond a group of young men together in opposition to those outside, rituals that marked a passage from protected youth to masculine adulthood."[36]

There are, of course, differences between Sappol's model of homosocial and homoerotic bonding and the relationship triangulated by Pancoast, Allen, and the Bunker twins' body. Even though Pancoast and Allen were not, at the time of this autopsy, students but physicians in the prime of their careers, this performance for their peers showed that their socialization in the early stages of professionalization carried over into everyday medical practices with their shared and simultaneous penetration, both physical and epistemological, of socially problematic bodies. A more important difference lay in the fact that the Bunkers were not surreptitiously snatched from their grave under the cover of night but won through a transparent and intricately orchestrated courtship of Sarah and Adelaide Bunker. The collaborative wooing of two middle-class white women on the part of the physicians was at times pleading and at other times coercive, qualities not altogether different from those of heterosocial romantic pursuit. If the incidences of grave robbery and dissection Sappol recounted carried with them connotations of "rape" and "sodomy"[37] when meted out on African Americans, indigenous people, immigrants, condemned criminals, and the poor, the successful and performatively consensual courtship of two "respectable ladies" made visible the class differences between the Bunker family and the others who more commonly found themselves on the anatomist's dissection table. However, the obvious pleasures of this conquest did not overshadow the more vexing frustrations surrounding the autopsy.

Separation Anxieties

Although reports of the autopsy performed on the Ballestero twins in sixteenth-century Hispaniola indicate that it had been conducted with the intention of determining whether the twins had one soul or two, the objectives of Chang and Eng Bunker's autopsy were defined secularly. The physicians were primarily interested in the anatomical specifics of how the two brothers were joined, their causes of death, and whether they could have been separated safely during their lifetimes. How Pancoast phrased his goal, however, suggests a rarified, even transcendent, quest for discovery with religious overtones—to "solve the mystery of their union"—and anticipates the involvement of the spiritual in this realm of the scientific.

Writing about highly publicized conjoined twin separations of the present day, medical ethicist Alice Domurat Dreger contends that these surgeries serve not the interests of conjoined siblings or their parents but those of the medical professionals who conduct them. The attention these high-profile procedures draw and the cultural capital they confer on medical teams and hospitals is not surprising given the long history of theatrical medicine. About these surgeries, Dreger writes:

> A major reason for the incredible sorts of surgeries attempted, with or without intentional sacrifice [of the physiologically weaker twin], is what I call the technological imperative—perhaps better, the technological inertia—of surgery. This is the situation in which increasingly fantastic and expensive surgeries are performed, without much pause to consider their propriety, in the interest of "progress" and "discovery." Technological inertia also tends to carry with it legitimacy inertia; that is, as more and more spectacular surgeries are attempted, they build up a heroic history which brings with it a tacit legitimacy and acceptance, and they cease to be fundamentally questioned.[38]

The contemporary state of medical science Dreger discusses in this passage, although markedly different from that of the late nineteenth century, shares striking similarities with the past when it comes to how physicians legitimize themselves to laypeople. Even though the present-day literature on Chang and Eng Bunker notes that today's technological advances would have been able to separate them successfully, a report authored by Pancoast a year after the autopsy concluded that attempts to have done so would most likely have proven fatal.

Despite the risks Pancoast identified, he paid an inordinate amount of attention to the nonmedical reasons a separation, if it had been feasible, should have been performed. Merely hinting at his inclinations in the early parts of the report, he expressed concerns that "upon moral and even physical considerations, it would have been well if the twins could have been separated."[39] This vague reference to "moral and . . . physical considerations" would become more obvious later when he referenced the Bunkers' household arrangements: "Though it seems most immoral and shocking that the two should occupy the same marital couch with the wife of one, yet so thorough was this understanding of alternate mastery, that, as I was told by one of the widows, there never had been any improper relations between the wives and the brothers."[40] If Pancoast was scandalized about the possibility of nonmonogamous contact among the twins and their wives, he seemed suspiciously relaxed with his own intrusive inquiries into the Bunkers' sexual activity even as he pressured them to consent to an autopsy—all while the widows mourned.

Pancoast retreated from his interventionist tendencies only once during the report to concede that perhaps a state of conjoinment might not have been a personal or moral tragedy. He expressed amazement at the level to which Chang and Eng were able to cooperate and negotiate with each other despite their differences: "They had learned to accommodate themselves to their situation; and probably they regarded themselves as equally, if not more favorably suited in respect to the necessities of life than if they had enjoyed a separate existence."[41] Signaling that the Commission on the Siamese Twins may, in fact, have seen its subjects as multidimensional people and not merely as medical specimens, this statement shows that medical science was less totalizing in its view of those with unusual anatomy than expected. Furthermore, Pancoast seemed to have admiration for the twins, saying, "They brought to the accomplishment of any undertaking; if needed, a double strength and a double will,"[42] even as he looked favorably on the idea of separation:

> Should such a case occur again, I would recommend the operation [to separate], and be willing to perform it, even if . . . one of the children died, for then at least the survivor would be able to enjoy a natural life. Even if both perished, the risk might be justified; the moral sense of the community, at least in a Christian country, would then not be shocked by the unnatural complication which otherwise would arise, and did arise in the case of the Siamese twins, proving the cause of so much criticism severe and unjust, when we consider the peculiar conditions under which the twins enjoyed their lives, the respectable families which they

> raised, and the good opinion in which both the Messrs. And the Mistresses Bunker were held in their neighborhood.[43]

As Pancoast wavered between moral outrage and empathy to admiration and respect, his conclusions were, by no means, straightforward. His report did not express definitively whether surgical intervention, on Christian rather than physiological grounds, should have been attempted even as he claimed he would have been willing to undertake the operation. In fact, he condemned the "severe and unjust" criticisms doled out by this "Christian country" that would impel a separation. This interplay of academic medicine's secular impulse with the sacred dictates of religion suggests that perhaps Pancoast, writing more than three hundred years after the autopsy of the Ballestero twins, did not find himself that far removed from the premises of that earlier time.

Died of Fright—or the Left versus the Right?

Even though the autopsy report stated that Chang's cause of death could not be conclusively verified, given that his brain was off limits, there was no evidence of a debate that he died of a cerebral clot. On the other hand, the question about Eng's cause of death generated two possibilities, the first of which survives in the medical and popular-cultural record most prominently. Pancoast and Allen's final report indicated that Eng's body showed several signs of the physiological response to fear: Eng's bladder was distended and in a raised position, and one of his testicles had retracted. However, within the same document, there were differing accounts as to which one of his testicles was retracted. At first, the report stated, "The right testicle of Eng was normal. The left testicle was not within the scrotum. Dissection from within the abdomen showed that the organ had been retracted."[44] In the end, the concluding remarks indicated "Eng died, in all probability, in a state of syncope induced by fright—a view which the over-distended bladder and the retraction of the *right* testicle would appear to corroborate."[45]

While this discrepancy may have been a mere copyediting error, it contributes to the haze of ambiguity surrounding Eng's death. The official cause of death that was recorded appears to reflect anxieties held by the normatively bodied when forced to confront the concept of interdependency. While it is true that the sympathetic nervous system can cause the testicles to retract in response to fright, Pancoast and Allen did not eliminate other causes, such as cold or pressure, for the same physiological effect. The Bunkers died during the winter, so temperature-related causes were possible. Given the significance the physicians assigned to the location of the testicle in determining cause of death, the sloppiness with which they recorded this observation raises suspicion. There seems to have been too much attention paid to Eng's testicle and yet too little attention paid to its accurate documentation.

This grand pronouncement of the cause of Eng's death, however ambivalent, arouses a considerable amount of salacious fascination in the collective imagination. A twentieth-century physician named Worth Daniels referenced this story in his presidential address to the American Clinical and Climatological Association, which ended with these words: "In Eng's case, I fully agree with Dr. Harrison Allen. Eng died of fright. If any of you doubt this try being joined to a dead xiphopagic twin!"[46] The exclamation point punctuating the close of Daniels's presidential address entreated his normatively bodied peers to place themselves in Eng's position, not inviting them to empathize with a different embodiment, as his words may suggest, but stoking fears about their inseparability from other individuals.

Along these lines, literary critic Leslie Fiedler devotes an entire chapter of his iconic book *Freaks: Myths and Images of the Secret Self* to the phenomenon of conjoined twins (or "Siamese twins," the terminology of the day). Like many other categories of "freaks," as Fiedler argues, these twins raise concerns about the sanctity and normalcy of those who remain unmarked, thereby generating an inner "secret self" that is simultaneously repudiated and embraced.

> The phrase "died of fright" resonates in my mind, evoking the terror of lifelong mutual dependency. In their relationship I feel caricatured symbiotic relations more familiar to me—not sealed in the flesh, like theirs, but quite as inescapable: parents and children, unjoined siblings, lovers, husbands and wives. Like Chang and Eng, such pairs, however equal in theory, are never equal in fact, since one of them inevitably leans a little harder, clings a little longer, demands a little more. And both live always with the threat of that ultimate disparity which will occur when one begins to die, and finally—the other still living—is dead.[47]

The dread of inseparability from a weaker, parasitic other that both is and is not oneself signals to normatively bodied people that their individuality may not be as complete as American ideals of liberal republicanism would imply. Perhaps Pancoast and Allen, anticipating Fielder, projected these fears onto Eng.[48]

At least two others have voiced opposing possibilities for Eng's cause of death, both focusing on Pancoast and Allen's observation that "the venous system of Chang was engorged, giving the appearance of those vessels having been injected after death; that of Eng was comparatively empty."[49] Kay Hunter's biography of the Bunkers finds that a family friend, a man named Issac Armfield, thought Eng died from blood loss as his circulatory system continued pumping blood through the vessels in the connecting band but received no blood back from Chang's side in return.[50] Hunter does not say whether Armfield was a trained medical professional, but his hypothesis has been corroborated by one other physician as reported in the biography by Irving Wallace and Amy Wallace. Physician Summerell indicated that a large part of the actual dissection had been assigned to a physician named Nash. Nash had been a dissenting presence on the Commission of the Siamese Twins who opposed the pronouncement of death from fright, indicating

> that the *arteries* of a dead body were completely empty of blood—and that the veins were more or less filled with it. This is a well-known fact. In making the dissection in this instance, [Nash] noted that the veins of No. 1 (that died) were full of blood—that his arteries contained some blood—that the arteries of No. 2 contained a small amount of blood—that his veins contained less blood than the amount to be expected.[51]

However, both biographies of the Bunkers ultimately reject these voices of disagreement. Wallace and Wallace concur with Pancoast and Allen, stating that "most likely, Dr. Allen's opinion was the correct one: On finding himself attached to a dead brother, Eng had literally been scared to death."[52] Hunter calls the claim that Eng bled to death through the ligament "another interesting theory" that "could perhaps have had some truth in it,"[53] but she downplays this conclusion. In the end, that Eng died of fright prevails not only in the medical record but also in the popular-cultural imagination.

Missing Pieces and Blurred Relations

The Bunker family's interactions with the Philadelphia medical men did not end with the completion of the autopsy. A son of Chang and a son of Eng sent this letter, dated April 1, 1874, to Harrison Allen:

> Sir
> Enclosed you will find the receipt for bringing the bodies of Papa and Uncle from Salem to our home. You will please send the Money by post-office order.
>
> My Mother and Aunt was very sorry that we did not bring the lungs and entrails of our Fathers with the bodies home. And as we did not bring them, you can keep them until further orders from the families.
>
> Respectfully,
> CW and SD Bunker[54]

After the physicians finished the autopsy, they returned the body to the Bunker family, presumably via rail to the train station at Salem, North Carolina (now Winston-Salem). Apparently, there were some parts of the twins that had gone missing. Speculating on the unsettling strangeness of the letter, Ella Wade, the former curator of the College of Physicians of Philadelphia Mütter Museum, wrote, "Its contents may seem amusing to us, reading it today, but I venture to say that it was a serious matter indeed to the survivors of the twins."[55] That these icons of medical authority may have cheated the Bunkers out of some internal organs most likely increased the disdain the family felt for the physicians. Wade goes on to say that while the College of Physicians maintains Chang and Eng's preserved liver on display at the museum, whether the lungs and intestines were ever returned to North Carolina or disposed of in Philadelphia remains unknown.

The letter shows that not only had Sarah and Adelaide been involved in communicating and negotiating with the Philadelphia doctors, but the children had taken an active role, too. Even so, the dismay over the missing body parts references the widows and their concern about being shortchanged, making Sarah and Adelaide the agents behind this missive. Ultimately, the letter reveals the sustained and continuing caution with which the Bunkers regarded medical authority. It is apparent that even after the body was returned, the Bunker family was not content to inter their loved ones' remains unquestioningly. They were either knowledgeable enough about anatomy, having discovered the absence of the organs themselves, or they had the foresight to hire an expert to make these observations before burial.

This letter not only reveals the Bunker family's distrust of the medical profession but indicates an interesting blurring of kinship lines between the two sides of the family. Signed by two Bunker children, the letter makes some slippages in the kinship relations among the family members. Although the wording of this letter would suggest that the undersigned are siblings from the same set of parents, when the initials of C. W. and S. D. are matched with the names of the Bunker children, they correspond to Christopher Wren (son of Chang and Stephen Decatur (son of Eng). Thus, the terms "Papa," "Uncle," "Mother," and "Aunt" in the letter would refer to different relations each for C. W. and S. D. However, this conflation appears fitting in that it indicates the extent to which traditional kinship ties were blurred in the Bunker family. Despite their fathers' decision to maintain separate households—an effort that approximated the heteronormative dictates of the conjugal family—the language in this letter suggests that the children at least may have maintained dual membership in each of the two families. It appears that the Bunker families were more fluid and the boundaries between each kinship unit more malleable than their separate residences would indicate.

This porosity, be it among the wives and children of Chang and Eng or between Chang and Eng themselves, is what remains most salient when we consider the artifacts that emerged from the Bunkers' exchanges with the College of Physicians of Philadelphia. It is unremarkable that medical discourses find their limits when examining a pair of conjoined twins, beings that defy traditional notions of individuality. In the postmortem medical reports on the Bunkers, there were moments when the taxonomic and corrective gaze gave way, indicating that nineteenth-century scientific medicine was not monolithic but rather a space that entertained multiple possibilities despite efforts to arrive at definitive conclusions. The coverage of the autopsy in these documents shows that the medicalization of these famous twins contained potential for open-ended play.

3

Strange Incursions into Medical Science at the Mütter Museum

When William Pancoast and Harrison Allen finished their postmortem examination of Chang and Eng Bunker, they made sure to record the body's presence at the College of Physicians of Philadelphia before returning it to North Carolina for burial. The incisions from the autopsy were sutured, and the twins were suspended upright so that postmortem photographs—one full length and another a close-up of the incised areas—could be taken.[1] Next, sculptor and artist John Casani was hired to produce a plaster cast of the twins from the hips up, and this is now displayed in the Mütter Museum, a gallery space inside the College of Physicians of Philadelphia that is open to the public.

The two-tiered Plexiglas case holding the Bunkers' cast sits prominently in the center of the ground floor of the museum. This placement in the center, rather than along a wall, with a clear 360-degree view of all sides, permits museum guests to circle the object. The first tier of the case displays the cast so that the eye level of the twins meets the eye level of the visitors; it is positioned so that the height of the twins' likenesses are more or less congruent with that of an average adult. The second tier holds a clear container filled with a preserving liquid in which the Bunkers' shared liver is submerged. This organ is perhaps what may have been mistakenly identified as the "lungs and entrails" in the letter (discussed in Chapter 2) that the Bunker family wrote to the College of Physicians of Philadelphia following the autopsy. Off to one side is a cabinet along a wall displaying a custom-designed double chair the twins used—a well-worn and tattered wood-framed piece with a rattan seat that resembles a settee. Together, these artifacts at the Mütter Museum extend the display of conjoined anatomy well beyond the natural life spans of Chang and Eng Bunker.

In an iconic essay about the social function of the museum, Duncan Cameron presents two models of understanding how this institution engages the public. In the first, the museum operates as a "temple"—that is, a hallowed center where official knowledge is transmitted top-down, from authoritative sources to a subject population. The museum acts not only as pedagogue but also as shrine, enabling both cultural and material preservation of canonical, rarefied texts. In contrast, the second model conceives of the museum as a "forum," a populist space that promotes multiple visions of truth and value. Rather than advancing a unitary narrative of history, the forum invites visitors to question not only the epistemological status of the objects on display but also the apparatus of the museum itself. Cameron regards favorably the democratizing potential of the latter model, but he does not propose abolishing the first in favor of the second. Instead, he sees these two models of museumship as separate but dependent on each other: "While our bona fide museums seek to become relevant, maintaining their role as temples, there must be concurrent creation of forums for confrontation, experimentation, and debate, where forums are related but discrete institutions."[2]

Although as anyone who has visited even only a few museums can attest, some museums appear to fit more readily into one category than the other. This chapter begins with the assumption that the lines between the temple and the forum are more porous than Cameron suggests. Rather than existing as interdependent entities at the same time that each maintains its distinctiveness, the temple and the forum can and do coexist within a single institution, as my analyses of the Chang and Eng Bunker artifacts at the Mütter demonstrate. Ritualized spaces of display inevitably serve both functions regardless of how any given museum might ostensibly lean. However, as is evident in the interplay of power among the Mütter Museum's stakeholders, the simultaneous existence of these two models occurs not without a significant amount of tension. My discussion of how the Bunker artifacts are presented at the Mütter places them within pressing conversations about the museum's role in civic society. These objects illuminate the complex ways museum staff, medical personnel, artists, and a range of laypeople—from the average museum visitor to Chang and Eng's descendants—interact to destabilize the opposing poles of temple and forum.

The Mütter Museum's Early Audience

Founded in 1786 at the urging of physician Benjamin Rush, the College of Physicians of Philadelphia is one of the earliest professional medical organizations in the United States. Inspired by similar medical societies in Europe—much of its early membership consisted of European-trained physicians—it sought to compete with the medical vanguard across the ocean as the United States came into its own after the American Revolution. Although the organization's name would seem to suggest an institution of higher learning, the term "college" during the time of its founding meant something different from what it does today.

Whitfield Bell reports in his history of the College of Physicians that Rush had two objectives for his organization:

> As a *college*, [Rush] said, the institution would address principally matters of public concern. Thus, it might undertake a national dispensatory and offer advice to legislative bodies on matters affecting the health and happiness of the citizens, as the Royal College of Physicians of London had. . . . As a *society*, Rush went on, a wide field lay open to the members to collect and publish medical observations and inquiries.[3]

Rush's vision for how a group of elite Philadelphia physicians would function combined public health advocacy with scientific research dissemination.

The accumulation of specimens at the College of Physicians of Philadelphia began in 1849 with the allotment of fifty dollars to purchase cabinets for exhibiting medical artifacts in the main hall. During the first three years after these cabinets were installed, Isaac Parrish, a member of the society, was largely responsible for the exhibit's growth. After his death in 1852, the acquisition of artifacts stalled for a while before Thomas Dent Mütter, also a member of the society and a physician nearing retirement, donated in 1856 his materials to the college, along with a $30,000 trust to expand the space, collections, and staff.[4] Among these materials were the many wax models depicting pathological conditions, then used as teaching materials, which are today interspersed throughout the gallery.

During these early years, the vast majority of the visitors to these medical displays were physicians. The Mütter's founding and growth progressed concurrently with the consolidation of medical training in the United States. Before this time, allopathic physicians had no more cultural authority than various other health practitioners who worked with a range of different philosophies and prescribed remedies, such as purges, sweats, and bloodletting. However, the standardization of medical credentialing in the latter part of the nineteenth century turned health care into an exclusive domain for a select elite and created a new form of legitimation for a growing class of specialists.[5] There were, at the time, other venues for laypeople to view unusual bodies; this was the era when the sideshow predominated as a form of entertainment. Medical museums, such as the Mütter, worked hard to distinguish themselves from these other commercial institutions. P. T. Barnum established his American Museum in New York in 1841, and he was accompanied by numerous competitors peddling similar attractions. This lucrative popular entertainment market flourished until the wane of the sideshow's golden age in the 1930s.[6] The display of artifacts of interest to medical professionals in the stately seriousness of the College of Physicians' main hall—as opposed to the raucous floor of the ten-in-one (that is, ten acts under a single tent)—went hand in hand with this major turn of events in medico-scientific history that framed, in esoteric ways, the viewing of anatomical pathology.

Up until 1943, all the curators at the Mütter Museum had been physicians themselves. Ella Wade's appointment to this position in that year marked the first time a nonphysician held the post. She was also the first woman curator. This change in the museum's leadership corresponded to a gradual shift from an audience composed largely of medical personnel to a lay audience, although the link between the individual at the helm and the museum visitor was not simplistically causal. Records indicate that Wade, who would have been well aware of the prejudice against women in positions of medical authority, actually regarded certain lay visitors to the Mütter Museum with disdain. Anthropologist Nora Jones writes of the curator's opinion of medical students' female companions who would invariably grace the museum:

> To respond with "how marvelously fascinating!" when viewing a skull with multiple face wounds from World War I was, Ms. Wade believed, the entirely wrong reaction, and the purpose of such a visitor's tour would have to be for a reason other than that of medical interest. One of these young ladies, in fact, is described as waiting for her "medical interest" while he was in the library studying.[7]

Nevertheless, these early regulars at the museum eventually paved the way for a different institutional culture at the Mütter that led to a more widespread change in the composition of its visitors.

Jones identifies the beginnings of this transformation in a 1969 column in *Philadelphia* magazine (a local arts and culture periodical) that featured the museum. The publicity increased the number of lay visitors, and the College of Physicians decided to generate further visibility for the museum by retooling some of its exhibits and creating new ones geared specifically toward this growing audience base.[8] This change in the style of museumship was not limited to the Mütter or to medical museums in particular, however. A paradigm shift was already in place within the United States whereby the museum—as a social institution—was turning from an insular fixture that focused on the maintenance of its collection into a service that advanced the public's educational interests.[9] Thus, the tensions between the Mütter stakeholders who wanted to maintain a clinically trained audience base and those who recognized a compelling interest in expanding the museum's reach were simply part of a larger cultural-professional sensibility that encouraged museums and museum-like institutions to rethink their role in society.

The Mütter Museum's Current Audience

The modern-day Mütter Museum is publicized in a variety of ways for the average lay visitor. It appears in a number of museum and travel guides, ranging from the steadfastly serious *Medical Landmarks U.S.A.*[10] to more playful volumes, such as *Offbeat Museums*[11] and *The New Roadside America*.[12] The

Mütter is housed in a stately brownstone on South Twenty-Second Street, between Market and Chestnut Streets, in downtown Philadelphia. Although it is not in the city's museum district per se, it is within walking distance from the Benjamin Franklin Parkway, where the Philadelphia Museum of Art, the Rodin Museum, the Academy of Natural Sciences, the Franklin Institute, and other well-known museums are roughly located. There is relatively little foot traffic on South Twenty-Second Street compared to the other nonresidential in-town areas, but the city's tourism signs point visitors to the Mütter. One approaches the building through a wrought iron gate with filigree detailing. On it hangs a cast metal sign with the college's insignia. Several steps lead to a set of tall wooden double doors that are framed by Doric columns and leaded-glass windows. Like other buildings that place a premium on the beauty of the entrance, the wheelchair ramp is not immediately visible.[13] The imposing facade of the building is matched only by the expansive marble foyer inside. To the right is the front desk, and behind it are the restrooms and coatroom. Straight ahead is a grand staircase that leads to the College of Physicians' library and archives on the second floor. A velvet rope hangs across the bottom of the staircase to signal to visitors that the area beyond is off limits, but those with advance appointments to use the library materials are asked by a staff member to step over the rope and walk up if they are ambulatory; otherwise, the second floor is accessible via an elevator located behind the staircase. To the left of the entrance is the Mütter Museum gift shop, which then leads to the gallery area.[14]

This area immediately beyond the gift shop is devoted to temporary exhibitions on specific themes and topics, while the area farther back and toward the rear of the building houses the permanent collection. When I visited the museum for the first time in 1999, the temporary gallery showcased the achievements of modern technology in treating pathogen-borne illnesses. The displays were simultaneously triumphant and instructive, featuring objects from protective suiting, gloves, and headgear worn by scientists studying Ebola to a life-sized diorama of a kitchen in a modern-day household interspersed with wall text educating visitors about proper sanitation in each area. Although this exhibition would appear to align with the model of the temple as conceived by Duncan Cameron, there was also an area that encouraged the debate and interchange of a forum. A chalkboard invited museum guests to participate in a short poll. Respondents answered yes or no to questions on slips of paper that were then deposited into a wooden box. The questions regarded topics such as the favorability of irradiating produce and the barring of people who are HIV positive from entry into the United States. The answers were tallied and updated on the chalkboard on a regular basis. During the time I spent at the Mütter, I saw people responding to the questions silently on their own, and I saw groups of visitors discussing the results on the chalkboard and the political implications of prevailing public opinion.

Even when opportunities for interactive engagement and critique were not consciously designed by curatorial staff, visitors created them spontaneously.

At one point, I noticed a small group of men and women, all of whom appeared to be in their early twenties, causing a minor commotion. They were pointing and snickering with delight at something in the kitchen diorama, calling out to one another, "Come here!" and "Look at this!" The group was laughing loudly at a specific wall text. Not wanting to seem nosy, I kept a distance while pretending to look at another display until the group moved on. When I approached the wall text that had generated the hilarity, I saw that it recommended the cleaning and disinfecting of refrigerators every two weeks. Certainly, the young adults' amusement at what appeared to be overly stringent standards for household hygiene communicated to them the sense of disconnect between normative lived experience and ideals set by scientists.

During a follow-up trip to the Mütter in 2009, I saw a show called *The Devouring Element* in the temporary exhibit space. Focusing on lead as a theme, the displays addressed the scientific uses of the metal element throughout history as well as the dangers and effects of lead poisoning. Artifacts on display included paint, toys, candy, and other items containing lead. What was most immediately striking about the exhibition was the impact of the bright red walls, which seemed unsettlingly incongruous in a medical museum or any other type of museum, for that matter. The dissonance between mode of presentation and referent was magnified by the ornate frames—conspicuously decorative objects that are more common in art museums—in which wall text was displayed. However, this borrowing from the visual rhetoric of the fine arts was not employed merely for dissident refashionings of medical museum spaces. A print of Francisco Goya's well-known *Saturn Devouring His Children* hung on the wall amid the more obviously science-themed objects (lead is associated with Saturn in ancient Greek mythology).

As guests leave the temporary gallery, they cross into the room that houses the permanent collection through an entryway that opens onto an expansive two-story space, which contains mahogany-toned wood-and-glass cabinets and red carpeting. The layout encourages visitors to circumnavigate the room along the wraparound balcony to see some specimens and a set of oil paintings of prominent nineteenth-century physicians before descending the staircase to the ground-floor exhibits. The contrast between the two gallery spaces—the former displaying contemporary materials that seem at home in the age of mechanical reproduction and the latter suggesting reverent conservation of older, one-of-a-kind specimens with their aura intact—is stark and self-consciously so.

The sequence of the route through the galleries is set up so that visitors' initial contact with the intellectual labor of present-day curators and consultants primes them for an informed engagement with the medical science of times past. Within this teleologically reversed chronology, the Chang and Eng Bunker materials sit alongside other nineteenth-century artifacts, such as a large collection of skulls from anatomist and phrenologist Joseph Hyrtl,[15] a tumor removed from Grover Cleveland's jaw, an enlarged colon, the tallest skeleton owned by a North American museum, and the exhumed corpse of a woman buried in soil, the chemical composition of which transformed her body fat into soap. Fetuses with rare physical traits float inside glass jars. An extensive set of verisimilar wax models portraying dermatological diseases, many of them once belonging to Thomas Dent Mütter, are displayed alongside organic anatomical specimens, thus, troubling the lines between the real and the fake.

The Real and the Fake: Science and Art at the Mütter Museum

In his social history of the freak show, Robert Bogdan finds it useful to blur the distinction between people with genuine anatomical rarities who worked in the industry and those who "gaffed" their conditions as part of their stage routine. The very appearance of any person in a mode of ritualized performance rendered his or her arresting physical difference an act or fabrication of some sort. "Every exhibit was, in the strict sense of the word, a fraud. . . . Every person exhibited was misrepresented to the public."[16] Inverting this logic, the Mütter's organic specimens and the wax models mimicking organic tissue—seen together as part of a museum display on nineteenth-century medical history—could both be regarded as "real" insofar as the two sets of artifacts are objects from the same time period and, therefore, are legitimate primary sources for historians researching this era. However, as Bogdan might agree, these artifacts' mere presence in a museum changes them palpably. The museum turns them from objects that in their former state had a particular function or utility into objects whose primary role is to be looked at. In his critique of the visual consumption of folk art, Néstor Garcia Canclini laments the fact that "museums make people forget that pans were meant for cooking, masks for celebration, *sarapes* for warmth."[17] The ontology of exhibits, be they human or inanimate, is shaken by their decontextualization and inclusion in a space where, paradoxically, they provide the illusion of unmediated knowledge transmission.[18]

Undoubtedly, we need to be sensitive to the political ramifications of object removal, particularly when it occurs in museums displaying human remains and/or artifacts whose acquisition resulted from conquest. The extent to which curatorial agency has been (and continues to be) implicated in colonial and other forms of violence is vast. The folk objects in Canclini's example testify to the ease with which museum visitors can ignore the circumstances of their removal and, thus, ignore their own participation in that ongoing decontextualization. Similarly, the freak show patrons in Bogdan's study can forget that the humans onstage are playing characters and that these actors lead complex lives outside of their employment in show business. However, I also want to recognize the politically enabling ways in which this decontextualization—as objects become artifacts, human actors become freaks—can also generate potential for challenging static, unitary master narratives occasioned by the model of museumship Duncan Cameron calls the "temple." When the museum grapples with its changing role in society, from arbiter of knowledge to a space of open-ended discussion and back again, the status and purpose of its artifacts become a point of contention. What may be an item of scientific interest to one person may be something else to another, and the presence of multiple, competing interpretations elicits conversation about medicine, health, and the body from a wider set of voices.

In the early 1960s, the Mütter began opening its doors to artists, although their presence at first was sparse. A notice issued in 1970 by the director of the museum committee assured College of Physicians of Philadelphia fellows that the strangely clad young adults in the gallery sketching the specimens were students from the nearby Moore College of Art and Design.[19] Apparently, the sight of artists occupying a space traditionally associated with medical knowledge was unsettling to the extent that the director felt compelled to explain their presence. However, it cannot be forgotten that a century earlier, painter Thomas Eakins had established a close relationship with the Philadelphia medical community.[20] Eakins's iconic *The Gross Clinic* (1875), which depicts the eminent surgeon Samuel Gross overseeing an operation in a medical theater, is one of the most recognizable pieces in the canon of American painting. *The Agnew Clinic* (1889) portrays a similar scene with David Hayes Agnew presiding and is another widely known painting in Eakins's oeuvre. These realist paintings, striking in their resemblance to photographs, instill their subjects with an imposing air of dignity.

The relationship between art and medicine predates even Eakins, as art historian Barbara Maria Stafford shows. Crucial to European Enlightenment–era advances in medico-scientific knowledge was a corresponding visual language that made that knowledge legible. This imaging of the anatomical body did not operate prediscursively, or beyond interpretation, as it were. The optic codes that conveyed medical knowledge needed to be accompanied by a set of hermeneutic conventions for the meanings to coalesce.[21] As expected, these somatic images often generated readings that were unpredictable and polysemic, escaping the intentions with which they were created. Long before the Mütter began grappling with the question of how best to preserve and transmit the language of science through the realm of the visual, these discussions about the relationship between art and medicine were already in place.

Despite these historical connections between the clinical and the aesthetic, what the College of Physicians may have feared about the growing popularity of the Mütter Museum among artists was that the participation of laypeople would change how physicians were accustomed to engaging with the public. If the museum encouraged ways of depicting unusual anatomy that differed from what these specialists learned in medical school, the legitimation that scientific medicine enjoyed would be, in their view, undermined. Rather than maintain the representational and hermeneutic sovereignty the Mütter may have had generations earlier with a more homogenous visitor base, the museum might have been compelled to divest some of its power to assign meaning to the thousands of objects in its collection. Nora Jones's book-length study of the Mütter Museum devotes a large amount of attention to anxieties among the society's membership that accompanied this turn of events. As the openness of the Mütter leadership to artistic renditions of the artifacts increased, so did the number and profile of the artists who worked with them. Although some College of Physicians fellows voiced support for the Mütter Museum calendar (the first appearing in 1993), which featured the products of this engagement with the art world, the prevailing resistance against the aestheticization of objects traditionally under medical purview was so strong that production of the calendar was halted in 1997 before making a comeback in 2000.[22] The fact that one of the artists whose work was published in the calendar decided to enroll in medical school did not assuage these tensions. In fact, there is evidence to suggest that the presence of an artist who was also a medical student threatened the traditional wielders of medical authority all the more.[23]

If a museum's removal of an object—any object—from its context so that it can be reborn as an artifact effects an act of decontextualization that is always power laden, would artists' further appropriation of these artifacts as creative fodder not re-create and further intensify that original moment when the object was displaced? This is, of course, always the danger. Although the opening of the Mütter to the art world brought these images to a broader public in ways that democratized and demystified encounters with the museum's collections, when artists participate in discussions about the extraordinary body, they may replicate power differentials that have always attended the practice of museumship. I do want to recognize the politically enabling forms of decontextualization that artists can effect in their resignification of objects from scientific medicine's domain. However, one needs also to be careful not to uphold art as the panacea to an authoritarian, static empiricism that often accompanies science. Despite the calendar's many detractors among the society's membership, the mere presence of clinicians' resistance is not adequate evidence of art's efficacy in challenging assumptions about unusual anatomy.[24] Art, too, can potentially flatten and elide the workings of a range of social inequalities and obscure the complexities of everyday life for unusual bodies.

Fine Art Portrayals of Chang and Eng at the Mütter Museum: Rosamond Purcell and William Wegman

It is not difficult to see even from a cursory encounter with the Mütter that Chang and Eng Bunker's plaster body cast is a flagship artifact of sorts. It has been reproduced on postcards, T-shirts, tote bags, and shot glasses available for sale in the gift shop. It features prominently on the museum's website and other publicity items. Quite possibly, no other specimen gets higher billing than this rendition of the twins' likenesses.[25] The artists who have worked with this object call attention to its beauty and uniqueness alike.

Rosamond Purcell, a photographer known for aestheticizing objects of medical and scientific interest, produced a piece titled simply *Chang and Eng* in 1990. Her relationship with the Mütter is among the most extensive and long ranging of all the artists who have photographed its collections. *Chang and Eng*, one of the earliest photographs she took at the museum, comes on the heels of the first of her collaborations with the late evolutionary biologist and popular science writer Stephen Jay Gould. *Illuminations: A Bestiary* (1987) highlights artifacts in cold storage, so to speak, in the backrooms of museums as opposed to the specimens on public display, lending visibility to "information lost in partial preservation."[26] This shows that, from the beginning, Purcell's photographic portrayals of the natural world were also about the acts of sorting that occur inside institutions dedicated to its preservation. She says that, where possible, she "tried to use backgrounds or settings that would normally accompany the specimens" and that "no specimen in liquid was photographed out of its liquid,"[27] which further calls attention to the museum's mediation of knowledge. Her words from this earlier work preemptively explain her choice to photograph the Chang and Eng body cast inside its case. The plaster cast's protective cabinet, a literal mediation/barrier between the artifact and the museum visitor, is impossible to ignore in Purcell's *Chang and Eng*. Its reflective properties contribute significantly to the spectacle Purcell creates in her photograph.

Like the images in *Illuminations*, Purcell's Mütter photographs of the human form are undeniably beautiful. The images of body parts tend to have a level of uniformity in presentation and characterization regardless of the material composition of the object pictured. Whether they are of wax, plaster, bone, or soft tissue, these anatomical forms as captured on film show similarities in style and arrangement. The physical properties of these wildly divergent materials are made to resemble one another, merging the organic with the synthetic and collapsing their differences. Purcell's camera tends to shoot her subjects up close, revealing in detail the texture of the surface and lending a tactile quality to the largely visual experience of looking at photographs.

Chang and Eng is a black-and-white image of the body cast from the shoulders up (see Figure 3.1). The contrasts in shade in this photograph are stark, even severe, as the blinding white of the surfaces on which light falls—such as Eng's upper chest and Chang's face—are set against a pitch-black background. The reflection of Eng's face is clearly visible as a faint specter against the rear panel of the Plexiglas case. Although there is no doubt that the object in the foreground is plaster—cold, white, and powdery dry—its reflection in the case resembles, in some inexplicable way, flesh. The color is a soft gray, and the "skin" on Eng's chest appears smooth, even warm. While the body cast's closed eyes suggest lifelessness, Eng's reflection seems eerily to be looking back at the viewer.

The optical effect Purcell produces is twofold. First, she creates the illusion through the Plexiglas's reflective properties of there being two objects in front of her lens when, in fact, there is only one. This is a visual pun on the conundrum of conjoined twins who are two individuals and, paradoxically, one body.

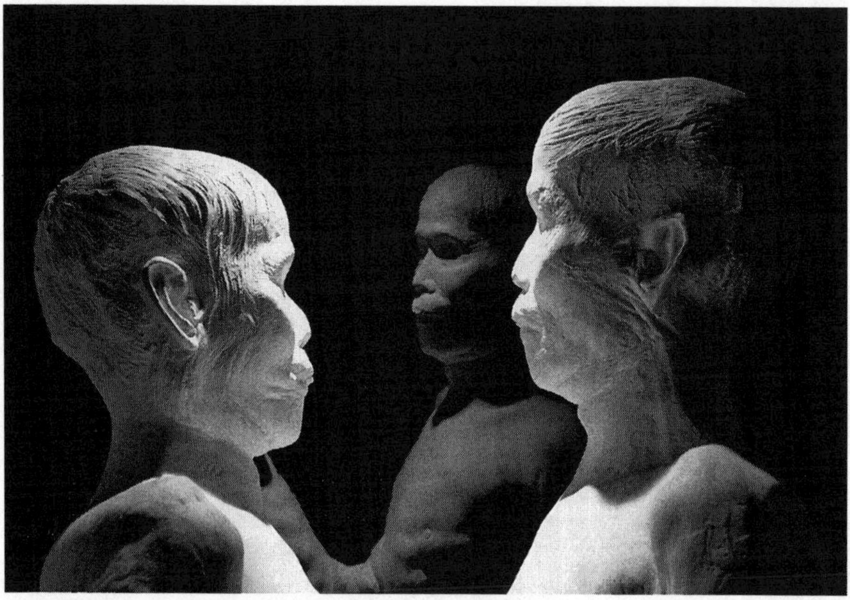

Figure 3.1 *Chang and Eng* by Rosamond Purcell. 1990. *(Reprinted by permission of the artist.)*

Second, she manages to make the immateriality of the twins' reflections seem more real, more alive, and more present than the material object depicted. It appears as if the flesh-and-blood twins, lurking behind their plaster likenesses, are keeping watch or holding a vigil to remind museum staff and visitors that they, too, have an interest in these dialogues about medical knowledge. The photograph summons the Bunkers' spectral attendance at the Mütter to ensure that these actual people behind the museum's artifact are not forgotten, that they in fact meet the "gaze" of the viewers.

At the time she photographed *Chang and Eng*, Rosamond Purcell had already established her credentials as a photographer of subjects pertaining to natural history, so it was not a stretch for her to collaborate with the Mütter in the fine art world. At the other end of this taste spectrum is William Wegman. Although Wegman has exhibited in numerous galleries internationally, he is widely regarded as a commercial photographer whose work is disseminated through the medium of decorative print culture. Many recognize his signature photographs of the posed and—often costumed—bodies of his Weimaraners not from art museums necessarily but from greeting cards, calendars, address books, photo albums, and other related consumer commodities. Given the resistance within the College of Physicians membership to what it perceived as the irreverent appropriation of the collections for nonmedical purposes, the Mütter's partnership with Wegman was probably a riskier venture than its association with Purcell. In contrast to the quiet, contemplative still lifes that

Figure 3.2 *Chang and Eng Get Together* by William Wegman. 2000. *(Reprinted by permission of the Christine Burgin Art Gallery.)*

mark Purcell's oeuvre, Wegman's photographs self-consciously exude humor and middlebrow kitsch, appealing to a different set of cultural tastes than those cultivated by Purcell and the other artists who have worked with the Mütter.

William Wegman's *Chang and Eng Get Together* (2000) also makes the reflective properties of the body cast's Plexiglas case do artistic work as it visually quotes Purcell's piece and embellishes on it (see Figure 3.2). Like Wegman's other photographs, this image is shot in color and features his posed Weimaraners. In the foreground is the plaster form, cropped a few inches below the twins' connecting ligament. The stark white of the plaster is softened by a light source that imparts a golden hue. Like Purcell, Wegman plays with how the camera can make inanimate and synthetic material resemble living organic tissue, but he does so differently from Purcell, using lighting instead of a strategically generated reflection. Wegman's canine models, identified in the caption as "Chip" and "Battina," are positioned bipedally upright behind the case and are visible in the background. The dogs are out of focus and appear in the negative space between Chang and Eng's upper chests and faces. The reflection of the body cast is superimposed on the image of Chip and Battina so that the reflection of the connecting ligament makes it seem as if the dogs are conjoined as well. In a postmodern stroke that reveals the conditions of the image's capture, Wegman himself appears in the shot. The bottom half of his face, as he shoots this photograph, is visible in the frame as a reflection on the front surface of the case.

The playful conjoining of Chip and Battina through a manipulation of the likenesses of Chang and Eng Bunker is classic Wegman, whose humor is expressed in the anthropomorphizing of his models. In fact, not only does this photograph render canine bodies as (conjoined) human bodies; it hybridizes these two species in the layering of reflective illusion on material object. The amalgamation of the canine with the human is a repetitive motif in Wegman's oeuvre as Weimaraner heads repeatedly and unsettlingly poke out of costuming that also drapes human arms and legs. Not surprisingly, the other two photographs Wegman created with Mütter artifacts similarly evoke interspecies fusion. In *Bad Foot*, Chip places a hind leg atop a sealed container displaying what is identified in the caption as a wax model of a typhus-afflicted ankle and foot. The wax form then appears to be an extension of the dog's foot. In *Kyphosified*, Battina dips her face into the pelvic girdle of a spine with degenerative kyphosis. The dull brownish gray of the skeletal specimen matches the signature hue of the Weimaraner coat, making one fade into the other. The pathological curvature of the spine is aestheticized by the placement of the dog's full-body profile in a way that complements the backbone's smooth, graceful lines. In these examples, the alive and the inanimate, the human and the dog merge. Together, they speak to the interdependency and interpenetrability between species, between the organic and the synthetic, between the living and the dead, and—ultimately—between science and art.[28]

In this sense, Wegman, who appeared on the art scene in the 1970s, seems to be anticipating, decades in advance, Donna Haraway's extended essay, "The Companion Species Manifesto," and its revised version in book-length form, *When Species Meet*, which were published in 2003 and 2007, respectively. Wegman's posthumanist play in the realm of visual/commercial art predates and, perhaps, creates the conditions for the posthumanist turn in critical theory in the academy. The first of these Haraway polemics makes intertextual reference to her earlier essay, "A Cyborg Manifesto," widely known for proposing a post-Enlightenment sensibility that privileges the interfacing of humans, animals, and machines.[29] Her later work extends this line of thinking by upholding the human-canine relationship as a model for a liberatory natural science about the symbiosis of humans with other animals—namely, domestic dogs. These challenges that recent critical theory has mounted to the anthropocentric, autonomous human suggest that Wegman, in noticeable ways, contributed to the catalyzing of these discussions organically before they entered the academy.

It is important to note that the photographer's reflection in *Chang and Eng Get Together* exposes the photograph's seams, revealing itself to be a crafted object. The visibility of the author in the image calls attention to the calculated staging that needed to happen before this image could be captured. This feature, given that it resists the conventions of realist photography, makes it impossible for the viewer to become lulled into a fantasy of having an unmediated encounter with the extraordinary body, a tendency so common when viewing anatomical images. Historian Martin Kemp writes about photography in science:

> In freak photography, the prodigious body has always drawn attention away from the image's status as an artifact, encouraging the viewer to conflate the photograph with its referent. Questions about lighting and composition inevitably diminish when the subject is conjoined twins, a microcephalic child, or a hermaphrodite. So interesting is the fact that these extraordinary figures once sat before the camera that the camera's intervention seems irrelevant. But, as we have seen, photographs never simply recorded the reality of freaks; they played an important part in creating a freakishness that represented itself as the real thing.[30]

Kemp regards the hyperrealist impetus behind the genre of "freak photography"—which hides both technology and author—as a key component in the discursive production of pathological anatomy.[31] If we take this reasoning to its logical conclusion in Wegman's *Chang and Eng Get Together*, we see that the insertion of the author into his work reveals his creative process and thus mitigates the photograph's potential to reproduce historical modes of representation that denigrate socially problematic bodies.

However, at the same time that Rosamond Purcell's and William Wegman's photographs enable post-Enlightenment, postmodern ways of looking at unusual anatomy that remove it from the hard empiricism of medical science, they may risk triggering a range of affective responses that reinscribe and reproduce historically entrenched ideas about physical difference. In Purcell's *Chang and Eng*, the ghostly image of Eng "gazing" back at the camera confronts retroactively the nineteenth-century physicians who, as I discuss in Chapter 2, used their authority in coercive ways to gain access to the Bunkers' body. But it also unsettles the layperson, one presumed to be physically normative, who is offered no contextual narrative with which to understand how twins thus configured can and do accommodate themselves to a world geared toward non-conjoined normativity. Likewise, Wegman's *Chang and Eng Get Together* elicits a lighthearted laugh in both title and visual image that makes the subjects of the photograph seem approachable, amiable, and sociable. However, the clever layering of the likenesses of the Bunkers onto Chip and Battina can also turn the real-life twins into the butt of a joke as opposed to a more serious interrogation of anatomical normalcy. Like the "Make mine a double" shot glass in the Mütter Museum gift shop, which at least one Bunker descendant finds off-putting in light of Chang's alcoholism, the humor is quick and easy. It comes at the expense of a pair of twins whose sociability with each other, contrary to what Wegman's tongue-in-cheek words suggest, was not elective.

The Nonartistry of Chang and Eng's Liver

There are no art photographs of Chang and Eng Bunker's conjoined liver. This is not to say that the liver, as humble and unassuming as it appears in its preserving fluid, is inherently incapable of being a muse—there have been quite a few art photographs taken at the Mütter that feature jarred organs—but only that the debates the liver has generated so far approach it as a different kind of object. These interchanges about the Bunkers' liver among the Mütter's different stakeholders hinge on the organ's ability to teeter-totter not between medical specimen and aesthetic object but between medical specimen and venerated ancestral remains.

For years, several descendants of Chang and Eng have been requesting that the museum relinquish the liver so that it can receive a proper burial. These appeals revive the sentiments behind Christopher Wren and Stephen Decatur Bunker's letter, discussed in Chapter 2, asking the College of Physicians for the return of their fathers' "lungs and entrails." When the Bunker family invited Mütter Museum curator Margaret Lyman to speak at its 2007 reunion, one of the issues she confronted was the feasibility of the liver's return. Footage from Josh Gibson's documentary *The Siamese Connection* shows Lyman dismissing this request as she fielded questions from the audience during a presentation:

> And it looks like [William Pancoast and Harrison Allen] kept the livers because that was the one [organ] that was unique. You just don't see many conjoined livers, and so they kept that so they could pull it out to show to their students. [*Noticeable edit at this point in the film.*] And when you think about it, you know, if you get your relative back from the mortician, and he's missing a few parts that you never see, anyway, what you would do with them if you got them back? At least I'm hoping that's the attitude you're going to adopt, because [*nervous laughter from audience*], well, there's nothing I can do.[32]

If she received a response to her stance defending the Mütter's possession of the liver or an actual answer to her rhetorical question, it seems to have been cut from the film. However, the footage does appear to show Lyman ending the question-and-answer period following her declaration that "there's nothing I can do" by turning away from the audience and proceeding to leave her position at the front of the theater.

This brief clip of Lyman's interaction with the Bunker family in *The Siamese Connection* echoes another scientific authority figure's words in the narration of what is quite possibly the most high-profile mobilization in history against museological ownership of human remains. Director Zola Maseko's *The Life and Times of Sara Baartman* was released in 1998 amid international efforts to have an indigenous Khoikhoi woman's remains returned to her ancestral home. Baartman was displayed throughout England and France in the nineteenth century under the derogatory name "the Hottentot Venus," after being lured from her native South Africa. Upon her death in 1816, the French anatomist Georges Cuvier conducted an autopsy and made a plaster cast of her body. Her brains, genitals, and skeleton were preserved and given to the Musée de l'Homme in Paris where they were on display until they were removed from public view in 1974. However, they were still housed at the museum, and it was not until 2002 that they were repatriated to South Africa and buried.

Not surprisingly, the scientific community did not initially welcome this challenge. Historian of science Sadiah Qureshi shows that the opposition to Baartman's repatriation defended the Musée de l'Homme's possession of her remains by raising concerns about the potential loss to scientific advancement.[33] Even Phillip Tobias, a scientist at the University of Witwatersrand in Johannesburg who allied himself with activists to lobby for Baartman's return, appears in Maseko's documentary qualifying his support:

> I'm not going to suggest that everybody who has ever been dug up should be put back into the ground. Science would come to a standstill if that were followed. But I believe that the government could erect a shrine for [Baartman], perhaps in Cape Town from which she was recruited to Britain, at which Khosian people could be the curators and custodians of her remains with panels reflecting this tragic history.[34]

The imperfect parallel between Baartman and other human specimens notwithstanding—Baartman was not "dug up" because she was never buried—Tobias's reluctance to support the wholesale repatriation and burial of all human remains attests to the unquestioned role of the museum in creating and disseminating information about science. Without these specimens, as the logic goes, there can be no knowledge. The tendency to preserve and guard high-profile artifacts dies hard even among those sympathetic to anticolonialist projects.

Interestingly enough, the palliative restitution Tobias suggests remains couched in the verbal and conceptual language of museumship. It appears that correcting the colonial relationship between the natural history museum and the racially charged specimen involves more appeals to other types of exhibitions. In Tobias's vision, indigenous South Africans—rather than Frenchmen—will become the "curators" of Baartman's remains held in a "shrine" and will themselves supply the narrative history that will be told through "panels" of wall text. This turns the apparatus of the museum into something that enables anticolonialist politics.

It is important not to confuse the example of Chang and Eng Bunker with that of Sara Baartman given that they occupied social locations that differed significantly from each other. Although, like Baartman, the Bunkers were recruited from their home under coercive circumstances and tapped into nineteenth-century transnational circuits of movement in the entertainment industry, Baartman never had the opportunity to assert a palpable level of control over her own display. Despite the multitude of revisionist imaginings of her story,[35] any agency ascribed to Baartman must be considered in the context of historical records. These records show a lived experience that was diametrically opposite to that of the small percentage of entertainers who were able to build a successful career in the sideshow industry.[36] Moreover, not only did Baartman and the Bunkers find themselves differently situated in the social and economic terrain of early-nineteenth-century Western Europe and the antebellum United States, respectively, but the contexts of their museological display also diverged. Baartman was exhibited in life and in death as part of a larger project prompted by nineteenth-century scientific racism. These discourses were explicitly gendered, as evidenced by the enormous amount of attention paid to her genitals. The Bunkers were racialized very differently, as I discuss in Chapter 1, particularly after their class assent and their marriage to white women.

Nevertheless, Tobias's words about Baartman imply that those who may take issue with museums about their display of venerated ancestral remains might potentially imbue these institutions with the ability to serve their interests, too. Returning to the issue of Chang and Eng's liver, this was indeed the case in at least one instance. In an e-mail communication between then–Mütter Museum curator Gretchen Worden (now deceased) and a Bunker descendant, the descendant can be observed inquiring about the possibility of conducting a DNA analysis of the body hair trapped in the plaster cast or the liver in hopes that this information will establish another record to supplement the genealogical work performed by family members.[37] There was also some mention about this data possibly assisting in the resolution of an intra-family debate over whether the twins fathered children with women they owned in their capacity as slaveholders. A forensic scientist with whom Worden consulted about the feasibility of obtaining usable DNA from an organ submerged for more than a century in preserving liquids (first, it was alcohol and formaldehyde and, later, ethanol and methanol) informed her it would not be possible. However, genetic material could be extracted from the hair.[38] These exchanges between a Bunker descendant, one who is actually a vocal proponent of having the liver returned to the family, and museum leadership show that the two sides are not at odds all the time.[39] In fact, not only can the descendant regard the museum's leadership as a resource; curator Worden—as she acts on behalf of the decendant's interests—appears to welcome the opportunity to be consulted by constituencies outside the medical world who may benefit from her scientific contacts.

Beyond the Brick and Mortar

Maintaining a commitment to dialogic interactivity between staff and visitors and among visitors themselves, the Mütter Museum has created a Facebook fan page. Among its fans are some present-day descendants of Chang and Eng Bunker. Facebook, an Internet social networking site launched in 2006, presents the Mütter with yet another means of interfacing with the public through a series of daily updates. Each member of the museum's fan page receives postings via a news feed, an area personalized for each Facebook user in which friends' activity is aggregated. A user can access the updates of any friend or fan page by clicking on the name of the person or fan site. This then directs the person to that account holder's "wall," a place where current and prior postings are displayed with the more recent ones at the top.[40] Some of the Mütter's messages provide interesting facts and figures about the museum and its collections. Others publicize upcoming events.

By far, the postings that receive the largest volume of responses on the Mütter Museum fan page are the guessing games. These present an image and a clue along with a challenge to identify the object pictured. Among the examples that have been used in these guessing games are: the tallest skeleton owned by a North American museum entreats fans to identify the medical diagnosis associated with it (acromegaly); an oil portrait from the balcony level of the permanent collection asks fans to name the subject (I volunteered William Pancoast, but it was actually Thomas Dent Mütter); and the ubiquitous specimens in jars beg identification (among these, Grover Cleveland's jaw tumor and Chief Justice John Marshall's bladder stones have made appearances). Once the Mütter's Facebook administrator initiates a challenge, fans can post their responses in comment boxes. Many of the guesses are serious attempts to answer the question, but some are made in the spirit of humor. For instance, on the day a picture of the brain of James Garfield's assassin was featured, someone responded to the question of what was in the jar by answering "the ingredients for menudo," a Latin American stew that contains tripe. Also, fans discuss together the plausibility of prior guesses and react to one another's jokes in the comment boxes.

These guessing games, yet another forum for Mütter fans to interact with one another, echo P. T. Barnum's popular *What Is It?* exhibit. From 1860 through the 1870s, a series of men of African descent (at least one of whom was intellectually disabled) performed in Barnum's American Museum as the purported "missing link" between human and ape. The costuming, props, background, and publicity for this act varied over the years, invoking not only Africa but also the indigenous Americas and other locales—even outer space—according to the whims of Barnum. Says historian James Cook, these performances invited the American public to consider how notions of civilization and savagery informed contemporaneous scientific ideas about racial difference. The performing character onstage was called a "nondescript," leaving him unnamed, and the very title of the exhibit—*What Is It?*—encouraged active participation and dialogue from audience members. Cook avers that the nondescript was a

> kind of anticategorical category whose novelty lay precisely in rendering the classification process itself equivocal, perpetual, subject to endless discussion and revision. While Barnum's audiences clearly understood What Is It? as their physical and cultural other, they also just as clearly reveled in the flexibility and open-endedness of their judgments, a somewhat paradoxical pattern which suggests that these viewers may have been up to something more than merely drawing fixed lines of racial distinction in the popular cultural sand.[41]

Although most of the framing of specimens at the Mütter is not racially inflected—for instance, Joseph Hyrtl's skull collection is really about an unfortunate moment in nineteenth-century history and not about reproducing the tenets of that history—there was one Facebook update that asked participants to identify the particular tribe from which a shrunken head had come.

A key difference between Barnum's exhibit and the Mütter's Facebook games may be that with the former, there was no final and dramatic unveiling of an ontologically correct answer. Cook finds that Barnum's coy refusal to provide his audience with an absolute definition for his nondescript was a crucial component of the act. With the Mütter's Facebook games, however, the ludic contract between the museum and its fans demands it. Thus, the Mütter's attempt at reaching out to the public through an open-ended, rhizomic, and seemingly populist forum—a social networking site—still tilts it in the direction of the model of museum as temple. Behind the question "What is it?" lies a correct answer. By taking these moments from the live performance space of Barnum's brick-and-mortar museum theater and into the very different live venue of the Internet, the Mütter implicitly references an earlier real-time participatory activity at a commercial museum, even while it maintains itself as the final arbiter of scientific knowledge. However, it is not without the expectation and urging of its fans that the Mütter exercises its authority in this way. Once, when its Facebook administrator forgot to post the answer to the daily puzzle, several fans, brimming with anticipation, cried out in mock-indignant protest.

On the Status of the Artifact

The issues accompanying the Mütter Museum's ongoing ownership and display of these Bunker artifacts ultimately speak to broader conversations about the role of museums and museum-like institutions in public life today. From earlier models of museumship that imagined the collecting, categorizing, and safeguarding of objects as a primary objective to more recent ones in which artifacts take a backseat to forms of outreach and education that rely on other means, these spaces continue to serve an important, albeit contested, social function.

Steven Conn's recent book *Do Museums Still Need Objects?* exposes a paradox about the status of the artifact in current museum practice. On the one hand, prevailing modes of museumship today may privilege interactive exhibits over objects in order to remain accountable to a wide constituency. This emphasis on democratization is partly a conscious way of ameliorating an older but still prevalent conception that museological spaces are elitist. It is also partly financial; museums are increasingly compelled to legitimate their existence to foundations and other sources of funding by stressing the broadness of their audience base. On the other hand, the diminished role that aura-imbued artifacts play in these institutions can run counter to a multiplicity that older, more traditional, models of museumship elicited. As Conn claims, "Fewer objects mean fewer opportunities for alternative stories to compete. When museum galleries were stuffed to the rafters with objects, they certainly conveyed a narrative, but with so many objects filling our visual field there well may have been more space for the accidental or unintentional for visitors."[42] The present-day downplaying of the object in museum practice may actually attest to an underlying anxiety about the loss of interpretive control—"that objects might get in the way of telling the stories they want to tell just the way they want to tell them. . . . Perhaps objects aren't presented in these museums because they can't be trusted."[43] This counterintuitive observation about the historical trajectory of the object complicates the tendency to think of changes in museums and their public reception in a linear and teleological fashion. They were never wholly temples, as in Duncan Cameron's formulation; nor are they fully forums despite their present-day proclamations of open-ended dialogism and pluralism.

The entrance of interlocutors drawn from the lay public appeared to create unease in the membership of the College of Physicians in mid-twentieth-century Philadelphia. However, the presence of these visitors from outside the ranks of medicine quickly became commonplace. As the Mütter's recent history shows, the museum is not just for physicians anymore. Stakeholders who tend to hold views diametrical to their staff can potentially see these medical authorities as resources who might advance their interests, too. Given how the Mütter and its diverse set of constituencies have interacted with one another around the Bunker exhibits and other artifacts, it is safe to say that the museum is not a monolith of scientific knowledge and does not aspire to be. Its immersion into fine art echoes much earlier connections between medicine and the visual arts even as this places the Mütter within a larger paradigm shift in museumship during the twentieth century. Although the increasing openness of the Mütter to artistic renderings of its collections reveals a certain flexibility in how it engages the public in the pursuit of medical knowledge, as the examples of Rosamond Purcell and William Wegman show, sometimes the art world is not that far removed from that of medicine when it comes to imagining physical difference. Art and medicine do not exactly go hand in hand, but scientific inquiry and the fine arts are similarly immersed in larger trends having to do with the anomalous body in society.[44]

Part II

Reading Literature and Visual Cultures

4

Late-Nineteenth-Century Visions of Conflict and Consensus

Chapters 2 and 3 cover how Chang and Eng Bunker's corporeal body was interpreted by professionals and laypeople alike within medically oriented spaces. From Harrison Allen and William Pancoast's report of their autopsy, to the experiences of visitors at the Mütter Museum, to the photography of Rosamond Purcell and William Wegman, a cacophony of voices and meanings crosscut the Bunker twins at every turn. We see that medicine, like all cultural institutions, is far from being a totalizing system of domination and regulation. Rather, it is a forum that entertains multiple voices, weighs and balances competing interests, and opens up space for debate even as it implicates itself in hierarchies that unevenly privilege and subjugate physicians, patients, and laypeople.

Part II, "Reading Literature and Visual Cultures," looks at the interplay of ideas and power, turning attention from the physical, anatomical presence of Chang and Eng Bunker to their ethereal traces in the arts and culture of the United States. Even if, as Robert Bogdan argues, the consolidation of medical training triggered a chain of events that all but put the freak show out of business,[1] laypeople continued to indulge their fascination with unusual bodies in other public venues.[2] One of these is the realm of print culture. These nonmedical portrayals of the Bunkers from the mid-nineteenth century to the present operate as a counterpoint to the medical sources referenced in previous chapters. The literary and visual texts here progress fuguelike alongside medical science, but these nonmedical sources do not necessarily rescue or reclaim the Bunkers from the clinical lenses through which they have so commonly been seen. The fact remains that physicians and laypeople informed each other in knowledge production about physical difference. Just as evidence of nonscientific concerns were apparent in medical tracts documenting Chang and Eng Bunker's body, the scientific at times would seep into the literary, and the two would show their interdependence.

This chapter presents portrayals of Chang and Eng Bunker by nineteenth-century white American authors who saw their symbolic potential for conceptualizing unity and collaboration in the face of disunity and disagreement. The range of print media in which representations of Chang and Eng are found in nineteenth-century American culture includes newspapers; advertising posters; souvenir booklets; trading cards; and other portrayals of the twins in verse, drama, and fictional prose. I examine two texts from this motley collection: Mark Twain's essay, "Personal Habits of the Siamese Twins" (1869), and Thomas Nast's political cartoon, "The American Twins" (1874). Although both texts invoke a reconciliatory politics during times of civil unrest, they demonstrate an uneasy ambivalence about the national unity they advocate. Both reveal an unspoken concern about the nation's inability to contain racial and other forms of difference while calling for harmonious interconnectedness among all Americans. The texts, appearing after the midpoint of the nineteenth century, acknowledge the presence of social upheaval and the inequalities behind it if only to offer or—perhaps—parody a resolution that falls short of its mark. These invocations of Chang and Eng Bunker in the literary and visual arts are unstable and ambiguous in ways similar to how their physical body escaped static definition by anatomists. Any attempt to harness this figure for significatory purposes always undoes itself in the gaps and indeterminacies that language opens up.

Racial Representation in the Nineteenth Century

The cover for one of Chang and Eng's publicity pamphlets sports a line drawing of the American eagle under which the words "United We Stand" are printed. The jingoism behind the pairing of these words with this image, a combination that elicits humor, is not lost on cultural critic Allison Pingree.[3] When the reader of the pamphlet turns the page, an image of the famous twins, the true subject of the text, comes into view. In this artifact, a tongue-in-cheek invocation of U.S. patriotism sells a pair of performers who, because of anatomical and racial difference, do not immediately come to mind as symbols of American national pride. Yet it is precisely the incongruity of word with image that begs further consideration. What happens when the inverse takes place, when Chang and Eng are deployed to sell an Anglo-American vision of nation? What are the implications for conceptualizing a cohesive America by alluding to these unusual twins?

Twain and Nast show that this dynamic necessitates the erasure of the Bunkers' racial difference. The twins, in effect, engage in whiteface performance through the use of their body as literary and visual metaphor, even as these metaphors continue to rest on their palpable and visible distance from whiteness. Not unexpectedly, this whitening underscores the subject's further difference from actual whiteness. For the twins to occupy this role as exemplars of U.S. national pride, they must be positioned in proximity to an Anglo-American universality. The process the Bunkers undergo to pass from one racial category to another is not incidental in Twain's "Personal Habits of the Siamese Twins" or in Nast's "The American Twins." Rather, it is crucial to the spirit of reform behind these texts. That the twins are transformed and reformed through becoming white signals the transformative and reformative potential they have as metaphor. At the same time, the inconsistency between Chang and Eng's actual racial categorization and their representation in arts and letters casts into higher relief the gulf between the races.

Mark Twain's essay and Thomas Nast's cartoon appeared during the postbellum events of reconstruction and industrial growth. The Bunkers' racialization in both texts rests on and reinforces ideas that were widely circulating about Asian-raced labor during this period. As ethnic Chinese subjects from what was then known as the kingdom of Siam, the Bunkers already would have been differentiated from other Chinese people living in the United States at the time. More important, their class identity was what set them apart. Across the United States and its territories, Chinese migrants functioned largely as exploited noncitizen labor, and their racial difference within the expanding economy was harnessed by capitalists to divide and conquer a racially and ethnically heterogeneous workforce. This economy positioned Chinese workers in ways that undermined the efforts of working-class whites and emancipated blacks in a variety of industries, such as the plantation, the railroad, and the laundry.[4]

Americans in the second half of the nineteenth century would have been familiar with the figure of the "Chinaman." It was a fairly recent construction at the time both Twain and Nast were writing. Images of Asian people underwent considerable transformation between the Jacksonian era and the period after the Civil War. Before the advent of Chinese immigration to California in 1849, "China," in the Anglo-American imagination, was associated with luxury and opulence. At this time, China dominated international trade, dealing in commodities such as spices, tea, silks, and porcelain that were the domain of the upper classes in the United States and other countries. Moreover, the ongoing projects of U.S. expansion in the early 1800s were motivated largely by a desire to compete with China, which was then the world's leading economic stronghold.[5] Perceptions of China in these years rested on what were then the country's primary exports to North America—not labor but luxury goods. When Chang and Eng Bunker first arrived in Boston in 1829, "China," for Anglo-Americans, did not yet signify the dirty, disease-ridden "coolie." Instead, it signified wealth. Not unexpectedly, this Asian conjoined body on public display in the 1830s was contextualized in a way that referenced the international flow of goods and capital that supported the consumption habits of the Anglo-American owning classes.

Some of the past scholarship in Asian American studies on Chang and Eng emphasizes their presence alongside another contemporaneous Chinese performer, Afong Moy, to show how nineteenth-century audiences received Asian-raced human curiosities.[6] Starting in 1834, U.S. urbanites had the opportunity to observe a young woman in popular venues, such as Barnum's American Museum and Peale's Museum. Of particular interest were her bound feet, a physical anomaly invoking highly sexualized fantasies of Chinese patriarchal rule and female submission. An 1835 lithograph depicts Moy dressed in a long silk gown and seated on a stage designed to look like a parlor containing random chinoiserie: painted scrolls, patterned curtains, large porcelain planters, a Chinese lantern, and an oriental rug. A turret evocative of North African architecture hangs over the stage, and beside Moy is a round table covered with a sheer lace tablecloth on which rest a dainty teapot and cup. Likewise, some of the contemporaneous lithographs of the young Chang and Eng show them similarly framed by the trappings of early-nineteenth-century class respectability.

Social historian John Kuo Wei Tchen points out that this widely circulated image of Afong Moy, presumably in her habitat, appears ironically to conform more accurately to the interior decor of class-privileged white Americans than to that of actual Chinese people. "Yet to the Anglo-American eye," notes Tchen, the setting appears to be according to "Chinese taste."[7] There is a paradox that accompanies these Chinese bodies as objects of mass consumption. On the one hand, a large part of the appeal of the Bunkers and Afong Moy stemmed from their association with the upper echelons of Anglo-American society and the exclusivity that accompanied this association. The stage resembling a parlor and the props of Chinese-originated decorative objects found in the sitting rooms of upper-class white Americans implied restricted access. On the other hand, the economically diverse cross section of American society that would have made up the spectators at events showcasing the Bunkers or Afong Moy allowed these performers to be available to anyone who could afford the nominal entry fee. As Rosemarie Garland-Thomson observes, nineteenth-century sideshows were populated largely by immigrants and the working classes.[8] However, by alluding to the upper classes in the Bunkers' and Afong Moy's public presentations, sideshows made the trappings of privilege vicariously accessible to almost all.

The juxtaposition of the Bunkers with Afong Moy is a logical and plausible maneuver given the many similarities between their venues and the stylization of their performances. However, I suggest that a more productive pairing may have been of Chang and Eng Bunker with another set of Chinese bodies also circulated for visual consumption in the nineteenth century. Historian Lucy Cohen reports that during the 1840s, Christian missionaries, particularly from the American South, were involved in evangelizing missions in China. On regular occasions, missionaries would return to the United States with converts in tow, and they would conduct tours with them to legitimize and raise more funds for their ongoing efforts abroad. Although these early Chinese visitors to the United States traveling with missionaries tended to return to their homeland after their tour was over, some converts remained in the United States as theology students and eventually became missionaries themselves.[9]

The spectacle of the heathen made civil—indeed, the heathen-turned-civilizing-agent—presents another way to read portrayals of Chang and Eng Bunker in the literary and visual record. The odd trajectory of their lives from Siamese village boys to Victorian-era Christian gentlemen was, for many, a fascinating transformation. Unlike Afong Moy, whose stage act relied on her fixed inscription as a foreign object as she spoke in Chinese and ate with chopsticks for the amusement of her spectators, the Bunkers performed interactively with their English-speaking audience members, telling jokes and engaging in light banter. Even though they were able to engage their audience in ways that suggested redemptive conversion and reform, their racial difference continued to haunt their depictions in nineteenth-century American arts and culture. This image of the redeemed yet troublingly irredeemable body became a useful trope for social commentary on the state of national affairs during this tumultuous period.

The history of immigration and naturalization law has shown that migrants from Asia were barred from U.S. citizenship, whereas Europeans were not. This is because of the belief that Asians were resistant to assimilation. However, these counternarratives featuring Chang and Eng Bunker reveal evidence of competing stories. It was precisely these allusions to the alleged redemptive and transformative potential of Asian people in these contexts that made representations of the Bunker twins ripe for literary and visual appropriation during the Industrial Revolution. As the nation grappled with the question of how to contain difference and dissent, Mark Twain and Thomas Nast found ways to adopt Chang and Eng as tropes that signal an uneasy unity across a heterogeneously constituted population.

Mark Twain: Fascination with Conjoinment during the American Renaissance

Neither Twain nor Nast was the first to look to Chang and Eng Bunker as muses for their work. The countless pamphlets promoting the twins' appearances that were authored pseudonymously or anonymously seem to be the earliest pieces of imaginative writing about them. The Bunkers make cameo appearances in Herman Melville's fiction; they are named in *The Confidence-Man* and "Billy Budd"; and they exist as thinly veiled allusions in *Moby-Dick*, as can be seen in the second epigraph I have chosen for this book. In a scene in *The Confidence-Man*, one man needing support to stand is invited by another to take his arm: "It was taken; and the two stood together; the old miser leaning against the herb-doctor with something of that air of trustful fraternity with which, when standing, the less strong of the Siamese twins habitually leans against the other."[10] In "Billy Budd," the notorious John Claggart, vexed with contrasting emotions toward his rival, Billy Budd, has his state of mind described by the omniscient narrator: "Now envy and antipathy, passions irreconcilable in reason nevertheless may spring conjoined like Chang and Eng in one birth. Is Envy then such a monster?"[11] Then in *Moby-Dick*, Ishmael's conjoinment with Queequeg, balancing precariously as he struggles to spear the whale, means that Ishmael would slip and perish, too, if the companion he anchored fell while engaged in his dangerous task.

The first passage, which references Chang's dependency on Eng,[12] portrays conjoinment as a parasitic state that is not altogether unfavorable to the stronger man given that the herb doctor then uses this gesture of charity to self-congratulatory advantage. The second passage sees conjoinment as dangerous and monstrous because it yokes together opposing forces that—as the conclusion to "Billy Budd" reveals—result in disastrous consequences. The third reinforces the homosocial/homoerotic interdependency of the racially mixed crew of the *Pequod*. The codes of honor of such a whale-spearing endeavor necessitate "that instead of cutting the cord, [the fall] should drag [Ishmael] down in its wake."[13] In these examples, Melville elicits a vast range of affect—sympathy, loathing, fear, and affection—showing that even within the work of a single author, there is considerable variance with which interconnectedness is perceived. It can be valued, exploited, disavowed, managed, or endured.

Mark Twain's fascination with Chang and Eng Bunker, and with twins in general, was more extensive than Melville's. In 1889, he introduced two writers, James Whitcomb Riley and Edgar Nye, at a Boston reading. Alluding to how they influenced each other creatively, Twain playfully called them "Mr. Eng Nye" and "Mr. Chang Riley." During a party on New Year's Eve 1907 in New York, Twain appeared onstage in a performance with an unnamed guest. The two men dressed in white, and a pink sash symbolizing Chang and Eng's connecting ligature tied them together.[14] These public antics postdate the death of the Bunkers in 1874 by fifteen and thirty-three years, respectively, showing that their household-name popularity survived long beyond the period during which they would have been available for live viewing.

The theme of doubling and twinning throughout Twain's work has already received much attention. His novels, *The Tragedy of Pudd'nhead Wilson* and *Those Extraordinary Twins* (both published in 1894), have generated a considerable amount of academic scholarship.[15] As Twain discusses in the preface to *Those Extraordinary Twins*, the inspiration for his characters, Angelo and Luigi, originated in a picture he saw of "a youthful Italian 'freak' or 'freaks'—which was—or were—on exhibition in our cities—a combination consisting of two heads and four arms joined to a single body and a single pair of legs."[16] Here, Twain refers to Giovanni and Giacomo Tocci, sideshow celebrities from Italy who toured throughout Europe and the United States. In a performative wrestle with object-verb agreement, Twain calls attention to the central conundrum about conjoined twins. Are they singular or are they plural? Even though he locates the germ of *Pudd'nhead Wilson* and *Those Extraordinary Twins* in his reaction to a photograph of the Toccis, who were actually born four years after the Bunkers died, his long-time fascination with twins predated his writing of these two novels. *Pudd'nhead Wilson* and *Those Extraordinary Twins* share striking similarities with "Personal Habits of the Siamese Twins," which seems to be a rough draft of sorts for these novels. All three texts foreground the inseparability of self and other and raise questions about how difference can be reconciled, be it with violence or with negotiation.

"Personal Habits of the Siamese Twins" appeared in *Packard's Monthly* in 1869 and was later republished in Twain's 1875 collection, *Sketches New and Old*, under the title "The Siamese Twins." This satiric piece, which playfully purports to be biographical, contains many anecdotes—some real, others embellished, and many purely fictional—about Chang and Eng Bunker that were widely circulated during their career. The jokes that prevail throughout Twain's essay are tongue in cheek as he writes of, among other things, the twins' contrasting dispositions, the fact that one is active and the other sedentary, their courtship of the same woman, and the trickiness of holding different religious beliefs when baptism is involved.

However, under the deadpan humor that is Twain's signature style, the essay acknowledges the existence of ongoing sectional strife in the wake of the Civil War and reveals mixed feelings about the occasion of Asian migration to the American continent. It makes a crucial link between the contemporaneous events of North/South reconciliation along the Eastern seaboard and the influx of noncitizen labor on the California coast. The rendering of the Bunkers' anatomy, two individuals cohabiting one body, into a metaphor that describes competing factions within one nation exemplifies the paradox of national unity with which many Americans struggled during the latter part of the nineteenth century. Similarly, the invocation of readily recognizable Asian stereotypes points to the contrasting sentiments middle-class white Americans held about a foreign race of workers who were transforming the economy of the continent.

The essay is a thinly veiled allegory about sectional factionalism during and in the wake of the Civil War. In an episode, Chang, described as fighting for the Confederate side, and Eng, fighting for the Union side, take each other prisoner, and a jury is summoned to decide who is legitimately the captor and who the captive.[17] The injunction that comes after prolonged deliberation considers them both prisoners of each other and orders their exchange. On the surface, this nonsensical solution to the definitive crisis of the nineteenth century appears to resolve itself in a facile way. However, the absurdity of this outcome suggests a reading of Twain's essay as a parody of the reconciliatory sentiment that prevailed at the time.[18] By making readers uneasy about the underlying tensions within a nation that continued to struggle with its internal divisions, the essay satirizes contemporaneous cultural productions about reunion. At the same time that the war is resolved in a way that does not upset the antebellum order, the differences between factions are trivialized so that they become no more significant than, for instance, the fact that Chang is an early riser while Eng prefers to sleep in. The essay goes on to describe a fictional fistfight between Chang and Eng. Several bystanders who witness the altercation try to separate the twins—writes Twain in his usual deadpan manner—but, of course, they are unsuccessful. They continue to fight each other and wind up hospitalized with severe injuries. Despite its skeptical stance toward facile celebrations of reconciliation, the essay shows there is real threat of injury in disunity. This scene serves as a cautionary tale during a moment of national crisis.

Since the essay invites itself to be read as an allegory between the Northern and Southern states, it also raises important questions about moral responsibility and accountability in other scenarios. Despite the difficulties and negotiations that accompany conjoined life, Twain notes that there are some advantages to being thus connected. Unusual anatomical constitution works in the twins' favor when Chang is sentenced to a jail term to which Eng protests unfair imprisonment. This loophole gets the both of them freed, and Chang escapes punishment. In another passage, Twain describes the predicament the twins face in their contrasting drinking habits, describing Chang as a staunch teetotaler and Eng as an alcoholic.[19] Chang's membership in a temperance society is questioned when members find him in a state of unruly inebriation, and the question of whether Chang should be held accountable for his drunkenness arises. Since it was Eng who had imbibed the alcohol, the temperance society concluded that Chang should be considered blameless even though his level of intoxication is equal to that of his brother's.[20] He did not choose to become drunk, and therefore, his "moral principles were unsullied, his conscience clear; and so all just men were forced to confess that he was not morally, but only physically, drunk."[21]

It is within a moral economy based on agency, or its lack thereof, that the distinction between moral drunkenness and physical drunkenness makes sense. Eng is drunk; both his breath and his behavior indicate it, but "by every right and moral evidence the man was strictly sober."[22] Here, personal choice and individual agency become the gold standard by which culpability is determined. If the teetotaler brother cannot be considered "morally" drunk when his conjoined sibling drinks, then he is absolved of any kind of blame in having the physical characteristics of drunkenness. Twain's portrayal of how the temperance society resolves this moral dilemma hints at the dissatisfaction with which decisions concerning blameworthiness are made. Not only can Chang be excused for his intoxication; he is—in fact—*victimized* by it. He is nevertheless affected by the alcohol in ways that are shameful, "caus[ing] his friends all the more anguish to see him shake hands with the pump and try to wind his watch with his night-key."[23]

When this moral dilemma is transposed onto the interconnectedness of the Northern and Southern economies, bloodstreams of a different sort, the implications of assigning blame and accountability become more pressing. Chang and Eng's situation, two individuals sharing one body, can then be correlated to that of the United States whereby Union and Confederate, one free and one slaveholding, share one nation. Although the Northern states had, one by one, abolished slavery in the late 1700s and early 1800s, industrial growth in Northern urban centers after emancipation was connected to slave economies that persisted in the South. Cotton harvested by the slaves was transported to milling factories in New England and other parts of the Union. These factories, in turn, spun the thread, wove the cloth, and sewed the garments to be shipped back and worn by the slaves. Shackles used to restrain slaves were forged in Northern foundries and sold to slaveholders in the South. The movement of goods and capital between the states fueled the Northern Industrial Revolution, implicating the North in the South's deployment of slave labor.[24] These channels of cross-regional trade raise the question of moral culpability in much the same way as the scenario Twain sets up in his essay.

The drunkenness scenario begs the question "How accountable should one be held for the effects of another's actions?" It is unclear whether Mark Twain himself was making the connection between the Northern states' complicity with slave labor and the leniency with which the judicial system and the temperance society place accountability in this fictional case. If "Personal Habits of the Siamese Twins," intentionally or not, exonerates the Union for its ongoing reliance on a slave economy, a similar incident in *Those Extraordinary Twins* would suggest the opposite. Angelo and Luigi, who share a pair of legs, become defendants in a trial when another character is kicked. The trial attempts to discern who did the kicking. Had the kick been initiated by one of the brothers, or had it been a joint kick? In the last scene of the novel, Luigi is sentenced to a hanging for an entirely different offense. However, unlike the way in which both Chang and Eng are freed when Eng protests unfair imprisonment, Angelo is hanged alongside Luigi in the novel's satiric-comic ending.

While "Personal Habits of the Siamese Twins" resolves these questions of complicity and accountability in ways that are purposefully unsettling, the more direct and overt message in this essay comes through rather unproblematically to a specific audience base. Although the Civil War and its immediate aftermath affected everyone living in the United States, the war is commonly conceptualized as a struggle between Northern white men and Southern landowning white men. Even though men of all racial categories were enlisted in the military efforts, the warring factions of the United States are assigned an Anglo-American subjectivity.[25] Accordingly, the intended reader to whom this essay speaks is assumed to be white.[26]

Twain addresses this audience directly several times. After praising the twins' ability to be accommodating in light of their conjoinment, he exclaims, "And yet these creatures were ignorant and unlettered—barbarians themselves and the offspring of barbarians, who knew not the light of philosophy and science. What a withering rebuke is this to our boasted civilization, with its quarrelings, its wrangling, and its separations of brothers!"[27] The Bunkers, as noble savages, sit on an opposing end of a binary that puts the intended addressee on the other. The first person plural in this passage hails an imagined community consisting of an Anglo-American polity, "our boasted civilization." Twain's target audience is one that is removed from the "barbarian" twins here, and it is a distinction he makes along hierarchical lines. However, as much as this portrayal of the Bunkers conjures pernicious colonialist fantasies, it is also these "barbarians" who must redeem Anglo-America as it struggles to restore itself in the wake of the Civil War. Despite, or because of, this distancing mechanism, Chang and Eng are able to function as role models in this capacity. Twain closes his essay with a pointed caution: "There is a moral in these solemn warnings—or, at least, a warning in these solemn morals; one or the other. No matter, it is somehow. Let us heed it; let us profit by it."[28] During this time of national healing, the white citizens of the United States needed to embrace this model of racial, cultural, and anatomical difference and bury the hatchet that threatened the goal of reunification.

Illustrations printed in the first edition of *Sketches New and Old* depict the Bunkers with European features. In one of the drawings, they are courting a young Southern belle. The image presents no phenotypical difference between the woman and the twins—a curious nondepiction of a potential act of miscegenation among three people (see Figure 4.1). The visual similarity between the twins and the white woman is disarming in light of the anecdotal evidence suggesting that before the Bunkers' wedding to Sarah and Adelaide, the townsfolk worried more about their racial difference than about their unusual anatomy.[29] Although Twain's essay relies on maintaining a racial split between the twins and the white readership it addresses, this lack of correlation between the written text (which upholds a racial divide between the twins and white people) and the visual text (which elides this difference) indicates that the twins' racialization was a slippery phenomenon, shifting even within the space of one short essay.[30] This image of Chang and Eng Bunker in whiteface shows how this figure of racialized conjoinment was used in nationalist narratives of conflict and reconciliation.

Three years after "Personal Habits of the Siamese Twins," Twain published *Roughing It*, a nonfictional travel account of his time spent in the western frontier. In it, he expresses outrage at the treatment of Chinese laborers in California by unsympathetic whites even as he perpetuates the racism behind that kind of abuse. However, the "Chinaman" figure in *Roughing It* is not framed as a role model as the Bunkers are in "Personal Habits of the Siamese Twins." Rather, he is an object of pity. The Chinaman allows the intended addressee—again, white middle-class America—to congratulate itself. "No Californian gentleman or lady," notes Twain, "ever abuses or oppresses a Chinaman, under any circumstances. . . . Only the scum of the population do it."[31] It is through an expression of tolerance that the white bourgeoisie distinguishes itself from the poorer whites (often coded as Irish), who are pitted against other disenfranchised groups by the interests of capital. Conversely, *Ah Sin: The Heathen Chinee* (1877), a play coauthored by Twain and Bret Harte, which premiered

Figure 4.1 Illustration from Mark Twain's *Sketches New and Old.* 1875. *(Courtesy of the Special Collections Library, University at Buffalo.)*

at the National Theater in Washington, D.C., is overtly (rather than quietly) racist. Written for Charles T. Parsloe, one of the most prominent Chinese impersonators at the time, the play makes no attempts to hide its reliance on the conventions of yellow-face minstrelsy or its hostile reification of male Chinese stereotypes.[32] As Twain's body of work shows, the lines between gentlemanly respectability and unrefined lower-class sensibility can easily be crossed. Because the Asian body, despite its redemptive potential during certain moments, was cast as an outsider in the nineteenth-century imagination, the national unity that Twain prescribes in "Personal Habits of the Siamese Twins" can be harnessed only by those for whom the privileges of a claim to the United States has already been cemented.

Chang and Eng Bunker were invoked as exemplary and universal examples for white America not only because of their racial and cultural foreignness but also because of their anatomical difference. Despite the fact that Twain never explicitly names the twins' physical constitution,[33] relying on his audience's familiarity with a pair of celebrities who achieved widespread fame, the rhetorical effectiveness of Twain's essay would have been lost, for example, had he featured nonconjoined twins with normative bodies. His valorization of the Bunkers is possible only insofar as they are presumed to be branded by the mark of overwhelming physical difference. More strikingly, the logic of Twain's essay runs counter to William Pancoast's conclusion about the moral imperative behind surgically separating the twins as I discuss in Chapter 2. While Pancoast would have been inclined to see such a medical intervention attempted despite its risks because of his disdain for the Bunkers' non-normative sexual practices, separation is most emphatically not an option in "Personal Habits of the Siamese Twins." Given the nation's concerns about the difficulties of reunification, the awkwardness surrounding Chang and Eng's romantic pursuits, which Twain touches on without shock or distaste, pales in comparison to the potential dangers of ongoing sectional strife.

Thomas Nast: Alluding to Conjoinment during the Labor Movement

Political cartoonist Thomas Nast took an interest in Chang and Eng Bunker during this same time period, but the competing factions that concern him are those of the working classes and the owning classes. Even though relations between the Northern and the Southern states remained tense long after the Civil War, another type of struggle for political ascendancy arose during the postbellum era. The Panic of 1873 abruptly ended the brief period of postwar industrial prosperity and left countless numbers of workers unemployed. Laborers clashed frequently and violently with the state and with owners of business and industry. Among the most infamous of events were the Tompkins Square rally in 1874, during which dozens of unemployed workers were injured by New York city police officers, and the Chicago Haymarket Square bombing of 1886, which resulted in eight fatalities. This period of class turmoil displaced the Reconstruction fantasy of national unity. Attempts to achieve reunion of North and South crumbled under the realization that there were once again two nations, one rich and one poor.[34]

Against this social and economic backdrop, Thomas Nast, one of the most vocal antagonists of socialism, published the political cartoon "The American Twins." It uses a patriotic logic similar to that of Twain's essay in an attempt to quell the rebellions that punctuated major industrial centers after the Civil War. Nast enjoyed a long, prolific career as an illustrator, and many readily recognizable images in American mass culture are credited to him. He created the image of Santa Claus as the rotund, bearded man that children in the United States have grown to recognize as well as the Tammany tiger and the Republican elephant. During the Civil War, he generated reelection posters for Abraham Lincoln, and in the years afterward, he developed a reputation for being one of the most fervent opponents of organized labor. His antisocialist cartoons regularly graced the pages of periodicals such as *Harper's Weekly.* "The American Twins," a cartoon carrying a loaded message about the undesirability of organized labor, appears in that publication on February 7, 1874. When read in conjunction with some of Nast's other antilabor cartoons, this reference to Chang and Eng Bunker appears to be part of a larger class-based sensibility that encouraged factions among the working poor in order to maintain economic hierarchies.

"The American Twins" depicts two white men standing side by side: one wearing a worker's apron and wielding a hammer in his well-muscled grasp and the other clad in a suit and top hat and carrying a bag of money (see Figure 4.2). Connecting the men at their chests at the location where Chang and

Figure 4.2 "The American Twins" cartoon by Thomas Nast. *Harper's Weekly,* February 7, 1874. *(Courtesy of the University of Michigan Libraries.)*

Eng were joined is a band containing the words "The Real Union." The words "Labor" and "Capital" are placed over the men's respective heads to stress what each figure represents. The caption reads, "United we stand, Divided we fall."[35] Whereas the words "United we stand" had once appeared alongside the American eagle in a publicity pamphlet for the Original Siamese Twins, invoking patriotism to sell Chang and Eng Bunker's onstage identities, the words return here in a text that inverts that relationship. The Bunkers now sell a particular brand of patriotism, one that serves industrial expansion.

The two men in Nast's cartoon appear to be middle-aged, and they resemble each other in physical appearance. Both have the same facial creases and jawline, deep-set eyes, and prominent nose, although the man representing capital is more rotund. Despite their physical similarities, they are definitely not identical twins; the noticeable differences in appearance between the worker and the capitalist force the reader to regard this illustration as strictly figurative. Both men wear the same calm, almost solemn, expression, indicating their acceptance of this interlocked condition. The man representing labor stands slightly taller, but the top hat worn by the man representing capital creates a semblance of symmetry in the image. The laborer more so than the factory owner seems to possess features that signify Irishness. This is a telling aspect of Nast's cartoon, given his overt hostility toward Irish immigrants in some of his other work, but the two men could conceivably be brothers even if they could not be (identical) conjoined twins.[36]

This image conjoining factory worker and factory owner appeared in *Harper's Weekly* five years after the first publication of Twain's "Personal Habits of the Siamese Twins" in *Packard's Monthly*. The temporal proximity of these two texts is no surprise. Like Twain's essay, "The American Twins" uses a metaphor of conjoined twinning to imagine unity across politically divisive lines, but rather than treating as the problem the continued faction between North and South, as Twain's essay does, "The American Twins" strives to bring together the interests of the working classes with those of the owning classes. Not really a benign vision of unity, the message this cartoon conveys invalidates the efforts of labor unions. Nast uses patriotic rhetoric in his caption "United we stand, Divided we fall" to mandate that workers form loyalties with their employers, effecting "The Real Union," rather than alliances with one another that would slow the pace of production.

The first person plural in the caption of "The American Twins" is similar to that in Twain's "Personal Habits of the Siamese Twins." Who is the "we" that stands in unity but falls when divided? Presumably, it is an imagined community consisting of an inclusive U.S. body politic. However, in Nast's case, the white specificity of his logic is even more explicit and less ambivalent than in Twain's text, which portrays Chang and Eng Bunker's race in uneven ways. The two human figures representing labor and capital in "The American Twins" are unambiguously white even though the labor force at this time of intense industrialization was racially mixed. Imagine for a moment the likelihood that

Nast would have drawn a cartoon depicting a Chinese worker connected to a white capitalist. The implausibility of that image suggests a white normativity in Nast's call for cross-class solidarity. Also, the gender specificity in "The American Twins" is significant given that a sizable number of women participated in the labor movements of the late 1800s. The white male laborer depicted in the cartoon, then, represents a working class that was, in reality, mixed with respect to race, ethnicity, and gender.

Like Twain, Nast positioned himself as a sympathetic supporter of Chinese laborers in the United States. As with the depictions of the Chinese in *Roughing It,* some of Nast's cartoons express outrage at the victimization of the Chinese by whites even as they similarly keep racist stereotypes intact. One reason Nast may have decried the treatment of the Chinese is that industrialists often used them as strikebreakers throughout the latter part of the nineteenth century. That the Chinese filled this need in capitalist expansion would have been regarded favorably in Nast's antiunion politics. In fact, one of his earlier cartoons depicts enthusiastically the first mass arrival of Chinese migrants to the East Coast, in 1870, to break a shoe factory strike in Lowell, Massachusetts. White-organized unions during this period were vocal in their support of the series of Chinese exclusion laws that the U.S. federal government signed into effect starting in 1882.[37] Many of these labor organizations actively excluded Mexican, black, and Asian workers from their membership, and this failure of intra-class solidarity allowed workers from different racial and ethnic categories to be pitted against one other. I am not claiming that Nast defended the well-being of the Chinese only because they functioned to thwart the efforts of the white working class. However, his sympathy conveniently situates itself within a sensibility that supports white capital. In the end, Nast's championing of Chinese workers' interests seems to be another way the white-owning class asserted its leverage. The utopian vision of cross-class solidarity that he prescribes in "The American Twins" bespeaks both a class-privileged and an Anglo-American masculine subjectivity.

As with Twain's "Personal Habits of the Siamese Twins," Nast's cartoon rests on an assumption that the anatomical anomaly depicted here, two bodies conjoined, cannot be considered something to be feared, gawked at, pitied, or medically altered by separation. The calm expressions on both factory owner and factory worker suggest that the interdependency of these economic positions is just part of the natural order of things. Nast calls the conjoining of these two contingents "The Real Union," riffing on the banter and open-ended debate that was part of spectatorship at sideshows ("Is it real, or is it fake?").[38] However, any kind of ambiguity that sideshow performers may have retained for their spectators is erased in this image, which impels the factory worker to locate a definitive source of "realness," stability, and patriotism in a connection with his often exploitative employer rather than with his economic allies.

However, the anatomical configuration on which the logic of "The American Twins" rests can serve to dismantle the ideas it represents. While Nast's antiunion sentiments are clearly conveyed, the image he uses to mobilize that stance had the potential to backfire. The rocky relationship Chang and Eng maintained with each other, particularly during their later years, was common knowledge. Given the contemporaneous mitigating narratives that presented conjoined twinning in unfavorable ways, Nast's text ran the risk of instilling fear rather than favor in the minds of those who would have been disadvantaged most by such a union. To a worker during this period of class turmoil, the problem was precisely that there was too much dependence on an employer who did not have the worker's best interests at heart. The connection that Nast advocates entailed some significant risks for these laborers in return for the questionable payoff of a jingoistic pride resting on industrial progress. Predictably, the upper classes, signified by the capitalist in this cartoon, had everything to gain from this union. In the end, "The American Twins" uses a figure of white labor to direct a message to a racially mixed working class to maintain the economic and psychic comfort of white capital.

Unity and Nation, or the Ongoing Persistence of Conjoinment

Thomas Nast's cartoon, which embraces anatomical difference and rejects prevailing notions of republican individualism and autonomy, is strikingly dissimilar to another image produced almost a century later, before the United States entered World War II. Theodor Seuss Geisel, who many youngsters know as Dr. Seuss, was a prolific political cartoonist as well as a children's book author. The resident cartoonist at *PM*, a New York–based daily newspaper, Geisel published an image that broached conjoined twinning on July 8, 1941 (see Figure 4.3). A banner reading "The Great U.S. Sideshow" appears above a stage on which two men are perched. On the left is a somewhat slim man standing relaxed with hands clasped and eyes closed. A calm smile spreads across his face, and the words "America First" are written across his jacket. The man on the right is considerably heavier and is crouched as if about to spring to attack. He sports a nefarious grin, and a large swastika appears on his chest. A long, grizzly beard connects the two men. In the foreground, a carnival barker wearing an Uncle Sam–style top hat makes this announcement to a crowd of curious onlookers: "And on this platform, folks, those most perplexing people . . . the Lads with the Siamese Beard! Unrelated by blood, they are joined in a manner that mystifies the mightiest minds in the land!"

Although Geisel uses a conjoined-twin metaphor to address conflict within the nation, he does so quite differently from Nast and Twain. In contrast to "The American Twins," Geisel's cartoon portrays this interconnectedness—between that of the America First movement, a collective of citizens who were against the United States entering the war, and the Nazis—not as an inborn trait but as an acquired and troubling condition. Oppose the war, Geisel warns his reader-

Figure 4.3 Untitled cartoon by Theodor Seuss Geisel. *PM*, July 8, 1941. *(Courtesy of the Mandeville Special Collections Library, University of California, San Diego.)*

ship, and be in cahoots with Hitler. However, his representation of this insidious conjoining also reassures the reader of the ease of its correction, which is unlike Twain's pronouncement that separation is neither feasible nor favorable and contrasts Nast's implicit refusal even to consider it. He calls the connection between America First and Nazism a Siamese beard—a beard being a secondary sex characteristic acquired years after birth (as opposed to a "Siamese" *twin* with whom one is born), and claims that the two human figures represented are "unrelated by blood." This suggests that the conjoining—because it is neither congenital nor hereditary—can and should be easily severed. This procedure, easy as it is, does not need the skilled labor of a surgeon or even that of a barber, and the beard between the two men dangles enticingly for any of the wide-eyed spectators to rise up and cut it in an act of audience participation.

It bears mentioning that along with Geisel's pro–U.S. intervention cartoons rallying support against Nazi anti-Semitism in Eastern Europe, he also penned cartoons that advocated federal action against Japanese Americans in the wake of Pearl Harbor's bombing. A cartoon published on December 10, 1941, shows a birdlike Uncle Sam frantically attempting to exterminate a large crowd of slant-eyed stray cats, one holding the Japanese flag, from a place called "Jap Alley." This reference to racial residential segregation, the "Jap Alley" in cities along the West Coast, suggests that further containment is in order, and the exclamation, "Maybe only alley cats, but Jeepers! a hell of a lot of 'em!" portrays the Japanese Americans as subhuman and dangerous in their unnatural multitudes. A second cartoon published on February 13, 1942, mirrors the visual rhetoric of the first. Here, it is human slant-eyed figures that stretch out into the horizon across California, Oregon, and Washington in the same manner as did the cats from the previous image. They line up at a booth labeled "Honorable 5th Column" to receive packages of dynamite. One man stands atop the booth peering into a telescope pointed west across the ocean, and the caption reads, "Waiting for the Signal From Home."[39]

Literary critic Kandice Chuh reminds us that concepts of transnationalism have historically been fraught for Asian Americans even as recent scholarship in ethnic studies has embraced this porosity of national boundaries. While Chuh places her own work within these transnational frameworks, she also warns that it was the very fear of a Japanese transnation that "enabled the justification of internment as necessary to contain that threat."[40] Hence, the "home" conjured in the second cartoon is not the "Jap Alley" ghetto found in U.S. cities that the first cartoon references but, rather, the enemy land across the Pacific.

Geisel's mid-twentieth-century "The Great U.S. Sideshow" echoes a concern that accompanies the late-nineteenth-century texts by Mark Twain and Thomas Nast: what is more dangerous, the mere fact of conjoinment or a complacent acceptance of it? It is this very uncertainty that causes the metaphor both Twain and Nast use to come apart. Twain's seamless reunification of North and South in "Personal Habits of the Siamese Twins" wavers back and forth between satire and earnestness in his calls for reconciliation through an embrace of racial and anatomical difference. In this embrace, however, is a conspicuous omission of the central points of conflict in the Civil War. Elsewhere, his replication of pernicious images of Asian bodies shows how even within the work of a single author, the idea of Asia is slippery, unpredictable, and malleable. Nast advocates for the formation of alliances between workers and capitalists, negating the heterogeneity among the working poor and the dangers that increased loyalties to factory owners pose for workers. The white specificity in "The American Twins" defers elsewhere in his oeuvre to a reification of Asian workers as they function in ways that exacerbate white working-class resentment.

This undoing of Mark Twain's and Thomas Nast's arguments acknowledges that despite the singularity of the nation, there are a multiplicity of dispositions, alliances, subjectivities, and value systems among its cultural citizenry. These contingents disagree and clash precisely because of the attempts to remove the evidence of the hierarchies that attend them. Here and elsewhere, the ideology of nation is one where difference and dissent are equated with danger and, thus, are subjected to containment and erasure. However, even as Twain and Nast see this variation in the national grain and even as they attempt to heal their ruptures, their calls for unity are troubled not only by the apolitical and ahistorical elision of social difference but also by the implicit exclusion of certain social groups and the aggrandizement of others. In the end, the white class-privileged masculine subject remains untouched and protected in these narratives of conflict and reconciliation.

5

Asian Americans Bare/Bear the Hyphen

The nineteenth-century Anglo-American texts in Chapter 4 invoke Chang and Eng Bunker to reference a union of competing political contingents for an abstracted collectivist good. Whether it is to ease sectional strife after the Civil War or to resolve the tensions of class revolt, Mark Twain and Thomas Nast use the anatomical body to make claims about the body politic. Moving ahead, contemporary Asian American texts taking up this figure of conjoinment see such unions differently. As they explore the significatory potential of Chang and Eng, these texts reveal more skepticism about the promise of national unity precisely because they are aware of power differentials within the nation-state. Multiple conflicting populations are channeled into an imperfectly imagined community of Americans, and this paradox of the nation-state in modernity is what comes to the surface in these invocations of Chang and Eng Bunker.

The double as recurring theme in Asian American literature is nothing new. A seminal text in the field of Asian American studies, Sau-ling Cynthia Wong's *Reading Asian American Literature: From Necessity to Extravagance*, devotes an entire chapter to tracing this trope's weave through the Asian American literary canon.[1] Wong locates her analysis in the field of European and American literature more broadly, especially within scholarship using psychoanalytic frameworks, to show how this figure of the double has been a key component of Western arts and letters from the Romantic period onward. She finds that the motif of the double, alternately referred to as "the alter ego, the shadow, the Doppelganger, the second self, the anti-self, the opposing self, and the secret self,"[2] asserts a particular draw for the authors she discusses. The specificity of the Asian American double, however, distinguishes it from most others in

Anglo-American or European literature because rather than functioning as an uncomplicated foil for the protagonist, it is a figure onto which undesirable or troubling aspects of racial identity are projected so that they can be disavowed. Wong convincingly places these sources in the Asian American literary canon within Enlightenment-issued literary traditions—which revolve around conflicts, negotiations, boundaries, and permeabilities between self and other—even as she demonstrates their racial specificity. However, I particularize the doubleness in these direct and indirect references to Chang and Eng Bunker differently. I call attention to how they engage, even if only fleetingly, with medical forms of authority and how their accommodation or resistance to such intervention continues to inform the rhetoric of nation building established by the nineteenth-century white authors discussed in Chapter 4.

I provide an examination of Chang and Eng Bunker's appearance in novelist Maxine Hong Kingston's *Tripmaster Monkey* as groundwork for this chapter's analysis of conjoinment in Asian America. Rather than the consensual affiliation or patriotic alliance seen in Mark Twain's or Thomas Nast's work, a nation-based unity among disparate social categories is burdensome for these authors. Autobiographer Monica Sone's *Nisei Daughter*, set during the World War II Japanese American internment, shows that within a space where Asian Americans' national affinities undergo constant scrutiny, to be doubly interpellated—in her case, to hold U.S. citizenship and to track into the category "enemy alien"—is dangerous. She refers to herself as a "two-headed freak" at key moments throughout her narrative to convey this sense of peril. Although Sone's protagonist describes her dissonant multiplicity by corporealizing it, Hualing Nieh interiorizes this theme of doubling in the face of state surveillance. Her novel, *Mulberry and Peach: Two Women of China*, features a protagonist who responds to repeated instances of state policing and violence in Asia and the United States by doubling her personality. Two women, each the other's professed opposite, share the same body, and the novel's resolution hints at the impending destruction of one and, therefore, the demise of both of them. Finally, two shorter texts by Cathy Park Hong and Karen Tei Yamashita play wittily with how Sone and Nieh work with the same metaphor. Showing a high level of self-referentiality as participants and interlocutors in the Asian American literary canon, these more recent texts call out that tradition's gaps, fissures, and possibilities.

The Hyphen and the Asian American

This chapter's title, "Asian Americans Bare/Bear the Hyphen," alludes to a passage from the mock-climactic scene of Maxine Hong Kingston's novel *Tripmaster Monkey: His Fake Book* (1989). In it, the cantankerous protagonist, Wittman Ah Sing, a recent Berkeley graduate and struggling playwright, effects a catharsis of self-actualization by producing a play in his own makeshift theater company. He takes the part of director, orchestrating a variety show that references and spoofs the debates about literary authenticity that accompanied the rise and consolidation of an Asian American arts and culture movement from the 1970s onward. Wittman's cast consists of minor characters he meets along his picaresque wanderings in Vietnam War–era San Francisco. The play's episodic form mimics structurally both the novel itself in a gesture of self-referentiality and the conventions of the sideshow as performers come onstage one after another in discrete, atomized appearances. One of the acts features socialite Lance Kamiyama (rumored to be modeled after literary critic Stephen H. Sumida) and a nameless, aging former Yale Younger Poet who Wittman encounters while working in the stockroom of a department store at the beginning of the novel. Together, they portray Chang and Eng Bunker.

Tripmaster Monkey, with its stream-of-consciousness narration and postmodern pastiche of literary traditions, is commonly read as Kingston's rebuttal to novelist/playwright Frank Chin's well-publicized attacks on her work, even though the author has coyly denied these allegations. Chin is known for his nonfiction essays criticizing Kingston for producing insufficiently authentic material geared toward Anglo-American audiences.[3] In *Tripmaster Monkey*, the intertextual references to a staggering number of U.S., European, and Asian cultural productions—cited playfully and often imperfectly and irreverently—performatively articulate the novel's polemics about the impossibility of delineating literary canons and the folly of claiming a primordial cultural purity.[4] That Chin is satirically renamed in Kingston's novel as the protagonist Wittman Ah Sing calls to mind not the feudal-era Chinese folklore of which Chin is fond but the American Renaissance and that tradition's iconic master of free verse poetry. The protagonist's last name, Ah Sing, could phonetically precede the direct object, "the body electric," referencing the multiple types of boundary transgression associated with one of Walt Whitman's most widely read poems.[5] However, it can just as easily conjure "Ah Sin," Whitman contemporary Bret Harte's racist caricature of Chinese immigrant men, an allusion that curbs tendencies against uncritical embraces of any and all literary traditions.

At the same time the protagonist's name invokes nineteenth-century Anglo-American literature, the novel's subtitle, *His Fake Book*, references both twentieth-century African American music and the Chinese epic mythology with which Chin identifies—specifically, the legend of the Monkey King, a trickster figure entrusted with the quest of restoring to China sacred scrolls whose authenticity (as they are blank) is doubted upon his return. Fake books, which circulate among jazz musicians, actively buck unitary notions of authorship as the chords and melodies of widely played songs are transcribed in shorthand and made available for infinite revision, improvisation, and collective *re-author-ization*. Kingston's reciting of U.S. and European cultural productions alongside Chinese myths and the *re-site-ing* of her detractor in the literary West forces a recognition that the hard-line cultural nationalism in Chin's criticisms overlook the inevitable hybridity and syncretism of any creative work.

It is this anxiety about cultural interpenetration and interdependency that Kingston unpacks in the scene in which Chang and Eng Bunker make their entrance: "Across the stage . . . forward-rolled acrobatic twins, tied together—four heels over two heads that did not gravity-drop katonk. They backflipped off. And re-entered—verbal twins in green velveteen connected suits. Yale Younger and Lance Kamiyama as Chang and Eng, the Double-Boys, pattering away in Carolina-Siamese. Chinkus and Pinkus."[6] Following lengthy improvisational banter between Chang and Eng that riffs on a series of factual and fictional anecdotes about the real-life Bunkers, a doctor comes onstage. He examines the ligament connecting the two men, which prompts them to attack. When the twins are jailed, Chang exclaims at the audience from behind bars: "We know damned well what you came out to see—the angle we're joined at, how we can have two sisters for wives and twenty-one Chinese Carolinian children between us. . . . You want to look at the hyphen. You want to look at it bare."[7] The connection between the twins—a band of flesh dissected and documented in the autopsy of the real-life twins—is decorporealized and transformed in Kingston's novel into a hyphen—a punctuation mark. Incidentally, this is the punctuation mark that has been the focus of some debate in the field of Asian American studies, and these interchanges about the hyphen probe at the crux of the contentions concerning aesthetics and politics between Kingston and Chin.[8]

The convention of hyphenating U.S. immigrant designations, especially those that are European in origin, references a Zangwillian teleological narrative of acculturation. In this model, the progression of generations allows the ethnically marked to overcome the perceived limitations of their social location and enter the universal embrace of a consensualist America. This ascension into an abstracted notion of America does not necessarily involve parting with one's ethnic or religious heritage. In fact, it relies on the ongoing evidence of this (depoliticized) immigrant past in order to affirm the success of the nation-building project of integration in the present. Given the established usage of the hyphen in the thinking through of European immigrant identities, the common practice of omitting the hyphen between the words "Asian" and "American" in recent decades signals a wish to problematize this model. First, refusing—per syntactical convention—to subordinate "Asian" as a modifier for "American," the dehyphenated "Asian American" indexes how the Asian diaspora in the United States represents a plurality of immigrant/colonial/refugee histories, citizenship statuses, migration trajectories, and homeland affinities. Their lived experiences do not necessarily follow the normative becoming-American narrative established at the height of European immigration to the United States.

Moreover, as David Palumbo-Liu stresses, the Asian continent—in its materiality and its idea—has always been part of the making of the U.S. nation-state so that the need for an apologia between "Asian" and "American" is a fallacy. For this reason, he prefers to use a solidus, or backslash, instead of a hyphen:

> The proximity of Asian Americans to that [immigrant] ideal should be read as a history of persistent reconfigurations and transgressions of the Asian/American "split," designated here by a solidus that signals those instances in which a liaison between "Asian" and "American," a *sliding over* between two seemingly disparate terms, is constituted. As in the construction "and/or," where the solidus at once instantiates a choice between two terms, their simultaneous and equal status, and an element of indecidability, that is, as it at once implies both exclusion and inclusion, "Asian/American" marks *both* the distinction installed between "Asian" and "American" and a dynamic, unsettled movement.[9]

These combined frictions of spanning-across and splitting-from-within that the rejection of the hyphen implies for Asian America is central to Maxine Hong Kingston's theatrical scene of strange interconnection.

This is the moment in *Tripmaster Monkey* when the figure of the conjoined twin appears onstage, purports to make itself available for epistemological ownership, and then resists legibility. In doing so, the ethnographic impulse that tends to accompany the consumption of ethnically or racially marked literatures becomes exposed and deflected.[10] The unsuspecting reader of these texts, represented by the doctor in Wittman's play, "want[s] to look at the hyphen . . . want[s] to look at it bare." However, the great reveal tells more about a naive or untutored readership than it does about the nature of Asian American difference, the hybridity and syncretism of which is and has always been commonplace. The baring of the hyphen, which then becomes another obfuscation, resembles the epistemological frustration that the autopsy of Chang and Eng Bunker generated for the sphere of medical knowledge. The doctor/reader in these cases, jolted with "the slap of refused intimacy,"[11] is enticed with the promise of discovering something new, unusual, or deviant—only to be eluded by a body or text that resists ethnographic or scientific possession. In Kingston's case, it is her invocation of postmodern literary conventions that erects a writerly wall against which the reader collides. It is all too fitting that Chang and Eng, as characters in a play played by characters in a novel, illustrate this conundrum.

Physical Difference and Containment in *Nisei Daughter*

Tripmaster Monkey highlights Asian America's refusal to be legible, but its opacity functions paradoxically as a hermeneutic key that can potentially make more difficult reading practices accessible. These reading practices that appeal to neither a salacious desire to be awestruck with difference nor a nationalist tendency to sanitize and erase variation are especially important for the generation of writers whose texts predated the consolidation of an Asian American literary movement in the late 1960s and 1970s. Monica Sone's *Nisei Daughter* is an autobiography about the author's experiences during a crucial moment in

U.S. history, the relocation and internment of 120,000 Americans of Japanese descent during World War II. Published in 1953, only a few years after the closing of the camps in 1946, it was reissued with an updated author's introduction in 1979, which reframed what appeared to be a relatively safe Cold War–era text for a new generation steeped in the civil rights logic of the Japanese American redress movement.

If Maxine Hong Kingston's performative opacity in *Tripmaster Monkey* stresses the necessity of recognizing how ethnic minority literatures may be strategically crafted to allow and inhibit epistemological access selectively, it anticipates literary critic Traise Yamamoto's reading of *Nisei Daughter.* Sone's autobiography is a text that has garnered its share of condemnation in Asian American literary studies for its purported assimilationism and docility. If read through Yamamoto's lens, however, which interprets Japanese American women's narratives through poststructuralist models of identity, we see that Sone's autobiography engages in a conscious negotiation between the needs of social justice and the limitations of its intended audience. It is this very dynamic, Yamamoto argues, that discursively produces a politicized Japanese American female subject.[12] The narrative strategies employed by authors like Sone alternatingly reveal and mask, vacillating not between essence and artifice but between social critique and "the conversion of white American awareness."[13]

Nisei Daughter begins with a chapter called "A Shocking Fact of Life," when Kazuko, the six-year-old protagonist, is confronted with her Japanese ancestry during a family meal. Although she acknowledges that "I never felt that it was strange"[14] before this conversation with her parents about their decision to enroll her in Japanese language classes after grammar school, she then considers her ancestry troublesome only after she begs an explanation for this incursion into her playtime. Her parents explain to her, "Just think you'll grow up to be a well-educated young lady, knowing two languages. One of these days, you'll thank us for giving you this opportunity."[15] The Issei, the first (or immigrant) generation of Japanese Americans, see bilingualism as a means through which to claim a favorable class-inflected identity, "well educated," which would presumably mitigate Japanese America's working-class roots. However, the Nisei, or second generation, see bilingualism as an occasion for internal conflict and estrangement. "It was like being born with two heads," muses Kazuko about her Japanese ancestry coming into contact with her American identity. "It sounded freakish and a lot of trouble. Above everything, I didn't want to go to Japanese school."[16]

This is the first of three moments in Sone's autobiography when the metaphor of two-headedness emerges. It is not a reference to literal conjoined twinning per se but a declaration of duality that uses the language of the sideshow. This doubling recognizes dissonance issuing from the immigrant generation's maintenance of cultural practices that the young Kazuko believes are at odds with her own childlike wishes. In a bathetic temper tantrum, she exclaims exasperatedly, "Terrible, terrible, terrible! So that's what it meant to be a Japanese—

to lose my afternoon play hours!"[17] Given that the theme of the generation gap in immigrant literature had already been established by European-descended writers at the beginning of the twentieth century, Sone's choice to open her narrative with a scene of conflict inside the household places it within this literary tradition despite its significant departure. More important, it prepares Sone's readership for the subsequent invocations of two-headedness that take more political risks because of their critique of the nation (private citizens' patriotic racism) and the state (official U.S. wartime action).

When Franklin D. Roosevelt issued Executive Order 9066, it authorized the relocation of people of Japanese descent from the West Coast. Kazuko, then a young adult, declares that "once more I felt like a despised, pathetic two-headed freak, a Japanese and an American, neither of which seemed to be doing me any good."[18] From her reading and rereading of the official decree in disbelief to hearing the racial slurs uttered freely in public places, Kazuko's sense of duality—first imagined nonthreateningly in the space of the home—then becomes transposed onto the contradictions of the nation-state's public sphere. She wryly notes that even though she has a U.S. birth certificate and can legally vote, she must endure wartime anti-Japanese sentiments and be subjected to internment. An openly pedagogical passage follows this one. In it, she reasons that although the internment was couched in terms of protecting national security, Japanese Americans living in Hawaii were not similarly evacuated because the islands' economy, largely reliant on their labor, would have crashed.

The final invocation of this recurring metaphor is what has drawn the most fire in the academic reception of *Nisei Daughter*, and it is worth citing at length. Released from camp early to attend college, Kazuko—on a trip back to visit her parents—declares:

> I don't resent my Japanese blood anymore. I'm proud of it, in fact, because of you and the Issei who've struggled so much for us. It's really nice to be born into two cultures, like getting a real bargain in life, two for the price of one. The hardest part, I guess, is the growing up, but after that, it can be interesting and stimulating. I used to feel like a two-headed monstrosity, but now I find that two heads are better than one.[19]

Sone's narrative then ends with this address to the reader:

> I had discovered a deeper, stronger pulse in the American scene. I was going back into its main stream, still with my Oriental eyes, but with an entirely different outlook, for now I felt more like a whole person instead of a sadly split personality. The Japanese and the American parts of me were now blended into one.[20]

One critic calls these words a "banal cliché,"[21] while another is more admonishing, condemning them as "a shockingly assimilationist cliché."[22] Yet another expresses the observation that this "blend seems externally imposed, and everything . . . is left in limbo"[23] rather than with the closure Sone's words attempt to effect. Still one more critic performs a reading of the gendered dimensions of a feminized Japan and a masculinized United States, arguing that "the price of this oneness of vision, the outlook of the American mainstream, is the repression of that part of the narrator's identity represented by her Japanese mother."[24]

Rather than beat the dead horse of a discussion about these often-cited passages in Sone's autobiography, I redirect these eruptions of figurative physical difference in *Nisei Daughter* toward one scene that portrays Kazuko's encounter with a literal stigmatized physical difference. This instance, in which she is diagnosed with tuberculosis and undergoes treatment, parallels and foreshadows her eventual internment during World War II. It is fitting that Kazuko is contained and interned for public health reasons immediately before she is contained and interned with the rationale of protecting national safety. Soon after she finishes high school, Kazuko is admitted to the North Pines Sanitarium, and even before she arrives at the facility, she is well aware of the fear her body generates. When a family friend offers to give her and her parents a ride to the sanitarium, he arrives with sheets draping the car seats, and Kazuko notices that he is dressed in old clothing that will undoubtedly be burned with the sheets after he delivers his cargo. Once admitted to the facility, she embraces and then mocks common perceptions of wilting tuberculosis patients: "I was prepared to start dying, but I found it wasn't such a simple matter to fade away into oblivion. Nurses and doctors kept on breaking my trance."[25] Significantly, it is not medical personnel who initiate an epiphany for Kazuko about coping with disease but her fellow patients. While she forms emotionally sustaining relationships with her roommates, she also experiences a disturbing moment of clarity about racial difference.

Kazuko's roommates, women who are not racially identified in the way that would make whiteness visible, are uplifting kindred spirits who refuse to allow tuberculosis to dampen their mood. This sense of camaraderie dispels the overbearing mythology about a disease that was demonized at the time these events occurred. For Kazuko, illness is not—as Susan Sontag might say—a metaphor for anything. Refreshingly, it does not signify something else but is simply a condition to be managed with available care. The nonchalance with which Sone portrays Kazuko's illness is striking given that *Nisei Daughter* was written and published at a time when tuberculosis was—following the development of reliable cures—just beginning to be viewed as a treatable bacterial infection, a recent shift from its representation as a grand-scale myth onto which cultural fears were projected.[26] The events in the sanitarium actually take place before that period. Despite the boldness with which disease is represented in *Nisei Daughter*, at a time when tubercular infection was just starting a process of destigmatization, Sone reveals the sanitarium as the site where racial self-loathing becomes a recognizable malaise.

Kazuko finds the energy of her white roommates sustaining, but she is jarred by what she registers as reserve and coldness when, one day, she attempts to befriend two Nisei women. Her awkwardness when attempting to engage them in conversation prompts her to recall a past incident. One of her roommates mentioned that a new patient (also presumably white) expressed that she had felt slighted by Kazuko. It then dawns on Kazuko that "the girls had not meant to be unkind even though they had made me feel as if I were a spy at large. Their response was Japanese, and that was the way I had behaved with Laura. No wonder Chris and Laura thought I had been deliberately impolite."[27] The realization that she is different in her expression of affect from the white women for whom she has grown to have much affection becomes obvious. Although this portion of Sone's autobiography contains enabling possibilities for how people with stigmatizing illnesses are cast, the author ultimately turns away from that aspect of the story. "The tragedy of having tuberculosis receded into the background,"[28] she reports, but only because this has instead become a tragedy about racial suffering. In fact, a groundbreaking acceptance of and comfort with illness becomes the grounds for further racial alienation.

Nisei Daughter raises complex questions about the nation-state through the same anatomical metaphor as the texts from the nineteenth century I examine in Chapter 4. Like Mark Twain and Thomas Nast, Sone attempts to resolve competing elements within the nation-state by imposing a clumsy unity that avoids conflict. However, if we revisit *Nisei Daughter* upon its 1979 reissue with a newly politicized Japanese American readership in mind, it lives alongside other contemporaneous events of the redress movement, such as Gerald Ford's rescinding of Executive Order 9066 under pressure from the Japanese American Citizens League. Although the quarantine and sequestering of people with tuberculosis fails to shake the protagonist of *Nisei Daughter*, the negative emotion surrounding the World War II internment lingers conspicuously in the text's conclusion despite attempts to banish it. In the end, Sone's autobiography is an intricate tangle of both stasis and promise.

Nation and Transnation in *Mulberry and Peach*

In the introduction to her analysis of Asian Pacific Rim film, Greta Aiyu Niu reworks Homi Bhabha's working term for colonial subjects who, as a result of imperialist histories, maintain multiple national networks: "people of the pagus." Drawing from the Greek suffix "-pagus" (to indicate fastening) in terminology for conjoined twins classified according to anatomical configuration,[29] Niu's harnessing of Bhabha's phrase pays heed to the dominant "discourses which contain and restrain Asian bodies and which view Asian bodies as contaminated, excessive, dangerous, out of bounds."[30] In Niu's reading of film, Chang and Eng Bunker not only function as a hermeneutic—referencing a bridging or a fastening that is both geographically and ideologically transgressive—but they also call attention to an ongoing cultural-imperialist history.

When we consider the flows, both inter- and intranational, of Asian bodies within a geopolitical critique of globalism, the embrace of an immigrant identity in *Nisei Daughter* after World War II shifts in the latter part of the twentieth century to a more carefully considered analysis of the forces behind migration—whether it is encouraged, coerced, or forced. Sone's *Nisei Daughter* generated an overabundance of academic scholarship in the formative years of Asian American literary studies, but Hualing Nieh's *Mulberry and Peach* appears to have been undertheorized and underread. This lack of attention may be because the text's liminality makes it difficult to categorize and, thus, locate in a single set of academic discussions.[31] The publication history of Nieh's novel provides an interesting counterpoint to the story contained in the novel itself. Both reveal a relentless and multilayered transnationalism years before the transnational turn in Asian American studies made these movements visible in the way they are now. That the material fruition of and themes contained in *Mulberry and Peach* predate the interpretive lenses used to analyze the novel signals the historical pervasiveness of a transnational analysis operating in Asian America even before the middle to late 1990s. Moreover, the circulation of the novel and the story portrayed in it take place at a time when the logic of Asian American civil rights organizing based itself on steadfast claims to the United States.

Nieh came to the United States from Taiwan in 1964 to accept a position at the Iowa Writers' Workshop at the University of Iowa. The novel emerged while she was living in the United States, but it was written in Chinese, rather than in English, and saw its first publication in serialized form in Taiwan in the 1970s. The editors of the Taiwanese *United Daily News* were forced to abandon the novel midway through its serialization when protests erupted against its sexual frankness and its criticisms of the Nationalist Party. Afterward, the novel found a less volatile readership in the British colony of Hong Kong, where it was serialized and printed in book form in 1976. An abridged version with the more controversial sections edited out was published in the People's Republic of China in 1980. In 1981, *Mulberry and Peach* was translated into English and appeared in English simultaneously in New York and Beijing, and it was not until 1989 that the original Chinese language text was published in its entirety on the mainland.[32]

The novel's germination in Chinese in a region of the United States correlated with "middle America" and its midwestern setting together challenge a crucial dichotomy between regionalism and transnationalism. If the local-color fiction of writers from previous generations captures the specificities of cultures rooted to region, Nieh's novel troubles that literary convention not only by showing how the global and geopolitical are enmeshed in these idyllic scenes of space and place but also by undermining the utopian fantasy of pastoral rootedness. Her character, a neuro-atypical Asian-raced woman with two personalities, relocates repeatedly to evade state surveillance. That the novel's English translation was made available in China before the unedited, unabridged original Chinese testifies not only to the continuing existence of imperialist-colonialist Anglophone dispersal in East Asia but also of the ways in which the interests of this settler population were cordoned off from the intranational political conflicts of the local Chinese.[33] This presence of an Anglophone reading public calls attention to the conspicuous absence in the plot of European settlers in Asia; scenes of political subjugation always portray an Asian person as the instigator of violence. Moreover, it is not envoys of the state who tend to mete out the most troubling abuses of power but opportunistic private citizens.

Unlike Monica Sone's protagonist, Nieh's Mulberry and Peach—two women who collectively inhabit one body—resist both state and national imperatives to consolidate their duality. Mulberry is timid and somewhat submissive, but Peach is openly defiant. Mulberry conforms to models of normative femininity, whereas Peach is sexually transgressive. As the narrative unfolds, it becomes more obvious that it is not the nation-state but Mulberry and Peach themselves, each through their hostility toward the other, who demand a unitary and consistent Cartesian correlation between mind and body. At one point, the narrative names explicitly what is apparent from the beginning, that the protagonist(s) "show signs of schizophrenia,"[34] but it seems to reference the popular, nonmedical usage of the term rather than the psychiatric definition.

It is not my intention to "diagnose" or otherwise medically describe the protagonist(s) based on her/their behavior, interior monologues, or other factors. What I address instead is how the novel mobilizes Mulberry/Peach's unusual embodiment, both similar to and different from that of a set of conjoined twins, to unpack the complex nature of U.S. federal surveillance at the time in which the narrative present is set. If the scenes of Mulberry/Peach's interrogation by immigration officials are unsettling for a readership inclined to sympathize with her plight as an illegal alien, the novel turns the tables on these moments of interrogation by making the processes of questioning the object of interrogation itself. However, in the process of doing so, the novel omits one salient component of inspection that has historically and overwhelmingly informed U.S. immigration screening—that is, a medical examination.

The fascination with what is today known as dissociative identity disorder and multiple personality disorder long predates the psychiatric recognition of these categories in 1980, the year they entered the *Diagnostic and Statistical Manual of Mental Disorders* and *International Statistical Classification of Diseases and Related Health Problems*. Robert Louis Stevenson's *Strange Case of Dr. Jekyll and Mr. Hyde* (1886), a novella popular at the time of its publication and one whose titular characters inspired a common idiomatic expression, is a case in point. Despite the fact that dissociative identity disorder and multiple personality disorder as clinical categories postdate the period in which the plot of *Mulberry and Peach* takes place, a set of historically entrenched U.S. immigration screening practices that have interpreted diseases and illnesses rather loosely would have flagged the protagonist(s) based on initial interchanges with the immigration officer when she/they respond in neuro-atypical ways to questioning.

In 1882, the United States passed the Chinese Exclusion Act after more than three decades of recruiting migrant labor from China. That same year also saw the passing of the Immigration Act of 1882, which barred the entry of "any convict, lunatic, idiot, or person unable to take care of himself or herself without becoming a public charge."[35] Although the law itself did not provide definitions for the above categories, the processes of screening and evaluation discursively produced them and provided the precedents through which medical officials from the U.S. Public Health Service would determine fitness. As medical historian Alan M. Kraut argues, anxieties about mental health within the context of immigration were just as great as, if not greater than, those about physical health. The two were often correlated in examination procedures such that physical symptoms were interpreted as evidence of mental or psychological impairment.[36] This long-standing idea, stretching back to at least the Middle Ages, that mental illness could be read on the body, is corroborated by Sander L. Gilman, who also points out a strong link between notions of madness and notions of racial difference, specifically blackness.[37] Through a series of physical examinations and cognitive tasks, immigrants would be screened and granted entry or returned to their countries of origin based on vague diagnoses such as "feeblemindedness," which was never a definitive disorder but an umbrella term for a wide variety of non-normative neurological and behavioral traits. As expected, other factors, such as language and cultural barriers, often gave the appearance of psychological aberrancy, and the stressful process of undergoing examination itself would sometimes lead to trauma.[38]

From the beginning of *Mulberry and Peach*, the lack of a mental health dimension to the surveillance by immigration is palpable by its absence. An exchange between Peach and an immigration officer grows increasingly tense:

> "I'm not Mulberry. Mulberry is dead!"
>
> "Well, what is your name, then?" asks the man from the Immigration Service. . . .
>
> He takes a form out of his briefcase. The form is covered with a cramped script in fountain pen. In the corner is the number: (Alien) number 89-785-462. In the other corner is a woman's photograph. The name Mulberry is written under the photo. One item on the form is checked in red: Application for Permanent Residency.
>
> He points at the woman's photograph. "This is you in the picture, right? There's a mole under her left eye and her right earlobe has a small notch. You . . ." he says, pointing at Peach, "have a mole under your eye and there's a notch in your right earlobe."
>
> Peach laughs. "Mr. Dark, you have a real good imagination. What you see isn't real. What I see is real. You know what I see when I look at you? A tiger with nine human heads."[39]

This dialogue, in which the state attempts to confirm the protagonist's identity first by name and then by visual evidence, indexes an older history of documenting Chinese immigrants during the time of exclusion. As social historian Anna Pegler-Gordon uncovers, the control of Chinese immigration took on a specifically visual dimension. Photographic documentation of prospective Chinese immigrants was implemented long before it was required of Europeans and Mexicans. While the Federal Immigration Bureau attempted to establish a reliable relationship between document and immigrant through the use of the photograph, the immigrants that photographic technologies were meant to regulate also actively manipulated the visual image themselves. In doing so, they worked within and reworked the discriminatory policies under which they were evaluated to challenge the primacy of photographic authority.[40]

When Peach defiantly refuses to claim the identity "Mulberry" while being questioned by the immigration officer, whether on the basis of the photograph or biographical details, she destabilizes that one-to-one correlation between self and document. She forces the immigration officer to conduct his investigation of her on her own terms when he breaks down and acquiesces, never resorting to accusations of mental instability: "Ok, Peach, you win. I need your cooperation. Please tell me everything you know about Mulberry."[41]

The subsequent interrogations Mulberry/Peach undergo(es) take on not only a racial cast but a gendered one as well, summoning historically entrenched beliefs about the sexual degeneracy of Chinese women. Although 1882 is widely cited as the beginning of a decades-long period of Chinese exclusion, it was actually earlier, with the passing of the Page Law in 1875, when exclusion took on a gendered dimension. At this time, women specifically were barred from entering the United States for fear that they would work as prostitutes. The law was not intended to protect Chinese women from exploitation; rather, it was meant to protect white America from foreign corrupting elements. Although there were also white and Latin American women in the sex trade serving a multiracial, largely male population in the port city of San Francisco, public discussions leading up to the passing of the Page Law preyed on fears that Chinese prostitutes in particular were carriers of infectious disease and moral corruptors of young white boys.[42] Given the discursive link between Chinese femininity and prostitution, this legislation greatly hampered the entry of Chinese women into the United States regardless of whether they could be identified as likely to support themselves through sex work.[43] In fact, as Eithne Luibhéid argues, given how the screening processes issuing from the Page Law played out, there was no inherent separation between wives legitimized through the heteronormative marriage contract who were attempting to join their husbands in the United States and women who sold or bartered sex.[44]

The painstaking attention paid by an immigration officer to the sexual activities of the protagonist(s) in *Mulberry and Peach* aligns with the gendered forms of surveillance that have historically been meted out on Chinese women:

> He leafs through to a page [in his files] that says according to the Landlady's report on the evening of 20 July, the very evening that the astronauts landed on the moon, Chiang I-po entered my apartment by way of the fire escape. He stares at me asks on the evening of July 20th did he or did he not have sexual intercourse with me I say yes, he asks how long did it last I say I can't say for sure, we weren't in bed we were in the bathtub . . . he asks how do you have sexual intercourse in a bathtub?[45]

Again, even though Mulberry/Peach's interrogation by the immigration officer reveals the United States' fears about the interlocked particularities of race and gender in cases involving Chinese women, the questioning she endures is conspicuously devoid of any consideration of disability. Her mental fitness, given that she actually transitions from Peach to Mulberry during this bout of questioning, is never considered by the officer. This irregularity is a nonissue in Nieh's novel; even while it critiques power relations in the maintenance of national borders, consideration of the immigrant's mental health is conspicuously absent.

The narrative present in *Mulberry and Peach* progresses synchronically to invoke a myriad of interrelated events in the late 1960s and early 1970s across broad geographical areas. It also moves diachronically back and forth in time to reference or allude to events taking place in the past. The episodic and nonlinear unfolding of the plot—the setting changes from China to Taiwan to the United States forward and backward, repeatedly—is one of the hallmarks of contemporary fiction in a number of literary canons. Specifically, this device in *Mulberry and Peach* calls into question the teleology of immigration's master narratives and the state-sanctioned interpellative legitimacy bestowed on those with privileged access to those stories.[46] Also, the novel's progression in a manner separate from the chronological ordering of events lends a proto-transnational sensibility to its narration. If the past in Asia constantly and abruptly surges into the present across multiple locations in the United States, it is because the social and political forces compelling this wandering nomad's movements traverse national boundaries. Time and space collapse not only for this female, Asian-raced subject monitored by the state but also for the imperialist-expansionist nation itself, whose cultural icons, as referenced by Mulberry/Peach, range from the nineteenth-century covered wagon pioneers stranded at Donner Pass to the narrative present's Vietnam War and Apollo space mission.

At the same time that *Mulberry and Peach* participates in critiques of the United States and other forms of empire, it also foregrounds the issue of reproductive rights that led to the passing of *Roe v. Wade* in 1973. The aggression between the two women who share the body of the protagonist escalates in this instance, and the narrative's foreboding conclusion hints not at a closure to the two sides of the abortion debate, as Mulberry and Peach now signify, but at a failure of resolution with tragic consequences. The novel's portrayals of medical personnel occur only in conjunction with Mulberry and Peach's contact with physicians who perform clandestine abortions and never with regard to the women's neuro-atypicality. In the final chapter, Peach is desperately attempting to schedule an abortion, even offering to pay triple the usual fee in order to bypass the long waiting lists at clinics, while Mulberry thwarts her efforts each time as she assumes control of their body before the scheduled appointment.

This dilemma of corporeal sovereignty eerily mirrors the scenarios Mark Twain composes in "Personal Habits of the Siamese Twins" and, later, in *Pudd'nhead Wilson* and *Those Extraordinary Twins*, which I discuss in Chapter 4. It undermines the fantasy of Cartesian agency and accountability not because Nieh's characters lack rationality—on the contrary, their actions show a high level of thinking and deliberation—but because there is a lack of any kind of negotiation between the two women. Twain's Chang and Eng must compromise with each other about imbibing alcohol and getting baptized, and Angelo and Luigi cope with similar interpersonal conflicts, often in life or death situations, as when they argue over their participation in a gun duel. However, while Twain's fiction and Thomas Nast's political cartooning have shown that negotiation and compromise ultimately benefit those in power, it is unclear who has the upper hand in the relationship between Mulberry and Peach. As Peach muses in an interior monologue/dialogue:

> You're dead, Mulberry. I have come to life. I've been alive all along. But now I have broken free. You don't know me, but I know you. I'm completely different from you. We are temporarily inhabiting the same body. How unfortunate. . . . You and I threaten each other like the world's two superpowers. Sometimes you are stronger; sometimes I am. When I'm stronger I can make you do things you don't want to do, for example the evening the astronauts landed on the moon, you teased and tormented I-po, when you acted like a slut with Teng in the ghost town graveyard. After those things happened you felt you were even more guilty—I like to do mischief with you like that. Because you limit my freedom.[47]

Her reference to "the world's two superpowers" inverts the relationship between tenor and vehicle established by Twain, Nast, and Theodor Seuss Geisel. In those earlier texts, the corporeal body functioned as a metaphor to articulate these authors' visions of "nation," but here, Cold War international conflict becomes a device that describes Peach's resentment over her embodiment. Like the show of U.S. bravado exemplified by the Apollo space mission at the height of the Cold War, Peach's sexual behaviors are calculated specifically to unnerve her opponent. Later, the sparring between Mulberry and Peach over the fate of their pregnancy becomes a metaphor for the dissent surrounding reproductive choice during the women's movement of the late 1960s and early 1970s. Each reacts to and anticipates the actions of the other, and the dynamic resembles U.S.-Soviet tactical maneuvers taking place contemporaneously with the gender politics of the era.

Chapter 6 delves into more detail about how conjoined twinning in late-twentieth-century texts echoes women's reproductivity, but first, it bears mentioning that unraveling medical science's role in *Mulberry and Peach* removes it from an authoritative discourse operating in tandem with the state. Again, health personnel are strangely absent from the protagonist's encounters with immigration officials, making her mental health status beside the point when her race, nation of origin, and gender are very palpably present. The only physicians portrayed in the novel are those who perform abortions beyond the purview of the law, and because of these choices, they also operate with a heightened sense of danger with respect to state authority. Paradoxically, these physicians share a considerable amount of social space with the protagonist(s), who exist(s) in legal limbo and whose actions throughout the novel serve to evade state officials—be it in China, Taiwan, or the United States. The physicians' precarious existence in the United States before *Roe v. Wade* undermines the cultural capital medical discourses have historically enjoyed.

It is fitting that the novel concludes with either Mulberry's or Peach's bucking of medical authority when the protagonist flees from the hospital where she was admitted after a car accident. The woman who does not have control of the body during the escape discovers what happened only afterward—along with the reader—when she buys a newspaper. The newspaper reports on this mysterious accident, and the last line of the column reads: "THE WOMAN'S IDENTITY IS NOT KNOWN."[48] This climatic moment, in which the reader's and the protagonist's perspectives merge with each other is preceded by an increasingly rapid and chaotic transitioning back and forth between the two women. Although the bulk of *Mulberry and Peach* places the reader in a position of relative omniscience in this double first person–narrated novel, the reader is left as much in the lurch as Mulberry or Peach is at the novel's end. One of the protagonists has escaped from the hospital, and she has also escaped the reader's ability to discern which one she is.

Nieh's often heavy-handed characterization of Mulberry and Peach as each other's adversarial opposite is consistent throughout most of the novel. However, the last few pages leading up to the accident accelerate the reader's confusion in distinguishing between the protagonists. Peach's defiance and flippancy erupt in what appears to be Mulberry's narration, and Mulberry's empathy and selflessness emerge in Peach's voice. The newspaper reports that the identity of this injured woman is not known, meaning that no government-issued card has been found in her possession and that there have been no other ways of discerning her name and other biographical details. However, it is most poignantly the indeterminate identities at the novel's end that drives home Nieh's treatise on the contingency of state-generated personhood and the politically and affectively charged complications of conforming to unitary models of cultural and juridical citizenship.

If Sone's two heads are "blended into one" in the cheery liberal-multiculturalist conclusion of *Nisei Daughter*, then Nieh's *Mulberry and Peach* contaminates one with the other in a gravely worded life-or-death call for a transnational consciousness critical of the normalizing functions of the nation-state. In both texts, the specter of medical authority looms in the background only to appear at moments when it seems to expunge the workings of race. However, this very process of erasing race—whether it is in Sone's account of having tuberculosis or Nieh's seemingly postracial refocusing of her narrative on reproductive rights—makes its significance all the more obvious as these protagonists continue to grapple with a U.S. cultural and juridical terrain that brings their racial alterity to the forefront.

One/Two, Asian/American

As if in conversation with each other about Chang and Eng Bunker's past roles in Asian American literature, two shorter, more recent texts reference them by name and revisit the theme of duality present in the work of Monica Sone and Hauling Nieh. Poet Cathy Park Hong's "Ontology of Chang and Eng, the Original Siamese Twins" is part of her chapbook, *Translating Mo'um*, her first collection of poetry. This poem is divided into two sections, the first portraying the Bunkers as polar opposites in ways similar to how Mark Twain begins "Personal Habits of the Siamese Twins." Like Twain, Hong ends her take on these famous twins by showing, after the section break in the poem, how they can also be in agreement about crucial issues when it matters. Moreover, their participation in opposing sets of activities need not be a burdensome barrier to negotiate.

> *Chang spoke / Eng paused.*
> *Chang threw a beach ball / Eng caught it.*[49]

Sometimes, as Hong's minimalist verse shows, this kind of give-and-take is absolutely necessary. Contrary to what the conclusion of Sone's autobiography suggests, homogenization is not needed or desirable.

Altogether, sideshows, carnivals, cabinets of curiosities, and similar entertainment venues appear with much frequency in *Translating Mo'um*. This poem about Chang and Eng Bunker finds its home in a collection where physical anomaly and racial difference are thematized to explore yet another sphere where difference emerges for Asian-raced subjects—that of language and speech. A number of Hong's poems in this collection wrestle with the cognitive and affective difficulty of language mastery, as one might expect from the word "translating" in the book's title. The first epigraph in *Translating Mo'um* is the often-cited passage from Mikhail Bakhtin's *Rabelais and His World*: "The grotesque body . . . is a body in the act of becoming. It is never finished, never completed; it is continually built, created, and builds and creates another body," and the second comes from visual artist and writer Theresa Hak Kyung Cha's mixed-genre text *Dictée*: "She mimics the speaking. That might resemble speech."[50] In getting Bakhtin and Cha to rub shoulders, Hong effects a maneuver similar to that of Maxine Hong Kingston's in *Tripmaster Monkey.* These two authors, one a Russian continental philosopher and the other a U.S. creative writer of the Korean diaspora, have both built their careers defamiliarizing language and body alike. They come into contact with each other unexpectedly across literary and theoretical canons.[51]

Karen Tei Yamashita's "Siamese Twins and Mongoloids: Cultural Appropriation and the Deconstruction of Stereotype via the Absurdity of Metaphor" appears in *Yellow Light: The Flowering of Asian American Arts*, an anthology of Asian American cultural production solicited by the late Amy Ling. Contributors were asked a set of questions about their role as artists in society and given free reign to respond in any way they saw fit. While many of the questions Ling posed were those that artists in general entertain repeatedly, the echoes of the debates between Maxine Hong Kingston and Frank Chin are clearly audible. This is a sampling of some of the questions on this list:

> What are the origins/genesis of your work?
> For what audience do you create your work?
> Are there risks and challenges peculiar to Asian American artists? If so, how do you attempt to resolve them?
> Must the multicultural writer/artist be answerable solely to his/her ethnic community, the community's spokesperson, or can s/he claim the right to express an individual vision and personal concerns and to modify the group's myths and legends for artistic purposes?
> If an Asian American writer/artist attracts a wide audience of non-Asian Americans, is this general acclaim in itself to be taken as evidence that the writer/artist has "sold out" and has become overly assimilated?[52]

Without naming the two authors whose contentious public dialogues dominated much of Asian American literary arts and culture in its earlier years, these questions expand the horizon of inquiry about artistic practice and politics beyond those two major figures and invite others to partake in a polylogic and playful manner.

Yamashita's response to Ling's queries is her mock literary-critical essay "Siamese Twins and Mongoloids," which is about an imaginary novel by Yamashita herself. What do we make of a piece of literary criticism about a primary text that does not exist? The essay's tongue-in-cheek humor pokes gentle fun at her interlocutor—Ling being a literary critic herself—and calls attention to the sometimes fraught relationships between fiction writers and critics. The excessively footnoted text, often with secondary sources that also do not exist, takes a jab at the practice of dissertation writing whereby authors situate themselves within an ocean of previous scholarship in attempts to find an original idea. Thus, it parodies notions of originality in academic work and therefore intellectual production of any kind.

The imaginary novel Yamashita's essay purports to analyze is about Sansei conjoined twins named Heco and Okada, and it takes the reader on a Kingstonian tour of Asian America as one cultural reference after another is hurled at the reader. Like *Tripmaster Monkey*, the climax of this imaginary novel is a variety show of sorts, except that it takes place at Heco and Okada's wedding rather than in Wittman's makeshift theater: "The list of performers is endless, short of being tedious; everyone from Dan Kwong to Cold Tofu and from Great Leap to Hiroshima is there to regale the nuptials. To the delight of everyone, Philip Gotanda comes dressed in a Godzilla costume, and David Henry Hwang as Madama Butterfly."[53] However, rather than the multinational and multiracial range of literary texts that appear in Kingston's novel, Yamashita's Asian American references—a few well-known, some more obscure—test the reader's facility with various names and show that a racially specific literary canon can also be heterogeneous.

These self-referential texts about duality in a complex and culturally mixed Asian-raced population impel a reconsideration of my initial assessments of *Nisei Daughter* and *Mulberry and Peach*. It is tempting to cast *Mulberry and Peach* as the "better" of the two ways of conceptualizing Asian America. However, creating a hierarchical distinction between an older assimilationist immigrant model that imposes unity and a newer transnationalist diasporic model that privileges multiplicity runs counter to the dismantling of dichotomous thinking that Asian Americanist theorists have worked hard to effect.

The awkward, forced resolution in *Nisei Daughter*, thus, is not the political or conceptual opposite of the relentless resistance to nation and self found in *Mulberry and Peach*. Rather, the sentiments expressed in each text run into and entangle with the other. At one point in her autobiography, Sone goes into considerable detail about an acquaintance who is a Kibei, a child born in the United States to Issei parents, who is sent to Japan for schooling. He returns to the United States in late adolescence and finds himself an outcast among the Nisei, many of whom are understandably sensitive about any further highlighting of their racial difference. This portrayal of a Japanese transnation at a time when it was still dangerous to acknowledge it complicates the widespread interpretation of *Nisei Daughter* as a text unaware of the clumsiness of its fit in a Eurocentric immigrant literary tradition. Although it is true that Sone's narrative voice colludes with the anti-Japanese Nisei sensibility repudiating this young man, the very fact of his appearance in her autobiography—if only as a foil—takes a significant risk.

The transnational turn in Asian American studies during the 1990s initiated a conceptual framework for thinking about the flows of labor, goods, capital, and cultures across national boundaries that departed from an earlier model based on civil rights and citizenship.[54] On the other hand, Jee Yoon Lee cautions that diasporic models are far from being uncritically liberating for a number of reasons, not least of which is the heterosexism behind their underlying assumptions about genealogical descent.[55] If anything, *Mulberry and Peach* suggests that a rethinking of sexual normativity is in order when it depicts the nomadic protagonist's first move—one that takes her away from home at the age of sixteen. Her departure hints at an unbearably conflict-ridden relationship with her biological family, and although one detail about her traveling companion, Lao-Shih, does not appear to contribute much to the plot, the novel indicates that she is a lesbian.

What is an already sophisticated vision of diaspora in Nieh's novel, one that contains multiple migrations and does not romanticize the homeland or propagate hereditary fantasies about it, becomes even more complicated when it opens itself to working within the strictures of the nation-state. After all, the protagonist's application for permanent residency, a process riddled with indignities at every turn, reminds us that there are material consequences for those without a legal status granted by the federal government. In a world where national boundaries are ever more permeable, it is not that the nation-state fades in significance. The patrolling and scrutiny its borders undergo in this new global system increase all the more.

6

Disciplining and Normalizing the Woman Subject in Contemporary Literature and Film

The sources I examine in Chapters 4 and 5 position racialized conjoinment as a recurrent metaphor in narratives about the composition of the nation and the state. These authors participate in compelling conversations about managing a polycultural public, either through negotiation or through coercion, in order to build an abstracted concept of "nation." Starting with the 1970s, the appearances of Chang and Eng Bunker in the literary/cultural record began to depart from that well-trodden logic and turned to concurrent debates about gender, domesticity, and the sexualized dimensions of kinship formations in the United States. The technological advances that led to the development and widespread availability of oral contraceptives in 1960; the passing of the Civil Rights Act of 1964, which forbade discrimination in the workplace on the basis of gender as well as race; and the Supreme Court's legalization of abortion in 1973—among other milestones—presented an ever-increasing set of options for middle-class women.

These advances for women were inflected not only with the particulars of economic class but also with race, and it is beyond the scope of this chapter to go into detail about how volitional nonreproductivities for white middle-class women came at the expense of women of color and women colonial subjects. This dynamic of controlling the reproductivity of nonwhite women to enhance the reproductive potential of white women stretches as far back as the antebellum era, when enslaved women endured unanesthetized vaginal surgery so that a reliable treatment could be developed for fistula.[1] Oral contraceptive trials in Puerto Rico during the 1950s went hand in hand with the United States' continued colonial investments on the island. Women who participated as subjects were commonly not informed of the risks and were not required to sign consent forms.[2] The experiments were part of a larger economic picture in which Puerto Ricans both on the island and on the mainland served the interests of an increasingly prosperous postwar United States.[3] In sum, a fraught history of medical experimentation provided the backdrop for the decreased biological reproductivity and increased economic power of white middle-class women.[4]

As an expanded range of meaningful choices about motherhood, access to cultural and material capital, and nonreproductive sex emerged in the 1960s and 1970s, conjoined men in fiction came to function as a trope around which prevailing anxieties about women's sexual excess coalesced.[5] This is not to say that public interest in the women who engaged sexually with Chang and Eng Bunker did not emerge until a full century after their deaths, with the sexual revolution. As noted previously, there was considerable speculation during their time about how the Bunkers managed to replicate the heteronormative dictates of the Victorian-era family. The projection of fears about white women's unchecked sexual behavior originated much earlier than the 1970s. In fact, they circulated at the time of the Bunkers' arrival to the West.

Some artifacts from the Bunkers' first tour in England flirt with the unavoidable question of women participating in sexual activity with them. An engraving from this period portrays a stir on a public street as four petticoat-clad women coquettishly surround them (see Figure 6.1). One woman embraces Chang with both arms and leans in to offer a reciprocated kiss, while another gazes lovingly at Eng from behind her fan. The other two women vie for the twins' attention as male onlookers at the extreme left corner of the image, their bodies largely obscured by the women, gasp in astonishment at the entire scene. The boyishness of the twins' faces in this illustration underscores the aggressiveness with which these women pursue them. Meanwhile, Chang and Eng's features—as they are drawn appearing to be white—mitigate what might be an unsettling image of cross-racial contact that would destroy the pleasure of viewing an otherwise cute and whimsical illustration.[6]

Another image from that period is a broadside, a printed sheet of lyrics titled "Siamese Youths, or, the Wonderful Prodigy of Nature!" The lyrics are meant to be sung to a popular tune of the day, rendering in song the same sexualized theme the engraving portrays. The illustration at the top of the broadside depicts Chang and Eng on their own without any female admirers (see Figure 6.2), which might explain the acceptability of their dark complexion and overtly racialized features. However, the penultimate verse of the lyrics makes it clear why conjoined men arrest the popular imagination:

When they to bed did go,
Upon last Friday night, sir,
They both kissed the Chambermaid,
But did not her affright, sir;
She fondly kissed them again,
Gave them their kisses back then,

Figure 6.1 Artist's rendition from Chang and Eng's first tour in England. Circa 1830. *(Courtesy of the History of Medicine Division at the National Library of Medicine.)*

And suppose she brings to town,
Next summer two young black men.

The figure of the sexually insatiable chambermaid here alludes to multiple levels of transgression. As a woman who is lax about both monogamy and miscegenation, her portrayal obscures the power imbalances that govern the often economically and sexually coercive/abusive interactions between actual domestic servants and their employers. While Chang and Eng's origins in Siam highlight the mysterious impenetrability of a nation never colonized, the "two young black men" the chambermaid is emboldened to court reference Britain's imperial reach in the Americas and its participation in the circum-Atlantic slave trade. Almost prophetically, this line also anticipates the Bunkers' slave ownership in the U.S. South years later.

This specter of interracial, nonmonogamous sex from the very beginnings of Chang and Eng's career complicates a commonly understood temporal trajectory about the gendering and racializing of sexual excess and transgression. While injunctions against interracial sex after emancipation in the United States hovered over purportedly hypersexual black men who were seen as threats to chaste and passive white women, social changes during the 1970s transposed concerns about sexual propriety onto white women. The artifacts from early nineteenth-century England, however, show that fears about white

The Siamese Twins.

Siamese Youths,

OR, THE WONDERFUL

Prodigy of Nature!

A NEW SONG.

DRAW near with one accord,
 Attention give I pray now,
While I to you unfold
 The wonders of the day now;
It's of the Siamese youths,
 As you shall quickly hear, sirs,
And Sir Astley Cooper says,
 There is no deception there, sirs.

CHORUS.

So off the people go,
 Through rain and windy weather,
To see the Siamese youths,
 By nature join'd together.

Now these two Siamese youths,
 Are eighteen years of age, sir,
If you wish them now to see,
 You quickly may engage, sir;
You have only for to go,
 I tell you just what I know,
To the Egyptian Hall,
 And tip them the ready rhino.

Mrs. Flinn went there to see,
 She waddled like a goose, sir,
Keep them fastened up, says she,
 And do not let them loose, sir;
Then to see them any more,
 I do not care a button,
Pray gentlemen, says she,
 Do you think they're fond of mutton.

Some say they came to town,
 It is true upon my life, sir,
To see if they could find,
 Each of themselves a wife, sir;
Some people say they came,
 Folks pockets for to fleece then,
But I think myself they came,
 To be made New Policemen.

A council there was held,
 About these curious fellows,
Some said their nose appeared
 Just like a blacksmith's bellows;
If Sir Ashley Cooper had his will,
 He would nimbly try to part it,
And stick one at Charing Cross,
 The other in Fleet Market.

While Sir Astley did them view,
 In hobbled Doctor Blunder,
Saying, "What God has join'd together
 "Let no man put asunder."
Well, well, Sir Astley said,
 You are altogether funny,
And you know the readiest way
 To gather in the money.

When they to bed did go,
 Upon last Friday night, sir,
They both kissed the Chambermaid,
 But did not her affright, sir;
She fondly kissed them again,
 Gave them their kisses back then,
And suppose she brings to town,
 Next summer two young black men.

They have had living skeletons,
 And hens with human faces,
Now these two Siamese youths,
 Are come to take their places;
To town we did expect,
 A Girl that had two heads, sir,
But her arrival is postponed,
 'Cause we understand she's dead, sir.

Printed by T. BIRT, No. 10, Great Andrew-Street, Seven Dials.

Figure 6.2 Broadside with illustration and lyrics. Circa 1830. *(Courtesy of the History of Medicine Division at the National Library of Medicine.)*

women's perceived sexual excess existed even before this period and that the Bunkers, in small ways, catalyzed these unsettling female figures in relation to blackness.

This chapter examines how repeated allusions to Chang and Eng Bunker articulate gendered whiteness in the culture of the late-twentieth and early-twenty-first centuries. There are numerous references in print and film to the Bunkers in particular and conjoined twins in general during this period.[7] I cover two movies and several novels here. David Cronenberg's *Dead Ringers* (1988) and Mark and Michael Polish's *Twin Falls Idaho* (1999) exemplify best the tension issuing from concerns about white women who exercise their economic and sexual independence. These characters, who have left the fold, so to speak, of normative femininity as a result of their reproductive, economic, and/or sexual histories, are "reformed" through medical mastery of the conjoined men with whom they share affective intimacies. Cronenberg's characters—a set of male identical twins who are both physicians—turn the medical gaze and instruments on themselves in a last-ditch effort to regulate female bodies at the moment when their medico-scientific regulative powers have been permanently lost. The Polish brothers' protagonists evade surgical intervention initially only to be subjected to it later so that the female lead can be redeemed. My treatment of these two films are bookended by a reading of Judith Rossner's *Attachments* (1977), a novel steeped in the historical moment of women's liberation, and a series of early-twenty-first-century narratives: Darin Strauss's *Chang and Eng* (2000), Mark Slouka's *God's Fool* (2002), and directors Peter and Bobby Farrelly's *Stuck on You* (2003). Applauded for their courage and vilified for their presumed sexual degeneracy, these women's transgressions of gendered social codes incite a range of affective responses that do not resolve in neat and clear-cut ways.

Attaching Judith Rossner

Judith Rossner's commercial success in the 1970s shows that the complex and, often, disturbing portrayals of the feared consequences of the U.S. women's movement resonated deeply with the American public. If *Attachments* was not the first text to broach the matter of women having sex with conjoined men—as the archive contemporaneous with the Bunkers' natural life span shows—it was arguably the first to use their figural legacy to foreground the development and disciplining of the white middle-class nonmonogamous female subject. Appearing two years after the author's vastly more popular *Looking for Mr. Goodbar*, the novel carries with it the polemical baggage of its predecessor even as it voices a somewhat more muted ambivalence over women's increasing sexual agency. There were few books that generated more popular attention in the 1970s than *Looking for Mr. Goodbar*. It appeared on *The New York Times* bestseller list for thirty-six weeks when it was published in 1975. The novel is a fictionalized account of the real-life murder of Roseann Quinn, a schoolteacher whose body was found in her New York apartment on January 3, 1973. The perpetrator was a man she had met in a bar the previous night.

Whether *Goodbar* is a reactionary treatise against the breakdown of codes that were paternalistically understood to protect women, it nevertheless is a representative artifact from a period when expectations for women were being reorganized and rethought, sometimes with great hope and at other times with pessimism. However, when paired with *Attachments*, which directly follows in the author's oeuvre, *Goodbar*'s rejection of normative kin and sexual relations does not find a happy resolution in its opposite—that is, a dogged replication of the two-parent conjugal family. The protagonist of *Attachments*, Nadine Tumulty, courts and marries one-half of a set of conjoined brothers and convinces her best friend, Dianne Shapiro, to wed the other for reasons that partly relate to Nadine's sexual attraction to Dianne. Nadine bears one child after considerable effort at conceiving, while Dianne has two quite easily, something that causes Nadine to become resentful. When husbands Amos and Eddie Smith, omphalopagus twins—joined in the same way as were Chang and Eng Bunker—undergo separation so that the family can maintain two different households, the underlying frictions present in this family come to the surface. The anatomical separation becomes an interpersonal one, too, fracturing the family. If *Goodbar* can be read in ways that caution against the wholesale bucking of gendered social codes dictating women's kin-related and sexual choices, *Attachments* warns readers of uncritical conformity to sanctioned models of domesticity at all costs.

Against the novel's story line of female same-sex desire triangulated through the conjoined men is its equally compelling questioning but ultimate reification of the genre of the human-interest documentary. The teenaged Nadine first becomes fascinated by Amos and Eddie after reading a *Life* magazine feature. She carefully saves the article along with every other news clipping she can find about them. Incidentally, this is the moment when Chang and Eng Bunker are explicitly named in the narrative. Although a present-day reader would be reminded of the 1996 *Life* photo essay on Abigail and Brittany Hensel, the appearance of a fictionalized *Life* feature situated in 1977 would not have been eerily prophetic. This is because the magazine has a history of generating stories about conjoined twins that predate Rossner's novel. Among these, in fact, was an article on the Bunkers.[8] Having *Life* magazine, as opposed to another periodical, introduce Nadine to Amos and Eddie is significant because it takes the conjoined men outside of the realm of spectacle and situates them in modes of representation that convey dignity and elicit empathy. As Rosemarie Garland-Thomson observes:

> *Life Magazine* was as far from a sideshow as the [Hensel] family could get. Known for decades as a venue for the best journalistic and art photography, *Life* was a popular, general interest magazine that told the story of America through photographs from the Great Depression to the

> Vietnam War. . . . The romance of national commonality, decency, and simplicity which animated the images in *Life* made it the perfect venue to work against the sensational entertainment narratives of monsters and freaks that defined the lives of most people in history who looked like Abigail and Brittany.[9]

Although Garland-Thomson's description of *Life* could spur one to problematize the magazine's role in generating homogenizing narratives of the Andersonian "imagined community" for print consumers, her refusal to mobilize this critique here suggests that there may be instances when such portrayals of unusual embodiment are more enabling than the alternative. The images from the lives of Abigail and Brittany Hensel are counterintuitive precisely because of their mundane familiarity to most middle-class readers. Nadine refers to the fictionalized *Life* article on Eddie and Amos as "sensational," but her descriptions of the photographs indicate quite the opposite: "the sixteen-year-old twins swimming in the pond near the state home where they'd been raised, fixing a car engine, eating at a long table in the home."[10] There is actually an indication that Nadine is frustrated by the very *lack* of sensationalism as she sees "the same sparse details relayed over and over again" in every media account.[11]

Despite these seemingly noninvasive and candid *Life* magazine images that obscure the conditions of their manufacture—the effect is that of witnessing the photographs' subjects as they experience quotidian life undisrupted by journalists—*Attachments* shows that the process of documenting anything can and will alter what is being recorded. This observer effect is foregrounded as the family struggles to hold up under public scrutiny while being filmed. At a certain point, Rossner's prose "jump cuts" to a lengthy twenty-five-page transcript of a documentary being produced about them, and Nadine challenges the filmmaker directly:

> NADINE: . . . You're a part of our lives, Ken, and you're making things happen just by being here and making a movie. . . .
> KEN: What have I made happen?
> NADINE (*thinking*): I don't know. It's not exactly that we're doing things we wouldn't have done . . . but it's as though we're going to. You're making things happen.[12]

Although it is tempting to side with Nadine as she questions modernist notions of ethnographic veracity, the fact that this footage is even included in the final cut shows that the documentarian himself, despite his mock innocence, is also challenging the conventions on which his practice rests. His choice to expose the seams of the film retroactively calls into question the seamless aesthetic of the *Life* magazine photo essay along with every other appearance Amos and Eddie have made in the media. This mode of analysis, however, is lost at the novel's end.

The publicity issuing from the documentary generates another movie deal, a fictionalized Hollywood-style account of their lives. Later, Nadine and Amos's discussion about these dual portrayals of the Smith family, the first nonfictional and the second fictional, concludes the novel. It is Nadine who most poignantly experiences the stress of being a subject of these narratives as she explains, exasperated, to Amos:

> "Even if I stayed with you I wouldn't have anything to do with the movie." Or the book. The movie would be a book which wouldn't quickly disappear. "I hate the fucking movie."
>
> "How can you hate it when you haven't even seen it?"
>
> "Where it's a lie," I said, "I hate it because I hate lies. And when it's truth . . . if it shows me as I really am . . . as we really are . . . were . . . then I'll hate it because I hate the way we were."[13]

Nadine takes Ken to task for the disruption he causes, which undermines the verisimilar effects that documentary films produce, but *Attachments* ultimately ends up reifying the line between fiction and fact. The ostensibly disinterested lens of the camera remains intact as a transmitter of culture and knowledge. This perception of unmediated vision, however, is shaken by the various contemporary films that follow in the wake of Rossner's novel.

Dead Ringers and *Twin Falls Idaho* attempt to offer a neat resolution: physically normalizing men in an attempt to behaviorally normalize women. But the films, in ways similar to *Attachments*, reveal the dangers behind these interventions. More important, how physical difference is manipulated in these films, whether it is through camera technology, costume design, or both, calls attention to the myriad levels of illusion behind the visual consumption of unusual bodies.

Unraveling Medical Authority in *Dead Ringers*

During the summer of 1975, Stewart and Cyril Marcus, twin brothers who lived together and shared a gynecology practice, were found dead in their New York City apartment, the body of one showing greater decomposition, by several days, than the other. It was never conclusively determined whether theirs was a murder-suicide, suicide pact, or joint accidental overdose of narcotics. Inspired by the story, *Dead Ringers* is quite possibly the motion picture that has attracted the most scholarly attention in director David Cronenberg's oeuvre. Although the film makes a series of unmistakable references to the true-life Marcus twins, it departs from the nonfictional story in several ways.[14]

The central characters in *Dead Ringers* are identical twins Beverly and Elliot Mantle, both portrayed by the British actor Jeremy Irons. For the first time in film history, soft-matte composite editing was used, which permits a single actor who plays twins to move more fluidly in the same frame. The technology employs a computerized camera system that pans and dollies in exactly the same way over multiple takes, producing a more seamless result. The female lead is Claire Niveau, portrayed by Geneviève Bujold. Claire, a film actor, enters the lives of the Mantle twins, both gynecologists, when she seeks medical intervention for a condition that is causing infertility. She has a uterus with three cervixes. Moving from the role of patient to girlfriend, she dates and sleeps with Elliot first and then later Beverly, who poses as Elliot, before discovering the brothers' ruse to share her between them. Whereas Elliot is cool, confident, and calculating, Beverly is gentle, sensitive, and introspective. It is Beverly who Claire chooses as her lover. In their shared medical practice, Elliot performs most of the research that garners public acclaim, while Beverly devotes his time to the less glamorous task of clinical practice. The central tensions that give this psychological thriller its momentum are the alternating degrees with which the women involved with Beverly and Elliot are able to tell them apart and the twins' own decreasing ability to make these same distinctions between themselves.

Although Beverly and Elliot are not anatomically conjoined, the film's direct and indirect references to Chang and Eng Bunker invoke anatomical metaphors to convey psychological and affective conjoinment. When Beverly collapses in a prescription drug overdose, Elliot takes great pains to keep blood from being drawn from Beverly in the emergency room so as to hide evidence of his chemical dependency. Once discharged, Beverly continues to receive care from Elliot at home, and in one poignant scene, Elliot responds to Beverly's resigned plea that he abandon him by referencing the Original Siamese Twins: "Remember how they died?" Beverly, still dazed and weak from his collapse, responds by lapsing into a sing-song chant reminiscent of the way children's rhymes are recited:

> *Chang died of a stroke in the middle of the night.*
> *He was always the sickly one.*
> *He was always the one who drank too much.*
> *When Eng woke up beside him*
> *and found that his brother was dead,*
> *he died of fright. Right there in the bed.*

It is right after Beverly's collapse and this reference to the Bunkers that Elliot, who has up until this point remained sober, starts abusing prescription medications along with his brother. Subsequently, during a conversation between Elliot and his girlfriend, Elliot defends his continued nursing of Beverly by appealing to the welfare of their livelihood: "My brother's research is the basis of my career. I need him. Besides, the truth is, nobody can tell us apart. We are perceived as one person. If Bev goes down the tubes, I go with him. . . . Whatever's in his bloodstream goes directly into mine."

This declaration about sharing a circulatory system appears late in the story, but it is not the first time the bond between Beverly and Elliot is articulated anatomically. In an earlier scene most reminiscent of Cronenberg's horror oeuvre, Beverly and Claire are snuggling in a darkened bedroom when he is startled and protests, "No. Don't look. He's here. I don't want him to see us." The third party in the room is Elliot, who stares intently at the couple as a jump-cut brings his face into sudden close-up. Next, a wider angle reveals that Beverly and Elliot are connected at the torso by a band of flesh at the same location where Chang and Eng Bunker were joined (see Figure 6.3). The special effects team was able to make the prosthetic connection admirably true to that of the Bunkers' in its placement on the body—down to the shared navel at its center. There is a mechanism inside the prosthesis that makes it appear to move on its own. The surface and texture of this prosthesis comes off as overdone—grotesque, even—compared to the original. Bold sinews sprouting from Beverly's side of the band lead into a thickly veined and purple mass of lumpy flesh. However, photographs of Chang and Eng Bunker and their death cast show the surrounding skin is smooth and tonally even—consistent with that of the attached ligament. This twitching, writhing appendage between Beverly and Elliot—which references but also embellishes on the Bunkers' anatomy—calls to mind in its gratuitous excess a giant penis. When Claire whispers, "I'll just separate you," before slowly lowering her head and sinking her mouth into the connection, it is unclear whether we are seeing an act of castration or fellatio.[15] The camera focuses on a close-up of Elliot's face as he closes his eyes and sighs before the nightmare jars Beverly awake in Claire's room.

As much as *Dead Ringers* is about troubling and blurring the status of the individual, it is also about troubling and blurring the status of medical artifacts as they threaten to morph into other categories of objects. In the film, medical instruments undergo a series of transformations from tool to trophy to sex toy

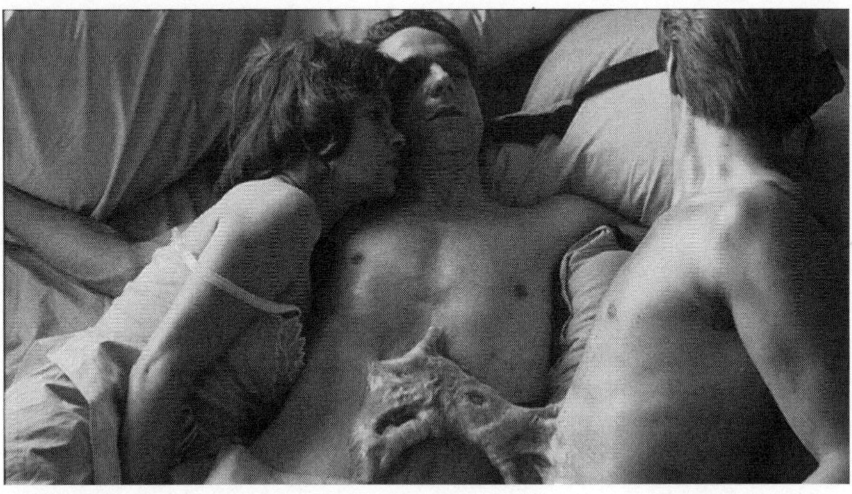

Figure 6.3 Still from *Dead Ringers*, directed by David Cronenberg (1988).

to aesthetic object to commodity and back again with each shift retaining the traces of the instruments' former status. These shifts in meaning take place despite and, sometimes because of, their handlers' attempts at fixing and stabilizing them. The strategically placed turns Cronenberg forces medical instruments to undergo are sometimes humorous and always clever, and they also reference an ongoing relationship between medicine and the fine arts that I discuss in Chapter 3. As the workings of the Mütter Museum show, the line between the aesthetic and the medico-scientific is and has always been porous. Meaningful interchanges between artists and physicians are consistently evident in the historical record even, and especially, when the latter group attempts to restrict access to the former. What may be, for instance, a preserved biological specimen to one person, may very well be a subject for fine art photography, to another.

One scene, in an art gallery, has Beverly bringing to a fine art metalsmith for casting a set of medical-instrument sketches he has drawn. When the metalsmith asks what they are for, Beverly tells him they are gynecological instruments meant for mutant women. Previously, we saw Beverly agitated by hallucinations about the patients he treats after Claire enters his life. He tells Elliot, "The patients are getting strange. They look all right on the outside. But their insides [*pausing*] are deformed." The metalsmith is fascinated by Beverly's idea and exclaims, "That's a great theme for a show!" This misunderstanding raises Beverly's ire. When the metalsmith advises him to approach a more appropriate manufacturer for the tools, Beverly rejects that possibility, claiming that he and Elliot have always been "too radical" for the conventions of medical science. On a later date, Beverly strolls past the same art gallery. In a moment that humorously mocks traditional notions of authorship, Beverly sees atop a pedestal the instruments he designed in their reincarnation as a work titled *Gynecological Instruments for Working on Mutant Women*. In a fit of rage, he grabs them. The gallery director struggles with him, letting him know that the work has already been sold, but Beverly is able to wrangle the pieces away.

Once Beverly brings his stolen goods home, Claire finds them, and she examines each one methodically. They possess an eerie beauty, invoking organic forms, such as vertebrae, claws, arachnids, and marine animals. As she holds one tool to her face for inspection, the camera pans so that we are looking at her head-on. The effect references a stock shot in cinematography—that of the viewer looking into the barrel of a pistol aimed by its handler. This close-up suggests the violence as well as the aesthetic pleasure that can be summoned by these pieces of metal that, just the previous day, were on display as art. Claire asks Beverly about the objects, and at this point—having undergone the shift from gynecological instrument to piece of contemporary sculpture to commodity—they transform themselves yet again. Beverly tells her that they are for the separation of Siamese twins, a claim that foreshadows how they will "operate," literally, in the twins' demise.

Although the extent to which *Dead Ringers* invokes race may lie in the overwhelming whiteness of its cast, as it is set in the racially mixed and transnational city of Toronto, there are two moments in which an ambiguously located, Asian-raced subject erupts into the narrative and around it. First, in an early scene, Elliot is picking up an order from a pharmacist and calls this Asian man Arthur, which is not his name. When the man interjects that his name is actually Dennis, Elliot responds flippantly, "I always get you confused." There is an ongoing theme in the film about the confusion and conflation of individuals, whether it is between Beverly and Elliot or between Claire the actor and the characters she portrays in her acting career. This seemingly gratuitous moment between Elliot and the pharmacist appears to exist for the purpose of establishing a thematic through line. Although we are not privy to any knowledge regarding the other pharmacists who work at the hospital where the Drs. Mantle have their practice—for all we know, Dennis could be the identical twin of another pharmacist named Arthur—this "get[ting] . . . confused" in the face of racial difference marks a history of fear over the presumed interchangeability and indistinguishability of Asian-raced bodies.[16]

The second eruption of an unstable Asian-raced subject takes place not in the film proper but in the intertextual effects of the connection between director David Cronenberg and actor Jeremy Irons. We need to move *Dead Ringers* forward in time to anticipate this encore pairing in *M. Butterfly* (1993). This film, released five years after *Dead Ringers*, is the adaptation of playwright David Henry Hwang's text by the same name. The play is Hwang's synthesis of Giacomo Puccini's opera *Madama Butterfly* with a fictionalized retelling of the real-life story of Bernard Boursicot and Shi Pei Pu. These two figures sparked international controversy, making headlines in 1986, when Boursicot, a French diplomat convicted of espionage, insisted he was unaware that Shi, the Chinese opera diva with whom he had maintained an eighteen-year romantic and sexual relationship, was—in fact—a man. Moreover, Shi had been a spy for the Chinese government and had stolen documents from Boursicot over the span of their relationship, resulting in the arrest, conviction, and imprisonment of both men in France. Renaming the central figures René Gallimard and Song Liling to fictionalize the story, Hwang calls his work a "deconstructivist" *Madama Butterfly*: in his story, it is not the white man who dupes an Asian woman to his sexual advantage but an Asian man disguised as a woman who sexually dupes a white man for professional leverage.[17]

I am not claiming, given the similarities between these male leads, Cronenberg was already thinking about casting Irons in the role of René Gallimard in *M. Butterfly* at the time that he was making *Dead Ringers*. This intentionalist reading would be impossibly anachronistic given that both Hwang's play and *Dead Ringers* premiered in 1988. However, a present-day consideration of *Dead Ringers* and *M. Butterfly* alongside each other incites an unsettling comparison of the roles that Irons plays in these two films. This linkage produces a disorienting intertextual occasion in which the traces of René Gallimard and his misreadings of this ambiguous Asian-raced figure can be seen retroactively in both Beverly and Elliot, not only in Elliot's brief interaction with the pharmacist but also in Beverly's doomed attempts to control and dominate Claire. Coincidentally, Song is—like Claire—a performer, and the ease with which both Song and Claire maintain embodied illusions appears to be a crucial similarity in how these respective narratives play out.

In their conflation of professional and sexual prowess, René/Beverly/Elliot regard their perceived heterosexual successes as a means through which they can advance in the largely homosocial world of their colleagues, be it in diplomacy or in medical science, and it is precisely the fear of their sexual shortcomings that leads to their professional demise. As men who "always get . . . confused" in ways that reveal the cracks in their painstakingly maintained claims on heteropatriarchy and professional mastery, René/Beverly/Elliot respond not by backpedaling, reassessing, and revising their misreads but by refashioning the terms on which their version of the truth exists. René turns himself into Puccini's suffering geisha, who is willing to die at her own hands for the benefit of white masculinity, while Beverly and Elliot sacrifice their own lives in a separation-surgery/murder-suicide atop a gynecological exam table to maintain their faith in the apparatus on which they have built careers surveilling female bodies. The elaborately arranged placement of Jeremy Irons—draped atop himself—in the closing shot of *Dead Ringers* anticipates his solo death scene, which is the denouement of *M. Butterfly* (see Figures 6.4 and 6.5). The final scene takes place during a prison performance of *Madama Butterfly*. René—in racial and gender drag—slices his throat with the sharp edge of a broken mirror, and the viewer is left with the same image as that which concludes Puccini's opera, a geisha sprawled on the stage, convulsing in death.

Cultural critic Mary Russo warns against reading the outcome of *Dead Ringers* as a satisfying reversal of gendered systems of medical control over female bodies, giving Beverly and Elliot their due. Because of the power differentials attending male and female bodies under the medical gaze, she calls heed to "the utter falseness of the presumed complementarity of the male and female bodies; the ludicrousness of the male body undergoing the gynecological drill shows up more than anything the asymmetry of gendered bodies in the same position."[18] David Henry Hwang makes this same critique within the diegesis of *M. Butterfly* when Song and René meet for the first time. Song launches into a monologue that begins, "What would you say if a blonde homecoming queen fell in love with a short Japanese businessman? He treats her cruelly, then goes home for three years, during which time she prays to his picture and turns down marriage from a young Kennedy. Then, when she learns he has remarried, she kills herself."[19] Rather than posit this reversal as a congruous exchange, Song's rhetorical question shows that these situations are not equivalent.

As much as *Dead Ringers* is most visibly about the doomed project of mediating self from other, it is also about the mediation of internal and external bodily surfaces, showing that they cannot be partitioned individually and safely from each other. Although Beverly's anxiety about his decreasing ability to differentiate himself from Elliot is corporealized in the dream sequence that

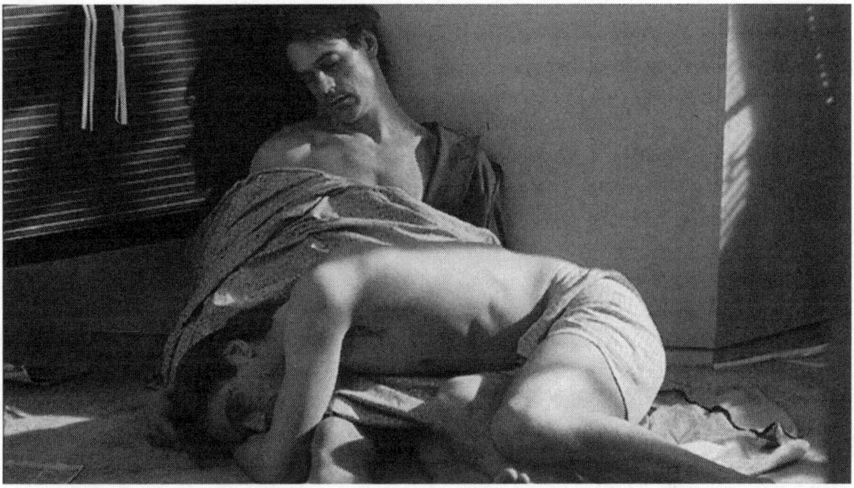

Figure 6.4 Still from *Dead Ringers*, directed by David Cronenberg (1988).

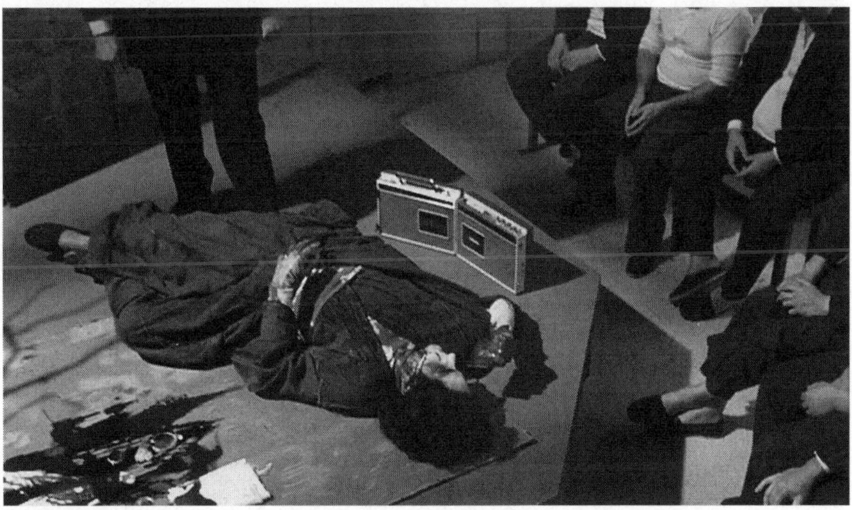

Figure 6.5 Still from *M. Butterfly*, directed by David Cronenberg (1993).

showcases the connecting ligament, the most unusual physical anomaly referenced in *Dead Ringers*—Claire's three-headed uterus—is never portrayed. The uterus is even more rare than conjoined twinning—given its nonexistence in the medical record—and yet it need not be seen by viewers for the narrative to be convincing. In fact, Cronenberg's decision not to show it is a crucial part of the film's logic. The decision to keep the uterus hidden is all the more notable given that Cronenberg rarely shies from portraying bodily interiors and other unsettling bodily images. Within his oeuvre, one can see, among other gruesome images, an exploding head, disemboweled abdominal cavities, a human-fly hybrid regurgitating digestive juices on its nemesis, mutant children hammering their teacher into a pulp, and giant leechlike parasites burrowing into human hosts. The list goes on. To say that Cronenberg is not for the squeamish is an understatement.

However, Claire's impossibly unusual uterus needs to be concealed from the audience so that the twins' undoing, while dramatic, remains incomplete. This organ is, after all, what sets the plot into motion, and its glaring absence from the screen means that the medical gaze retains some measure of privileged access to bodily interiors that it will not readily surrender to the lay audience's eyes. The extraordinary insides of Claire's body, to which only her gynecologists have epistemological ownership, never reveal themselves to anyone else, whether it is another character or the viewer. On the other hand, if we consider the film's referencing of older scientific concepts of sex difference,[20] Claire's female body, as it inverts itself from those of males, presents a conundrum that threatens the men around her. As cultural critic Terri Kapsalis notes, Claire is the triply phallic woman, one whose power is all the more unsettling because it is hidden, and Claire's "three" ultimately defeats Beverly and Elliot's "two."[21] Although the much-hyped uterus remains hidden in ways that signal the exclusiveness of the medical gaze, the film's ending leaves little doubt as to who is being vanquished in this unfortunate triangle.

Biological Mothers and Disabled Sons in *Twin Falls Idaho*

The narrative in *Dead Ringers* is inaugurated by a woman's quest for biological motherhood, an activity that positions her in terms of lack (infertility) and excess (the presence of three cervixes). On the other hand, a pathologized refusal to parent in the wake of biological reproductivity defines the female lead in *Twin Falls Idaho*. Directors Mark and Michael Polish play the lead roles of Blake and Francis Falls in this independent film. The female protagonist is Penny, a sex worker portrayed by Michele Hicks, who meets these conjoined twins while on assignment. As Penny enters a room in a dingy residential hotel, Francis—who has requested her services—greets her from the bathroom, door slightly ajar, and politely asks her to wait a moment. "You know, this hotel is full of freaks," Penny says. "You look pretty normal for a place like this though." When she notices a moment later that Francis is attached to another person he introduces as "Blake," Penny leaves the hotel room in a panic. It is only because she forgot her purse that she returns, and her reentry into the lives of Blake and Francis sets the plot in motion.

The narrative tension that propels *Twin Falls Idaho* is the age-old love triangle. Although Francis had called for her in her capacity as a sex worker, it is Blake with whom Penny develops an affectively compelling bond. Penny is touched by Blake's care for his ailing brother. For instance, when Francis is unable to swallow his medicine, Blake takes it for him. The courtship Penny and Blake strike up appears to resemble any other: they flirt and banter in a diner booth late at night; they attend a Halloween party together (where Blake and Francis blend in discreetly for most of its duration); they paint each other's toenails. A moment that would have made sexual activity possible, however, is cut short when Francis, who Blake and Penny believe to be asleep, wakes up beside them and eyes them coldly.

We know from the onset that Penny is a down-and-out sex worker, but what she lacks in both economic and cultural capital she makes up for in social capital, through her network of clients. At one point, she calls a lawyer to intervene in her impending eviction. In a gesture of concern, she contacts Miles, a physician, to examine Francis when he is sick. This action, taken on behalf of someone whose class status is at least slightly higher (Francis, after all, is able to afford the services of a sex worker despite the conditions of his living quarters), elevates Penny into a more recognizable model of bourgeois white womanhood even as she lives outside its boundaries of respectability. It is through a type of care coded as maternal that Penny initiates her transformation from sex worker to sympathetic protagonist. Miles, who helped place Penny's intellectually disabled son in an adoptive family, offers during his checkup of Francis to provide her the details of her son's adoption, but she refuses. This link between the disabled characters in *Twin Falls Idaho* becomes more explicit later when an entertainment industry agent taunts Penny with the suggestion that her loyalty to Blake and Francis stems from a desire to reclaim what he calls her "retarded" son.

The film's engagement with physical difference is somewhat heavy-handed; nevertheless, it demonstrates that disability in its various forms guides the viewer's opinion of the film's characters. The opening scene shows Penny and her friend, Sissy, sharing a cab ride. At their destination, the driver hands them change with a prosthetic hook. The sudden appearance of the metal appendage, which fills Sissy with disgust, does not faze Penny, as she accepts what she soon realizes is a two-dollar bill. Already, it is established that Penny is the more sympathetic of the two, an assumption that is confirmed throughout the film. This moment that makes the cabbie's prosthesis visible returns in another form at the film's conclusion, when Penny visits Blake in his trailer. As he sleeps, the camera cuts to a close up of the prosthetic leg he acquired after his separation from Francis. Again, not feeling any disgust for this hybrid flesh and synthetic body, Penny climbs into bed and drapes her arm around him.

Miles is also portrayed sympathetically, even though he is a physician, a fraught figure in narratives of conjoined twinning. Upon meeting the Falls brothers and asking them to lift their clothing so he can examine them, his attention is directed solely to palliating Francis's sickness and not to their unusual anatomy (see Figure 6.6). He cracks the joke, "Relax, I'm not a surgeon," to dispel the tension in a way that references for the film's late-twentieth-century audience the proliferation of triumphalist medical documentaries

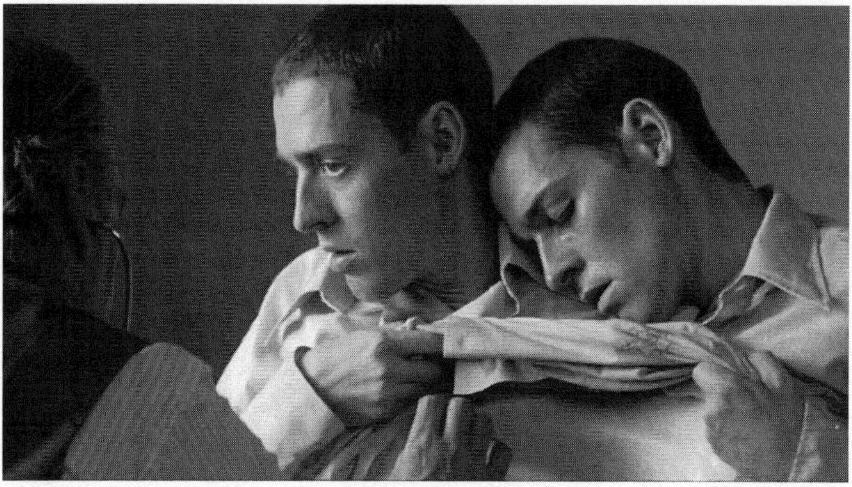

Figure 6.6 Still from *Twin Falls Idaho*, directed by Mark Polish and Michael Polish (1999).

about conjoined twin separations.[22] A heartbeat becomes audible as he places a stethoscope to Francis's chest, and this moment cements for the film's viewer an identification with Miles. We, the audience, hear what he hears, and later, we believe what he believes when he speaks of the importance of respecting Blake and Francis's intention to die together. However, the twins' wishes are never realized because other physicians intervene. While Blake and Francis are being conveyed on a gurney into the operating room, the camera—mounted on a dolly at the level of their faces—focuses on the twins' looks of anguish as an off-camera voice from the surgical team recites medical information in a clipped tone, starkly contrasting Miles's gentle bedside manner. In a last ditch effort to preserve the bond between them, Blake struggles as they approach the doors to the operating room but is swiftly subdued.

As I mention in the Introduction, much of the seminal work in disability studies established how disabled characters in fiction regulate a reader's affect by invoking fear, disgust, pity, and other related feelings. However, it appears that something different is happening in *Twin Falls Idaho*. Rather than disciplining the intended viewer in ways that enable identification with an idealized, nondisabled protagonist, it actually encourages the opposite. The characters who actively buck standards of physical normativity are the most sympathetic and multidimensional. The film's resolution makes this clear.

In the final scene, Penny arrives on the grounds of a defunct circus to visit Francis for the first time since his surgery. When she greets one of the residents, the camera's strategic aim obscures this woman's anatomical difference from the viewer. Penny, of average height, appears dwarfed by June, a little person, as she is filmed from below, the camera angling upward. It is only after June descends the steps of her trailer and stands alongside Penny that we see the extent of the height discrepancy between them.

For the first time in a film whose cinematography is dominated by the dark browns, grays, and olives in the characters' attire and in the urban locales where much of the plot unfolds, the viewer is treated to the lush greens of rural scenery on a sunny day. Whereas the somewhat claustrophobic camera work in the city rarely places subjects more than several feet away from the lens, the bright colors, natural light, and wide-angle views of the expansive circus grounds set the conclusion apart from the bulk of the story that preceded it. That Blake and Francis's prior career with the circus remains hidden until this denouement instantiates a twist ending, given that a key plot turn involves the twins' abandonment of Penny once she allows an entertainment industry agent to gain access to them. Rather than the indignities endured by sideshow performers this earlier scene would have us imagine, the film's conclusion gestures toward quite the opposite. The circus is set in a landscape coded with the visual rhetoric of "freedom"—complete with the Rockies in the background—easily recognizable as such to American viewers. From June, we learn that Blake and Francis were the circus's stars. "They were the best in the show," she beams. "I wish you could have seen them." The sense of pride with which she speaks of her profession, softened by her somewhat mournful nostalgia for the circus's prime ("Most of the performers have left. A few still live on the land, but it's not like it used to be"), elicits positive affect for this physical space and its inhabitants, even as they are understood to be forever relegated to a nostalgic past.

June's characterization as a self-identified circus artist aligns with social historian Robert Bogdan's thesis that although sideshow performers were often portrayed in ways perceived as degrading, the performers themselves tended not to think negatively about their means of livelihood. Many welcomed the opportunity not only to earn an income but also to join a tightly knit, exclusive subculture that stood defiantly outside the perimeter of middle-class conformity.[23] Although June's enthusiasm may indicate that Bogdan is correct, conversation between Blake and Penny complicates this rather celebratory recuperation of an often misunderstood form of entertainment. Directly rebutting Bogdan, historian David Gerber argues that any attempt to read volition into the actions of performers employed in sideshows must always be tempered by the fact that there are limited economic opportunities for disabled people. Until these material inequalities are remedied, as Gerber contends, disabled people's hypervisibility in popular entertainment cannot be considered empowering in the way that Bogdan claims.[24] Certainly, Blake's own opinion about his work with the circus is less positive than June's. As he and Penny sit facing each other on a set of rails, he recounts the times when, as children, he and Francis would fantasize about lying in the path of a train so that they could be separated. This anecdote explains retroactively the train whistle heard at the moment the twins were wheeled, while Blake fights and resists, into the operating room. "But as we grew older, we realized that we didn't have a problem with who we were,"

Blake continues. "Just the audience that came to see us did. We never wanted to be apart for any other reason than being gawked at."

The film's ambivalent assessment of circus life, compressed into the last few minutes, lends it a complexity absent from both Bogdan's and Gerber's analyses. In fact, it convincingly yokes their opposing arguments together. Neither an idealized community happily subverting the constraints of the class politics of the industrial era nor a form of exploitation that produces victims with little or no agency, show business for disabled people is ultimately somewhere in between, something of both.

At the same time, the film's twist ending, of which the final shot is of Penny and Blake (with cane) walking and embracing each other in the sunset before the credits roll, is an entirely conventional and clichéd marriage-plot resolution that finds its teleological closure through appeals to heteronormativity. Although the twins' separation is successful insofar as it keeps Blake from dying alongside his terminally ill brother, the operation actually saves Penny, for her ascension into forms of sanctioned heterosexuality are entirely dependent on it. In fact, the narrative logic of the film reveals that the real patient to be cured in this surgery is Penny and not the twins. This type of ending would not be possible if, say, Francis had recovered from his unnamed illness and the twins continued to live conjoined, interdependent lives. Not only has Penny recuperated herself as a marriageable partner for Blake; she has already proven her maternal potential with her nursing of Francis. Finally, her career change from sex worker to food worker (as she is portrayed in a server's uniform in the penultimate scene) renders her gender-specific transformation complete.

It is no surprise that fathers are conspicuously absent from this gendered narrative of redemption for biological mothers. Predictably, the father of Penny's intellectually disabled son is never mentioned, although the viewer knows that it could potentially be Miles. It is even less clear what role the adoptive parent is supposed to play in a film that otherwise seems to reify biological motherhood. Shown in Blake and Francis's possession, in brief close-up, is a document with the heading "Certificate of Adoption." Their birth mother's information is revealed but any information about the adoptive parent(s) is outside the frame. Since Blake speaks to Penny during the film's conclusion about having worked in the circus from a young age, it is possible that June may be the adoptive parent, but this connection is never made explicit. It is just as likely that June is a colleague. Similarly, when Miles succeeds in convincing Penny to make contact with her biological son's adoptive family, he hands her an envelope—presumably containing the family's records—and keys so that she can borrow his car. We never find out how (or if) this meeting ensues as the next scene shows her arriving at the circus grounds for the film's resolution. Although *Twin Falls Idaho* seems to indict and then redeem biological mothers who part with disabled children, even if that redemption is as simple as Blake and Francis's mother reconnecting with her sons before their surgery and Francis's immanent death, the work of kinship that maintains the parent-child bond is never portrayed. No information is ever provided about Penny's biological son in his adoptive family, and there is only scant information presented to the viewer about Blake and Francis's experience in their adoptive home in the circus.

Conjoined Self-Referentiality

Dead Ringers and *Twin Falls Idaho*—films featuring white women who refuse heteronormative models of kinship—resolve themselves through the disciplining and normalization of women characters. They do so by returning these women to the fold of heterosexuality's presumed redemptive potential and destroying the conjoined men with whom they have developed intimacies. Thus, the separation surgeries these men undergo serve to normalize not only them but also the women with whom they are sexually and affectively engaged. In fact, both of these films suggest that the vanquishing of physical difference in these men is essential and necessary for the rehabilitation of women. As a commentary on this logic, the following contemporary stories—two are novels, one is a film—comprise a metanarrative about conjoinment when considered in conjunction with one another. These stories show that the literary and visual trope of the conjoined twin persists into the twenty-first century and continues to turn on nineteenth-century ideas of bourgeois womanly virtue.

Darin Strauss's *Chang and Eng: A Novel*, a fictionalized story of the Bunkers told from Eng's perspective, narrativizes the sexual transgression of Sarah and Adelaide Yates in their marriage to these famous twins by invoking the figure of the black rapist. The novel begins in medias res as newcomers Chang and Eng Bunker arrive in North Carolina. Upon seeing them for the first time, Sarah and Adelaide's mother, abruptly and without fanfare, says to her son, "Jefferson. . . . Go get your father. . . . Tell him I found a pair of husbands for your sisters."[25] As time wears on, Eng's resentment of his wife, Sarah, is compounded by his increasing suspicion about an event in her history. An enslaved man was lynched for purportedly raping her, but Eng suspects the situation may have been a consensual sexual relationship Sarah initiated. Strauss's narrative implies that this incident has rendered the Yates sisters unmarriageable in their nineteenth-century North Carolina farm town. The question of why two middle-class white women would wed a set of Asian conjoined men is explained by invoking an even more unspeakable sexual transgression—a white woman's sexual involvement with black men.

As if in response to Strauss's novel, which tells the story through Eng's first-person narration, Mark Slouka's *God's Fool* reimagines those same lives through Chang's eyes. In contrast to the elaborately portrayed scenes of sexual activity in *Chang and Eng*, which are preceded by much narrative anticipation, *God's Fool* presents the reader with a scant and matter-of-fact description of sex, dispelling it as a nonissue: "Addy came to our bed that week, but though we pleased each other, sweating in the darkness, neither of us took much comfort in the thing. It was a weapon, nothing more—something to wield against the grief [of losing their son]—and both of us knew it."[26] As with the other mundane tasks of maintaining a household, activities in the marital bed are no more spectacular than, for instance, keeping watch on how the tobacco crop is doing.

Of these three contemporary stories, *Stuck on You* is the most blatantly parodic of conjoined-twin narratives. The Farrelly brothers often reference disability in their films, and this comedy is no exception, speaking as it does to how Peter and Bobby Farrelly thematize the multifaceted elements of human difference.[27] The narrative chronicles a brief period in the lives of Bob and Walt Tenor, portrayed by Matt Damon and Greg Kinnear, respectively. They are short-order cooks making a trip westward to pursue their dreams. Bob's Internet girlfriend, who lives in Los Angeles, has agreed to meet him in person, while Walt attempts to launch a Hollywood acting career. Bob has not informed his girlfriend, May (Wen Yann Shih), that he has a conjoined twin brother. The plot advances according to the increasing measures—laughably ludicrous—he takes to conceal that he and Walt, who chaperones their dates, are attached to each other. Along the way, Walt meets April (Eva Mendes), who immediately establishes that his anatomical configuration is not an issue, but it is unclear to Bob whether May might react in a similar way.

It is worth mentioning that neither of the two female love interests matched with Bob and Walt occupies the category of whiteness without tension. Shih portrays May with accented English, and Mendes—although portraying April as the quintessential all-American girl in *Stuck on You*—bears the traces of roles she has played in films such as *Training Day* and *Once upon a Time in Mexico*, in which her Latin roots are more apparent. Although May's and April's nonwhiteness alone may not be that significant, when juxtaposed against the racially specific standards of virtue to which white women in the texts this chapter discusses are held, it is a conspicuous anomaly. The playful nonchalance of April's reference to the twins' connecting ligament and May's ultimate acceptance of Bob's physical difference indicate perhaps the greater flexibility with which Asian and Latina women can transgress the boundaries of respectability that have historically been maintained for white women. Also, that Bob and Walt—unlike the twins in the texts that precede *Stuck on You*—do not die or become separated at the film's conclusion is apt within this logic.

Stuck on You is a difficult film to watch for the tedious repetitiveness with which jokes about conjoinment are cracked, and any possibility of it mounting a politically enabling critique is withheld until after the end. The song that plays as the credits roll is a cover of Reba McEntire's "The Fear of Being Alone," sung ironically by Reba Schappell, the conjoined sister to Lori Schappell. The Schappells are subjects in the documentary *Face to Face*, in which a story line develops around Reba's aspirations to become a country music singer (she claimed McEntire's first name after being known as "Dori" for much of her younger life). This aural component of *Stuck on You*, coming only after the narrative proper, turns the slapstick of the Farrelly brothers' comedy into a more serious intervention. It makes an intertextual reference recognizable to consumers of conjoined-twin narratives. These consumers recognize it as the song to which *Face to Face* unfolds as they see, in the documentary, Reba Schappell recording it in the studio and then performing the song in the music video that closes out *Face to Face*.[28]

However, if this song marks a moment of self-determination for the nonfictional conjoined twins Reba and Lori Schappell, it reinscribes the physical difference of the fictional characters in *Stuck on You*. One of its visibly disabled actors, Ray "Rocket" Valliere, appears after the credits, thanking the team of actors, crew, and producers that made the film possible. Although this postscript—tempting viewers to regard it as an endorsement of *Stuck on You* by disabled people—lends a credibility and authenticity to the film, we need to remember that the narrative has already self-consciously mocked how physical difference can be generated on screen, whether it is to hide or fake it. The casting of two actors who are not identical twins, given that all conjoined twins are identical, is the most obvious clue that physical difference is meant to be tongue in cheek. Moreover, the prosthesis connecting Bob and Walt does not make any attempt to look real. In one memorable scene, Cher (playing herself) is trying to break a television contract because she is dissatisfied with her role. Invoking the line from her agreement that indicates she will have free reign to choose her male lead, she picks Walt, the aspiring actor, who, of course, is conjoined with Bob. To Cher's dismay, the director simply uses blue screen technology to erase Bob from scenes that are shot, rendering her act of protest moot.

The Farrelly brothers' self-conscious parodying of onscreen visual manipulation then calls any filmic portrayals of unusual embodiment into question. However, the seemingly candid and unscripted footage of Valliere speaking into a microphone to a crowd outside the frame elides the discrepancy between the massive financial backing that a directorial duo such as Peter and Bobby Farrelly are able to command and the limited and often demeaning capacities people like Valliere tend to serve in the film industry. Valliere's moment of bridled success mediates, again, between Robert Bogdan's and David Gerber's respective theses. Disabled entertainers may achieve enabling forms of self-fashioning through their visibility in mass culture industries, but at the same time, they also find themselves circumscribed by the conditions of employment discrimination against disabled people in the workforce more generally.

In the filmic portrayals of conjoined twinning discussed in this chapter, it is technology—rather than anatomy—that is on dramatic scopophilic display. Be they high- or low-tech special effects, the panoply of computerized camera work, latex prosthetics, and pancake makeup becomes a visually stunning surrogate for the flesh-and-blood extraordinary body onstage from generations past. Jeremy Irons's portrayal of the dual roles in *Dead Ringers* is commendably convincing as he deftly conveys these two dissimilar characters not only through the delivery of his lines but also through facial expressions and body language. However, it is those moments in which the viewer steps back and understands the mechanics of how this actor works with a never-before used technology that the fullness of his virtuosity is realized. With a moving camera capturing both the A and B sides of a twin scene, Irons not only must be attuned to the timing of each cue when the characters are engaged in dialogue; he must also be mindful of his blocking—paying close attention to the pace and position of his movements—to keep the two images from overlapping in any shot. Although the prosthesis that Mark and Michael Polish wear in *Twin Falls Idaho* may seem low-tech when compared to the unprecedented cinematic equipment unveiled in *Dead Ringers*, part of what is so astounding for the viewer is imagining how these actors endured the physical discomfort for hours at a time during the process of filming. The impairment of Blake and Francis's movements rendered onscreen is facilitated by the actual burdensome nature of the actors' costume.[29]

All the texts in this chapter hinge on the changing nature of kinship for white women in contemporary culture. Beginning in the 1960s in North America, debates about the expanded range of life choices for middle-class women took place on a national and very public scale, even if the processes of working through them in fiction relegated these concerns to the space of the domestic. The strong sense of uncertainty with which the American public greeted these changes were focalized in representations of white women perceived as needing a return to gender's regulatory fold even as they welcomed the increasing options resulting from these developments. The white woman in these narratives, as a symbol onto which the nation's ambivalence is projected, is portrayed as someone who is divided within herself about the relative benefits and drawbacks of these freedoms.

Part III

Observing and Participating

7

Our Esteemed Ancestors

We have seen how the figure of the white woman functions in contemporary fictional narratives about the flexibility and malleability of kinship. These moments that unravel heteropatriarchal models of the family in late-twentieth- and early-twenty-first-century fiction and film show how conjoined men trouble modernity's atomized kin unit through the destabilization of liberal humanist concepts of personhood. The women companions of these twins then become the lynchpins on which critiques of normative family structures turn. Whether it is Nadine in *Attachments*, Claire in *Dead Ringers*, Penny in *Twin Falls Idaho*, or the fictionalized Sarah and Adelaide in *Chang and Eng* and *God's Fool*, these figurations of white womanhood deflect the shock associated with anatomical difference. Our attention is then redirected to the imperative to reimagine sexualized kinship formations in ways that more realistically accommodate the range of differences in everyday life.

Part III: "Observing and Participating" is composed of a single chapter shaped with ethnographic techniques. I examine the kin-making practices of Chang and Eng Bunker's descendants, which are yet another take on the importance of rethinking familial structures. Like the cultural producers from Chapter 6, the Bunker descendants see both pleasure and danger in creating kin relationships that deviate from traditional notions of family. Through a process that is simultaneously tightly structured and improvisational, the Bunker descendants shape a family identity that begins with their relationship to these exceptional ancestors but arrives at objectives that extend well beyond their investment in Chang and Eng. These ties—both binding and loose—are ultimately not much different from how most families maintain themselves in the face of changing perceptions about kinship.

The bonds the Bunker descendants have created are accommodating and fluid on several different levels. On the one hand, the activity of documenting consanguineous relationships to Chang and Eng has been a very visible and cherished part of the process through which the Bunker family has consolidated itself. To be able to claim direct lineage to these nineteenth-century entertainers and to find others similarly related is something these descendants hold dear. On the other hand, the valuing of genetic descent and wedded relation also gives way to more expansive notions of kinship that issue forth opportunistically from what initially started as research into biologically based familial relations.

Inventing the Bunker Family

During the summer of 2003, I drove 1,100 miles from what was then my home in Saint Paul, Minnesota, to reach Mount Airy, North Carolina, which is near Winston-Salem. This small town is best known as the birthplace of Andy Griffith and the inspiration for *The Andy Griffith Show*'s fictional town of Mayberry. Having arrived a day early for the anticipated Bunker family reunion, I spent my free time hiking the trails around the summit of Pilot Mountain and acquainting myself with the area by visiting the Mount Airy Visitor's Center and the Mount Airy Museum of Regional History. Then, on a characteristically hot and humid July afternoon, I joined nearly two hundred other people at the First United Methodist Church in the adjacent town of Pilot Knob. In the crowded space of a reception hall heavy with the aromas of baked beans, macaroni and cheese, ham hocks, and fried chicken, I became an honorary Bunker.

In the early 1980s, Warren and Nancy Bunker Atkins of Dobson, North Carolina—near Mount Airy, the original homestead of Chang and Eng—began hosting family reunions.[1] Nancy is one of Eng's great-great-granddaughters. What began as a modest and informal gathering of about sixty-five relatives eventually grew into a larger yearly event. In recent years, the last Saturday of July has been solidified as the annual date of the reunion banquet. Other activities are scheduled for the Friday beforehand and the Sunday afterward, but the maintenance of kinship relations merge into the rest of the year so as to become a part of everyday life for some of these family members. Many of Chang and Eng's descendants have remained in the western part of North Carolina. Others were born elsewhere or have moved out of the area but sustain affective ties to the region through their avowed connection to these famous ancestors.

Nothing I am claiming about the Bunker family's concept of kinship—flexible even as it glamorizes consanguinity—is new for anyone versed in the anthropological literature that addresses this issue. The topic of kinship has long been a central focus for qualitative social scientists studying the subjective dimensions of human life, and the discipline of anthropology built much of its early methodologies around an examination of family units. David Schneider's foundational scholarship is a key example. Published in 1968, the findings in *American Kinship* have been problematized in recent decades, but nevertheless, Schneider lays useful groundwork for thinking about familial relations in the United States. According to Schneider, subjects in what he calls "primitive" or "peasant" societies have their understanding of kin relations integrated into the entirety of their social relations. There is no such thing as kinship as opposed to something else. However, Schneider claims that Americans invest in the promise of self-determination in all aspects of public life (i.e., holding political office, owning property, engaging in business transactions, and so on) in ways that are imagined as unaided and unfettered by family of origin.[2] Thus, to suggest that kinship might be of significant import in U.S. civic society already cuts across the grain of popular opinion.

The very study of kinship in the United States, as Schneider recognizes, is touchy because of the ethos of individualism in American culture. As Alexis de Tocqueville's words in the first epigraph to *Chang and Eng Reconnected* suggest, what distinguishes Americans from their European forebears is the premium they place on notions of merit presumed to exist apart from the influence of ancestry. However, Schneider claims that the sustained primacy of kin relations to many Americans has not harmed the sanctity of self-fashioning on which their culture is organized. Rather, it is the very adaptability of American kinship structures that has allowed concepts of personal independence, self-actualization, and agency to flourish.[3] Although *American Kinship* confirms the importance of hereditary lineage and marriage in processes of kin making among his informants, Schneider is careful to state from the onset that there is a corresponding emphasis that Americans assign to familial networks outside of these bonds. These seemingly rigid frameworks frequently expand to more elastic relationships across a range of his informants' experiences.

As one of postmodern anthropology's earliest voices, Schneider went on to complicate his analysis further in *A Critique of the Study of Kinship*, stressing that kinship is not an empirical entity, one simply waiting to be uncovered, measured, explained, and documented. Rather, it is an ethnographic invention. By extension, the meanings that North American and European anthropologists impart to family are imposed on the processes of observation in other societies. These observers craft analogous models of understanding social organization in their field locations, which are then summarily categorized under the rubric of "kinship." Although—as Schneider described earlier in *American Kinship*—U.S.-based societies see great importance in the linkages between (heterosexual) pair-bonding, (hetero)sexual intercourse, gestation, birth, and childrearing, the significance that emerges from this chain of biologically reproductive functions is not necessarily the same one assigned by other societies.[4]

As would be expected of a population based in the United States, the means through which the Bunker family has consolidated itself is based on the principles of kinship that Schneider laid out in his study. The tracing of wedded, biologically generative pairs from Chang and Eng to their present-day descendants may normalize the processes of reproductive life Schneider described in his 1968 study, but it also makes it impossible to overlook the non-normativity of Chang and Eng Bunker's sexual arrangements, a vexing issue that the uninitiated may find difficult to accept. As I mention in Chapter 2, the question of how these couples managed to replicate the dictates of Victorian domesticity is so boggling that even the anatomists, who were pleading for permission to conduct an autopsy on Chang and Eng, could not resist asking their widows about their sexual habits during what was a time of mourning for the family. During my 2003 visit to the family reunion, I overheard a reporter from a local paper at the banquet (to which the press is regularly invited) express incredulity that these twins could have fathered children. Despite being surrounded by much evidence of the twins' procreative activities, the reporter was compelled to voice her disbelief. A descendant seated at the same table, who was probably used to such comments, shrugged nonchalantly and said, "You're too visual."

Growing the Bunker Family Tree

The filling in of the Bunker family tree had humble origins. Jessie Bunker Bryant, a great-granddaughter of Eng, was one of the original guests at Warren and Nancy Bunker Atkins's gatherings in the 1980s. At these informal reunions, Bryant began recording the names and addresses of guests and assembling them into booklets she distributed as Christmas gifts.[5] Because family members marveled at the usefulness of having an address and phone list that made it easy to keep in touch with others throughout the year, Bryant decided to widen her scope to include not only the core group of sixty-five or so at the Atkins' reunions but other relatives as well.

First, Bryant started compiling data by snowball sampling—asking known relatives for information on their relatives, asking these new contacts for their contacts, and so on. Even during the project's earliest stages, she was able to connect many families who previously had been unknown to one another. A large proportion of the descendants had remained in the western part of North Carolina, but she was able to find numerous others far away. Bryant later supplemented this organically culled data by making trips to the Surry County Courthouse for birth, death, and marriage records and the Surry County Genealogical Association Library at Surry Community College in Dobson. The information Bryant amassed eventually took the form of an ambitious self-published book titled *The Connected Bunkers*, a pun that references Chang and Eng's anatomical conjoining and their descendants' familial ties to one another. *The Connected Bunkers* is a manuscript that tracks the progression of generations issuing from the original twins. Copies are offered for sale each year at the reunion. The entries in the book include basic information about descendants who were known to Bryant at the time the project was finished. Facsimiles of photographs, press accounts, letters, and other items interspersed throughout the volume lend a human face to the otherwise generic facts and figures. About her writing process, Bryant—who was seventy-five years old at the time the project was completed in 2001—declares proudly, "I do not have e-mail or a computer. I did my book without it! People cannot believe it."[6]

There is friction between processes of kin making imagined as primordial and those associated with modernity in Bryant's piecing together of the branches of Chang and Eng Bunker's descendants. Her rhizomic method of surveying those with whom she was acquainted face-to-face later merged with, but was not overtaken by, her consultation with the record-keeping apparatus of the state and its juridical hold over various rites of passage. Although composing on a typewriter may simply be how Bryant is most comfortable writing, her communication with me—at the time just shy of my thirtieth birthday—about her lack of a computer indicates her understanding of the technological gulf that separates her from those in my peer group. Moreover, Bryant's documenting of these consanguineous links may be a way of, as she puts it, "connecting" families, but it is also a process of *creating* families—that is, of inaugurating interpersonal ties that did not exist before her genealogical project. The Bunker family was not simply "there," waiting to be uncovered by the right research tools. It was called into being by Bryant's work.

Taking in a different direction Schneider's argument that kinship is a discursive production on the part of anthropologists, I claim the Bunker family concept as it exists today was literally created by the ethnographic gaze. Although Warren and Nancy Bunker Atkins's reunions in the 1980s took root organically, cultural and intellectual producers sparked by public interest in Chang and Eng's legacy have catalyzed some of the activities associated with family that descendants now recognize as part of their rituals. When the Atkins's gatherings began to take place, the guests were drawn only from Eng and Sarah's side of the family. It was not until 1990 that descendants from Chang and Adelaide's line joined with them. Jessie Bunker Bryant recounts that filmmakers from Thailand had wanted to assemble the twins' descendants for a documentary about the country's most well-known expatriates. Because of this request from the Thai popular media, Bryant met with Milton Haynes, a Chang great-grandson, and collaborated with him to get both sides of the family together for the filming.[7]

The contact these Thai documentarians made with key descendants, thus, has solidified in family lore as the pivotal event that created the ritual of the Bunker family reunion. These filmmakers are credited as such in the explanation about the beginnings of this annual tradition. On the program of the reunion banquet distributed to each reunion guest are these words:

> In December 1990, family members were invited to the Wallburg Baptist Church, located in Wallburg, NC; which is between Winston-Salem and High Point. The purpose was the filming of a documentary by the Kantana Company, a television production company located in Bangkok,

> Thailand. The documentary was about the lives of the Twins and included their life in America and the families that followed.
>
> Since that time, descendants from both families, Sarah and Eng, and Adelaide and Chang, have come together for a reunion to get to know their extended family better and to learn more about their unique heritage.[8]

Perhaps this acknowledgement of the Bunker family's origins is why descendants have readily welcomed the press and other researchers, both in and outside of the academy, who are interested in speaking with them. Although comfort with reporters and scholars varies from person to person, there tends to be a general consensus that the presence of these nondescendant guests is part of the terrain of consorting with family in this venue. During my first visit in 2003, Helen Zia, author and former editor of *Ms. Magazine*, was there to find material for a manuscript on Asian American families. In subsequent years, I have also been in attendance with medical historian Alice Domurat Dreger, author of *One of Us*, and documentarian Josh Gibson, director of *The Siamese Connection*. Reporters from local papers, such as the *Mount Airy News* and the *Winston-Salem Journal*, come each year. In addition, a History Channel feature on the Bunker family and an article in *National Geographic* include material garnered at the reunion. Thus, the very materiality of kinship is an actual ethnographic invention, but it is by no means solely a creation of these cultural and intellectual producers. Rather, this high-profile family coalesces in tandem with the processes of knowledge production about it.

The Last Weekend in July

The number of people attending Bunker reunions tends to be fairly even—with an occasional blip. In my first year visiting, the crowd was larger than what I later understood is a typical turnout of about one hundred. In 2010, attendance was down slightly; when the program began, about half the tables in the reception hall were still empty. By my own estimation, there were seventy to eighty people present, and the change could have been due to the heavy rains that day keeping would-be travelers at home. Another reason may have been that the following year would be a milestone, the two hundredth anniversary of Chang and Eng's birth, and priority for some family members had gone toward anticipating the years when there would be more fanfare. As expected, the anniversary year saw a spike in attendance—possibly one hundred fifty—with a large number of first-time attendees. There are approximately fifteen hundred known descendants, and the reunion turnout represents a small fraction of that population. There is a core group of regulars who attend every or almost every reunion, and then there are those who attend only occasionally.

A typical banquet involves both informal mingling and a structured sequence of events. Doors open at 11:00 A.M., one hour before the official start of the program. As participants arrive, they are checked in and provided name tags by the greeter staffing the entrance. The name tags show not only the wearer's name but from which side of the family they hail. The documentation of lineage on the name tags is quite detailed, depicting each branch of the family tree so that, for instance, "C-6-9-3-1" would indicate the holder of the tag is Chang's great-great-grandchild issuing from his sixth child's ninth child's third child's first child. This style of recording descent, initially developed in Jessie Bunker Bryant's *The Connected Bunkers*, allows attendees to see how genealogically near or far cousins are to themselves. After registering with the greeter, family members encounter, just beyond the entryway, several rectangular tables where dishes for the potluck buffet are placed. Beyond that is the reception hall filled with round tables that accommodate approximately eight guests each.

During the hour of informal socializing, guests trickle in steadily and mill about in the buffet area and in the reception hall. The seating is unassigned, and guests tend to congregate according to nuclear family of origin. Researchers and the press integrate themselves into one of the tables. A station is set up just opposite the buffet area displaying items provided by family members, such as vintage photographs, current photo albums, and other mementos. One of the most prominently displayed photographs at the 2010 reunion was of present-day conjoined brothers Ronnie and Donnie Galyon, who had visited Mount Airy earlier that year. The Galyons are attempting to break the Bunker twins' record for being the world's longest-lived conjoined twins. They had been visiting Mount Airy to see Andy Griffith's birthplace when they discovered that it was also home to Chang and Eng Bunker, and they managed to connect with some family members during their stay.

During this period of unstructured time before the start of the reunion program, family members can be seen perusing the photographs and other memorabilia, as well as greeting and embracing. Conversation between relatives seeing one another after a hiatus tends toward personal and family news, and there may be subjects that arise over and over about specific descendants. For instance, at the time of the reunion in 2010, Florida polls showed that Adelaide "Alex" Sink—a Chang great-granddaughter who grew up on Chang's original farm—was the favored candidate in the upcoming Democratic Party's primary for the gubernatorial election.[9] This was a popular topic of conversation at the reunion that year. The informal socializing winds down as lines form at the buffet tables and guests return to their tables with full plates.

Jim Haynes is the usual master of ceremonies at the reunion. After he calls the banquet hall to order at noon, he introduces Gary York, a close family friend and former Surry County commissioner, who is identified in the program as an "Honorary Bunker" to lead the room in the saying of grace. As guests begin dining, the program continues with items such as a remembrance of the lives of family members who have died the previous year, a roll call of descendants whereby each nuclear family unit is asked to stand and recite the branches from which they hail, and recognition of the youngest family member (there are usually several infants present and stiff competition ensues for this honor), the oldest family member, and the family member who traveled the farthest distance to the reunion. During my first attendance in 2003, which was right after the United States' invasion of Iraq, a moment of silence was reserved for descendants who were deployed at the time. There is also "housekeeping business," such as a financial report by the family treasurer and calls for successors to take on leadership roles vacated by officers who have stepped down. Eventually, first-time attendees are asked to form a line behind a microphone at one end of the banquet hall and introduce themselves. Nondescendants, such as close friends or researchers, are then welcomed into the family as honorary Bunkers.

These activities, which are directly related to the development and management of kinship ties, are supplemented by additional programming that makes it difficult to ignore what distinguishes these gatherings from more run-of-the-mill family reunions. The celebrity status of these ancestors is continually thematized and emphasized in the weekend's scheduling. A researcher event usually takes place on the Friday before the banquet to allow the family to become acquainted with the intellectual producers who take interest in them.[10] A production of playwright Burton Cohen's *The Wedding of the Siamese Twins* coincides annually with reunion weekend. There are Friday matinee and Saturday evening performances, which are held at the Surry Arts Council, a facility that houses—among other things—the Andy Griffith Museum and the Chang and Eng Bunker Gallery, which together showcase Mount Airy's most well-known entertainers. Informal pilgrimages to Chang and Eng's plot in the cemetery of the White Plains Baptist Church take place on the Sunday after the banquet.

At the same time, organizers plan the reunion in ways that accommodate the more conventional needs of guests, some who travel from afar, to connect with family not readily available face-to-face at other times of the year. A lunch at a modestly priced restaurant on Friday allows reunion participants to socialize informally in anticipation of the more structured events ahead. Designating the Mount Airy Hampton Inn—owned by Eng great-granddaughter Betty Bunker Blackmon—as official reunion headquarters means that out-of-town guests, who receive a discount for the weekend, can partake in spontaneous encounters with one another in the hotel lobby, pool, gym, and breakfast area. A service at the First Baptist Church on Sunday appears on the itinerary for those who would like to worship with others within the context of reunion weekend.

Since these kin-making activities can be affectively pleasurable and difficult alike—as they are for most families—a guest speaker was invited one year to address how to anticipate and handle interpersonal dynamics that emerge when multiple generations and nuclear units converge. Laurence Basirico, professor of sociology at Elon University in Elon, North Carolina, provided this guidance and distributed copies of his book *The Family Reunion Survival*

Guide, in which he stresses the importance of good advance planning and the acknowledgement of "family culture[s]" that can differ from one nuclear unit to the next.[11] Although the organization of family reunion activities around a set of exceptional ancestors may make the Bunker descendants stand out, when viewed from the perspective of Basirico's field observations of many family gatherings, this example appears less an aberration from and more in line with other reunions that are often similarly structured around a central theme: be it a particular ancestor, a holiday of great importance to the family, or some other cherished commonality.[12] Despite one descendant's wry observation that the reunion has a bit of a "Chang and Eng fan club" feel to it, rather than operating in the way she figured a more conventional family reunion would, it appears that the Bunkers share their kin-making practices with numerous other families across the country.

Lineage, Descent, and Hypodescent

As I lay out in Chapter 1, the presence of the Asian diaspora in the American South revealed the tensions and contradictions within the black-white dichotomy that accompanied regulatory systems surrounding race. As a group that existed, at times, between or apart from those binary poles and, at other times, closer to one than the other, Asians mediated the opposing contrasts of black and white and called attention to the existing social order's inadequacies. These ruptures that Asians produced were especially palpable in how mixed-race children of Asian and white parentage were accounted for within existing frameworks.

The American South's "fiction of law and custom" mandated that mixed-race children of black-white parentage be classified as black, a practice of hypodescent that valorized exclusively white familial lineages. Although the collective imagination conceives of this taxonomic standard in the fashion of the "one drop rule," as it is commonly known, classificatory practices played themselves out differently at the micro level, whereby individual states quantified in varying ways how much African ancestry made an individual legally black.[13] Historian David Hollinger notes that hypodescent is not racially neutral but isolates blackness as the entity that begs management and containment. Using the case of Native Americans as a counterexample, Hollinger reveals the discrepancies with which being of mixed racial heritage is perceived. Although the claiming of indigenous ancestry has been romanticized and has, in fact, proceeded alongside settler colonialism, there is no correspondence when it comes to the recognition of black heritage:

> We do not see a multitude of ostensibly white Americans reclassifying themselves as part black. . . . The stigma carried by blackness is unique. . . . One has not been able to say "I'm one-eighth African American" without giving up socially, if not legally, the seven-eighths part of

> one self that is not. You can be one-eighth Cherokee and still be seven-eighths something else, but if you are one-eighth black you are not likely to be counted as white at all.[14]

Given the black-specific abjection the American practice of hypodescent performs, it is not surprising that juridical and cultural forces bearing on children of Asian-white parentage were different from those that accompanied children of black-white parentage. The U.S. census did not have a separate category for Chinese people until 1870; before that, the Chinese were counted as white. Historian Lucy Cohen finds that there was no standardized practice as to how children of Chinese and non-Chinese parents were classified with the advent of this new category. Among the Chinese men living in Louisiana with white wives, some had their children listed as white and others had their offspring listed as Chinese on the 1880 census.[15] The wedding of Chang and Eng Bunker to Adelaide and Sarah Yates in 1843, and their subsequent fathering of children from the years 1844 to 1868, would have predated the 1870 census. Nevertheless, Bunker family lore and one of Chang and Eng's biographies suggests that there was displeasure in the local community over the twins' double wedding to white women.[16]

The vast majority of attendees at the Bunker family reunion are phenotypically white. There is a level of consistency with which Bunker descendants make sense of their Asian ancestry when describing a subjectivity that arises from their genealogical connection to Chang and Eng. Family members tend to declare their pride for this unusual feature, an interesting embellishment on an otherwise uncomplicated white identity, which functions as an interesting topic of conversation and icebreaker when meeting new people. At the same time, they stress that not all descendants have been similarly minded or that they themselves have not always had a positive opinion about that ancestry. A descendant once expressed to me that when she was a child, her uncle—himself a Bunker descendant—teased her because she was darker complexioned than her fair-haired sibling. The nickname her uncle gave her was "Chinky," a historically specific racial epithet that he modified into a diminutive term of endearment for his niece. Although she understood that the joking was meant to be affectionate, she found it hurtful, particularly because no one else in her immediate family resembled her in appearance.[17] Among present-day descendants, many stories abound of relatives from previous generations who disavowed their connections to Chang and Eng—because of racial difference, anatomical difference, or both.

There is a double-edged maneuver that such proclamations create. The embrace of nonwhite lineage, proudly called "hybrid vigor" by one descendant and "a different thread running through that tapestry [of northern European stock]" by another, undoubtedly provides delight for my informants. However, it could also potentially romanticize the difference of shadowy and idealized distant ancestors without taking full account of their circumstances.

Likewise, this often ahistorical embrace of a distant nonwhite relation may overlook the particularities of racialized lived experience in the present time and day. My interactions with various Bunker descendants, however, show that their identification with these famous ancestors tends to be more complex than that. The recurring teleological narrative that announces an overcoming of the negative affect associated with racial difference itself acknowledges the workings of a racist society and the privileges of whiteness. The "hybrid vigor" brandished at one moment could easily become the shock of receiving an epithet such as "Chinky," and these two opposing affective poles are dependent on each other for their legibility.

It is tempting to claim that despite the Bunker family's almost totemistic embrace of ancestors who migrated from Asia, their actual access to an Asian American identity is limited. According to social historians who have documented the emergence of something called "Asian America," this political coalition emerged from the interlock of race-based civil rights organizing and anti–Vietnam War protest based largely (but by no means exclusively) in the San Francisco Bay Area during the late 1960s and early 1970s.[18] It may be the case that many Bunker descendants, living in western North Carolina, would have had little access to the activities and effects of these changes in the United States. There are certain Bunkers who may claim Asian ancestry without having adopted or even having been aware of the existence of an Asian American subjectivity as defined here.

However, it is important to remember that many other examples abound of people of Asian descent living in the United States—temporarily, longer-term, or even permanently—for whom this is the case. The Bunkers should not be considered an exception from an imagined norm in which ancestry, racial categorization, and political sensibility correlate neatly. As the transnational turn in ethnic studies has shown, these entities more often than not play themselves out in unexpected and unpredictable ways. From Aihwa Ong's study of class-privileged East Asian subjects who migrate repeatedly across the global north, to Vicente Rafael's research on Filipino overseas contract workers, to a host of other examples, we see that numerous people of Asian descent who land in the United States do not necessarily come to sympathize with the modes of social critique that gave rise to something known as "Asian America."[19] This paradigm shift in the field of Asian American studies—which privileges flow and movement rather than static models of identity—is one that dislocates space, race, culture, and nation from one another.

Most Bunker family members are not, by and large, directly enabled or oppressively controlled by the global flows of labor, capital, and/or culture in quite the same way as the subjects discussed in the aforementioned studies. However, the conceptual framework invoked by Ong, Rafael, and others riding the transnational turn makes it easier to see the Bunkers through a lens that does not regard their seeming incongruities as atypical. That racialized embodiment necessary engenders pan-ethnic, cross-racial, and transnational subjectivities or that subjectivity arises only out of racialized embodiment is what this body of work has repeatedly debunked. This is far from saying that the critique developed by Asian American rights movements and other civil rights movements has escaped the Bunker family. In fact, my interactions with them, in the form of structured interviews and casual conversations alike, have shown that descendants possess a nuanced understanding of racial inequality in the United States. Moreover, they show that they are able to understand their place and that of their ancestors within these racial dynamics.

Chang and Eng Bunker's Descendants and Asian Ancestry

Margaret Kansa is a descendant of the Bunkers through her maternal line. Her mother, Margo Miles-Carney, is a great-great-granddaughter of Eng. Ironically, it was not Kansa's mother but her father, a nondescendant history buff, who first informed her in her childhood that she was related to these nineteenth-century celebrities. Kansa says this in an interview about first discovering the connection:

> I was probably thirteen or fourteen. . . . My dad was taking my brother and I back to my mom's—my parents are divorced—and we were talking about an area where I lived. . . . He was saying that we were related to both the families that these landmarks [seen along the drive] are from . . . on his side of the family. And somehow it came up, "Well, what about Mom's side? Isn't there anything interesting from Mom's side?" And he said, "Well, you guys got the twins." And my brother and I had no idea what he was talking about. He's like, "Your mom hasn't told you?"[20]

Many of the older relatives from Kansa's maternal line had downplayed their relationship to Chang and Eng Bunker. When asked about the source of this reticence, Kansa speculates that it may have been behavior passed down by George Ashby, a grandson of Eng who was Kansa's great-grandfather. Ashby was, at one point, president of the Union Pacific Railroad, and the irony of a man such as him holding the highest executive position in an industry that has historically exploited Chinese immigrant workers is not lost on Kansa. She surmises that Ashby was mum about his heritage because he worried about what this connection to a race associated with demeaning, underpaid labor would do to his career.[21]

When Kansa discusses whether she considers herself Asian American, there is a bit of active processing before she makes an attempt to speak:

> I don't think being part [*pausing*]—I can't even say I'm part Asian, like it's such a small amount, right? Like, no one would believe me. . . . I think that [my ancestry] is good to know, because I could have had thalassemia, for example, and a doctor wouldn't have even thought to have

> tested me for it. And even when I asked my doctor to test me for it, she kind of brushed me off, and I had to say, "No, I am part Asian."[22]

Thalassemia is a genetically inherited blood disorder found in populations originating close to the equator where it provides some degree of protection against malaria. A number of the Bunker descendants have already been diagnosed, and it is believed among some that the gene came from Chang and Eng. Here, Kansa expresses that awareness about her genetic lineage is a prudent way of keeping abreast of any medical matters that are linked to heredity. At the same time, she resists laying claim to an Asian heritage:

> I don't have any culturally—there's nothing that's been passed down through my family of any kind, of any thing that I know of that's an Asian trait or way of doing something or words. There's nothing continual in that regard. . . . I don't think it would be fair to Asian people, to people with a greater percentage of Asian-ness or background. I think it would be rude of me to say that I was Asian. . . . I went through a period where I thought I could say that I was Asian, but I don't think I can.[23]

Kansa's words make visible the friction between the fact of a direct genetic Asian ancestor and the absence of a set of signifying practices that can be considered identifiably Asian. By pointing out that there is a difference between the transmission of a biological link and the transmission of languages, rituals, and customs, Kansa astutely observes that racial categorization and cultural practices have long been yoked together in United States even as this connection has been tenuous.[24] Recognizing that race weaves in and out of the shifting interplay among social disadvantage, heredity, and quotidian life, her musings about her own claim or lack thereof to something called "Asian American" reveal how complex these identifications can be.

Also, family members' insights about race in U.S. society are articulated in less formal interactions. As I visited Eng great-great-granddaughter Kathy Bryant Proctor in her home on the day after the 2010 reunion, our conversation drifted from the specifics of her nuclear family to social changes that took place during her childhood. About *Brown v. Board of Education*, Proctor says that the rural area where she was raised was predominantly white, and therefore, the Supreme Court decision did not have a material impact on her community. She recognizes that despite her ancestry, she was able to melt effortlessly into her environment. Proctor's mother—the aforementioned Jessie Bunker Bryant—was present during my visit and volunteered the information that before *Brown*, some school districts in North Carolina had a three-way segregation system that separated whites, blacks, and Lumbee Indians from one another.[25] However, the circumstances of Proctor's own schooling did not change after the Supreme Court ruling because of her social position. She recounts that at the time, it seemed as if nothing had happened. Likewise, she mentions being isolated from events in nearby Greensboro (where the landmark Woolworth's counter sit-in occurred in 1960). In her self-aware account of events in her past, it appears that the primary social gulf revolved not around differing racial categories but around the urban/rural divide, this being a case in which demographic and cultural differences were greater than the modest geographical distance between the city of Greensboro and its outlying areas.[26]

Asked about her ancestors' racial significance, Chang descendant Tanya Jones channels her thinking through the vantage point of wives Adelaide and Sarah Bunker. As the executive director of the Surry Arts Council, where the Chang and Eng Gallery is located, she is used to talking about her famous ancestors:

> A lot of times, people ask me questions because the exhibit is in there, and, you know, Chang and Eng and their accomplishments were incredibly huge. But their partners were huge contributors. . . . Their wives were an important factor, because they had to be—for that time period—extremely open-minded and extremely forward thinking. And, you know. . . . I think it's incredible. And I'm hugely proud.[27]

Her words about Adelaide and Sarah's role in the twins' lives do two things. First, Jones performs a gendered analysis that debunks popular assumptions of male careerist success. Her emphasis that "their partners were huge contributors" cautions one not to overlook the invisible work that women have historically performed to allow their spouses to flourish. The extraordinary names Chang and Eng made for themselves in the entertainment industry cannot, as Jones suggests, be viewed separately from the family members who worked behind the scenes. Second, she reasons that Adelaide and Sarah performed *discursive* work in addition to the material work of managing the household while their husbands were away. Alluding to widespread fears about racial mixing that existed during Chang and Eng's lifetime, Jones concludes that their wives must also have been extraordinary themselves, "open-minded" and "forward thinking," to have been willing to act against prevailing social taboos. The declaration—"I'm hugely proud"—with which this descendant sums up her sentiments about Asian ancestry references the accomplishments of the white women as well as the men in these two pairings.

In-Laws and Other Nonconsanguineous Bunkers

If knowledge of a direct hereditary relationship to Chang and Eng is alternately anxiety provoking and prized—or prized because its anxiety has been triumphantly overcome—the place of nonconsanguineous kin sheds a different kind of light on how family ties are generated and maintained. There are the honorary Bunkers, such as researchers and other guests, attending the Bunker family reunion, and then there are others who establish themselves in the family through affective and domestic ties with descendants. As evident in Margaret Kansa's account about discovering her lineage, sometimes nondescendant family members—in Kansa's case, her father—take an equal or more active role in the nurturing of a Bunker identity. The roles nonhereditary Bunkers play, often set within the context of a parent-child bond, are crucial to how this family passes down its sense of tradition from generation to generation.

Like Kansa's father, Sherry Blackmon also married into the Bunker family. As the spouse of Zack Blackmon, great-great-grandson of Eng, she has become one of the most active and visible members of the network of extended kin relations. She is the mother of a son and daughter who are twins themselves, and she sees it as her parental duty to foster in them pride about their lineage, whether it comes from her own side of the family or from Zack's. In her living room is a display cabinet full of Chang and Eng memorabilia, and framing the piano is a set of formal family portraits from generations past. Her enthusiasm for fostering a sense of familial belonging around Chang and Eng is so strong that, at times, it appears to bypass that of her spouse. One story she tells about the experience of seeing the twins' plaster body cast at the Mütter Museum suggests this may so. While accompanying her husband on a business trip to Philadelphia, Blackmon wandered into the Mütter because she had heard about the Bunker artifacts there. Encountering the cast, she was so moved by the experience that she called Zack immediately and impressed on him that he could not end his trip without seeing it himself. In this anecdote, Blackmon passionately stresses that she, a nondescendant, was actually more invested in this object than was her descendant spouse and that if it had not been for her urging, Zack may have missed the opportunity to visit the Mütter while he was in the city.[28]

Another nonconsanguineous family member who is as steadfastly regular at the family reunions is Margaret Boland, stepdaughter of Chang great-grandson Milton Haynes. The stepparent-stepchild relation seems to be an under-recognized family connection in general, but it appears to be an affectively enabling one for Boland and Haynes. The closeness of this stepdaughter-stepfather bond can be seen in Boland's initiative in the inner workings of the reunion. Both Milton Haynes and Boland's mother, Chase Haynes, are active consistently as reunion organizers. The Hayneses maintain the mailing list of invitees, and they always arrive early to and leave late from the banquet to oversee the setup and cleaning. Boland accompanies her parents enthusiastically in their leadership roles within the Bunker family. At the 2010 reunion, she staffed the registration table and passed the collection plate.

Quite possibly, the most visible nondescendant family member is Kester Sink, who married into the Bunkers through Adelaide Bunker Sink (now deceased). He resides on Chang's original homestead, which remains a quiet farm hidden from view by trees on one of Mount Airy's major thoroughfares. The entrance to the farm is an unobtrusive, narrow driveway next to a car dealership at the point where the progression of strip malls and large chain stores abruptly turns into old growth forest and the two-lane, traffic signal–studded road becomes a highway. Despite Sink's initiation into the family through marriage, there is some debate among the Bunkers over whether Chang's original property is still in the family's hands. One descendant can be seen in documentarian Josh Gibson's *The Siamese Connection* touring the grounds with an air of wistful nostalgia and lamenting that the family no longer owns it. Meanwhile, another descendant expresses the wish that this part of the film be edited out because Sink *is* family and, moreover, his status as father to the aforementioned gubernatorial candidate Alex Sink further legitimizes his claim to kinship. Although few among the Bunker descendants would disagree that Sink is passionately committed to caring for the land that is cherished by the family, this debate about the authenticity of Sink's ties to the Bunkers underscores how even the contract of marriage is sometimes perceived to be insufficient in securing family membership.

The reluctance to think of Chang's original homestead as being in the Bunker family's hands may stem in part from the fact that Sink's grown children—who are the ones with genetic ties to Chang—no longer live there, and the property is now occupied by Sink (who inherited it when his wife died) and his current spouse, both nondescendants. The placement of Sink in this liminal space, as family and not-family, speaks to the extent to which hereditary linkages assert their primacy when determining kinship. As David Schneider claims: "In American cultural conception, kinship is defined as biogenetic"[29] and, therefore, permanent in contrast to the ties that are formed by marriage. "It follows that it is never possible to have an ex-father or an ex-mother, an ex-sister or an ex-brother, an ex-son or an ex-daughter. An ex-husband or ex-wife is possible, and so is an ex-mother-in-law. But an ex-mother is not."[30] According to Schneider, the hereditary bond lies in a realm considered to be apart from all others, and regardless of the affective ties or lack thereof between two individuals related genetically, that relationship is imagined to be immutable while wedded kin bonds are not.

The roles played by the Bunkers whose family ties are actualized through marriage cannot be overlooked. They provide an insight into the crucial factor of nonhereditary relations serving in the creation and maintenance of family tradition. Their claims to a Bunker identity tend to be imagined in terms of parent-child relationships—be they biogenetic (as with Sherry Bunker Blackmon) or not (as with Margaret Boland). At times, it appears that these nondescendant kin delight in their relationship to the Bunkers all the more fiercely and protectively precisely because it is one that the conventions of kinship in the United States regard as being less stable and fixed than the hereditary bond.

"We Could Be Family": Beyond Chang and Eng

Although the Bunker family reunion is foremost a celebratory gathering of descendants claiming a hereditary or other familial relationship to Chang and

Eng Bunker, considerable effort goes into forging family connections that transcend the fact of this heredity. There are some who attend the reunion primarily out of an interest in genealogy, their relationship to their famous ancestors taking a back seat, and then there are others whose status as descendants inaugurates their interest in learning more about extended family.

In 2007, the Yates descendants—from the siblings of Adelaide and Sarah Yates—joined in the festivities for the first time. They were contacted after a bit of genealogical sleuthing on the part of some Bunkers. The presence of a small number of reunion participants from the Yates side of the family was complemented by a Bunker descendant's suggestion that a grave marker be created, through a collection of donations, for Adelaide and Sarah's parents—Chang and Eng's in-laws. The fund-raising goal was met and the grave marker purchased. During the Yateses' first year attending the banquet, I was seated with them. Similarly to how Bunker descendants tend to regard their famous ancestors with a measure of respectful awe, the Yates family spoke highly of their distant aunts. Adelaide and Sarah were, in their words, "courageous" for having risked social disapprobation for their choice of spouse and for inventing a domestic routine for which they had no prior models. Even though only a small number of the Yateses were in attendance—they filled a single table with room to spare—their very presence signaled a larger wish on the part of some Bunkers to extend their genealogical research and networks of family more broadly.

For another descendant, the expansion of potential familial relations is taken to a different level, one that is more conceptual than it is genealogical. Martha Hill Moore, a great-great-granddaughter of Chang, maintains the Bunker descendants page on an online social networking site. It is an activity she says has deepened her intergenerational relationships, particularly with her younger computer-savvy relatives. During our interview, Moore recounted her reaction upon seeing townspeople with whom she was already familiar when she attended a Bunker reunion for the first time. Unlike Margaret Kansa, who had spent her entire life outside of western North Carolina and encountered completely new faces with her first experience, Moore—who grew up in Mount Airy—was surprised to see people she knew from church and other local activities at the reunion.

Her realization that she was genetically related to people she already knew led her to this conclusion:

> You have to be really careful who you talk about and who you befriend or who you make an enemy [with] because we're probably related [*laughing*]. You know, there's probably some connection. . . . So I'm going to be very careful, and you know, just not judge until I get to know better, and then *not judge*, because we could be related. We could be family. And I've sort of adopted that as my philosophy of how I interact with others—is that we could be family.[31]

In describing an ethics of person-to-person contact borne out of this pivotal moment, Moore's words, "We could be family," reference what Schneider observed about an exalted level of intimacy Americans expect to have with those who share a genetic link. Her style of sociality, treating everyone as if they "could be family," acknowledges not only that these hereditary connections can and do exist without the knowledge of those involved but that, paradoxically, the very absence of this knowledge is what makes this relationality possible. Her sentiment uses "family" as a rhetorical tool to propose that the distinction between biological relation and not-biological relation be abandoned altogether. In a sense, Moore's mode of conceptualizing kinship is closer to that of the societies Schneider references, where kin connections are integrated holistically into all forms of sociality rather than reserved for a small set of relationships that are narrowly defined.

Moore's commitment to regard everyone as potentially family, genetic or not, has opened interesting doors for her. One of her former colleagues is an immigrant from Thailand who makes regular trips back to see relatives. She told me about an exchange she had with him early in their acquaintanceship with each other:

> I said [to him], "I could be related to you." And I told him the story about Eng and Chang, and he said, "You have to come." He said, "You have to come." He said, "We'll find the village." He said, "I'll take you to Bangkok." . . . He was so sincere about wanting to show me and share with me part of *my* culture, part of *my* heritage that he knew well. And I thought, "This is so cool." . . . We're so vastly different on the surface and the way we were raised and all that but yet there is this connection that I could [*pausing*]—that I have something that he shares. And that made us very good friends, very fast friends.[32]

Although another descendant who had already visited Thailand expressed to me her regret that no official records exist of the descendants of Chang and Eng's siblings, this absence of information about the Thai side of the family appears as though it would be more enabling for Moore than not. The lack of birth and marriage records from that historical period would potentially allow her to treat everyone in Thailand as family. Even though Jessie Bunker Bryant syncretized the record-keeping mechanisms of the state with the organic knowledge culled from already-known Bunkers in her genealogy project, this dearth of state-issued documentation is precisely what makes Moore's concept of kinship possible. As she claims Thailand—"*my* culture" and "*my* heritage"—as her own, it appears that something more is taking place than simply a facile appropriation of exoticized difference. I encouraged her to take her colleague up on his offer to visit.

Moore's ethics of sociality, one in which establishing a hereditary bond is beside the point, could potentially mediate a thorny issue for the Bunkers.

In 2003, a descendant of a woman Chang and Eng owned in their capacity as slaveholders attended the reunion for the first time while undertaking her own genealogical research. During the ritual of welcoming honorary Bunkers into the family, Brenda Ethridge introduced herself as a descendant of "Aunt Grace." Her knowledge of this connection was passed down through family lore, and she was seeking any information the Bunkers had about her ancestor. This request produced an immediate and eager show of hands from the crowd, and Ethridge—not having expected such a wealth of material—was visibly delighted and overwhelmed by how many of Chang and Eng's descendants had heard stories about her distant relation and wanted to share them with her.

Aunt Grace holds a special place in the family. She is buried in White Plains Baptist Church in the same cemetery as Chang and Eng, Adelaide and Sarah, and their children. A photograph of her is kept in the Chang and Eng Bunker papers at the University of North Carolina's Southern Historical Collection (see Figure 7.1), materials that were donated to the archive by a descendant. The subject in the photograph is posed in ways reminiscent of formal portraiture—positioned in quarter profile, seated erect and leaning slightly forward, eyes confronting the camera—despite her very informal attire of ragged clothing and boots that seem too large for her feet. A handwritten inscription on the back of the photograph identifies her as the nurse to Chang and Eng's children. There are no pictures in this archive of any other enslaved people Chang and Eng owned. This portrait of Aunt Grace appears to be so highly valorized that it has been enlarged and hung in the hotel regularly used as the reunion headquarters—the Bunker-owned Mount Airy Hampton Inn. There is a Chang

Figure 7.1 Photograph of a woman identified as the nurse in the Bunker household. Date unknown. *(Courtesy of the Southern Historical Collection, Louis Round Wilson Special Collections Library, University of North Carolina, Chapel Hill.)*

and Eng–themed conference room inside called the Bunker Room that contains framed portraits of the twins along with other family members. Aunt Grace's likeness resides alongside the others.

The convention of referring to enslaved house servants as aunts or uncles in the pre–Civil War South performs a frictive embrace and disavowal of family relation. As the nurse to the Bunker children, Aunt Grace's responsibilities would have included the parental tasks of nursing, bathing, diapering, dressing, and so on. This is a role within the intimate spaces of the domestic home that would have set her apart from the Bunkers' other slaves, who did agricultural work on their tobacco plantation. The appellations "aunt" and "uncle" in these contexts allude to a familial relation with human property at the same time that the South's preoccupation with racial purity precludes formalizing such appellations. At the very moment that enslaved servants were domesticated into the white household through this suggestion of a family tie, any acknowledgement of possible hereditary connections with them was actively suppressed. Hence, these aunts who were family (engaged in caretaking within the home) could not really be *family* (solemnized as relations with the inhabitants of that home) but were also "family" (genetically mixing with the home's inhabitants).

The debate among the Bunker descendants over whether Chang and Eng fathered children with women they owned is a thorny one, as it is for all families issuing from the landed gentry in the former Confederacy. The sensitivity with which the Bunker family regards the possibility that Ethridge may be a descendant is understandable, given the ways in which the Old South has been demonized for slavery's atrocities when, in fact, the United States in sum was complicit in that history. Much of the disdain for the South's sustained reliance on enslaved labor well into the nineteenth century revolves around the sexual violation of black women and the distortion of hereditary relationships as the genetic children of the plantation owner were turned into commodities.

This dispute in the Bunker family about Ethridge's biogenetic status individualizes what was an injury perpetrated nationally. It does not matter whether the sexual violence that attended slavery was present in any given plantation household because it took place on a collective level. These genetic legacies borne out of diametric gender and racial power differentials—regardless of their presence or absence in individual homes—are nevertheless part of the U.S. national grain and inextricably bound with the shared history of slavery that all Americans have inherited. The existence of children of enslaved women who were fathered by their owners throws a wrench into the practice of establishing family ties precisely because the gold standard for determining kinship, the hereditary relation, is actively denied. Whereas nonbiogenetic family member Kester Sink was able to solemnize his relation to the Bunkers by entering into the legal contract of marriage, in cases involving the children of enslaved women, their hereditary ties to the families that owned them could not receive social or juridical recognition even if they were silently and tacitly understood.

Several Bunker descendants have made inquiries to staff at the College of Physicians of Philadelphia about the possibility of testing hair trapped in the plaster of Chang and Eng's body cast to confirm anecdotes about hereditary lineages that issued from their slaves. From a series of e-mail communications archived at the College of Physicians of Philadelphia, it appears that in May of 2002, two descendants dropped in on Gretchen Worden, then the curator of the Mütter Museum, to make an in-person plea. Growing up, they had heard from an aunt about how Patrick Bunker, Eng's son, used to play with his half-sisters and half-brothers who were enslaved, and if possible, they wanted to corroborate family lore with science. Worden forwarded the contact information for these two sisters to the editor of the Bunker family newsletter, and they were added to the mailing list and attended the reunion the following year, in 2003.

Although I was seated at the same table as these two women at that year's reunion, my vantage point did not allow me to see what transpired. Much of our conversation revolved around their wonder and amazement at discovering so many distant relations they had not previously known. It was not until I read a follow-up e-mail message another Bunker descendant wrote to Worden after the reunion that the intensity with which the sisters sought a genetic link through African American descendants came to light:

> [One of these women was] really stirring stuff up about it [at the reunion]. I don't think she was well received with this. She latched onto Brenda Ethridge and is determined to "find out the truth" about this. I think she thinks that we need to DNA test Brenda and someone else in the family and see if we're related. . . . [S]he's asking if I think you'd allow us to have some hair from the cast at the museum for a dna test. . . . Of course if Brenda is a descendant that would be nice to know. . . . What do you think? I'm telling you all of this because I want you to be aware of the interest [among some Bunkers in genetic testing]. . . . I know through our previous discussions that you have really high regard for Eng and Chang and aren't interested in slander or works of fiction about them—when their lives were interesting enough.[33]

The unease in this message is palpable, and it is emblematic of how delicately descendants of slaveholding families treat the topic of hereditary relations with present-day African Americans. Despite the trepidation this message conveys, however, it seems this descendant's wish to accept Ethridge as a genetic relative is sincere if Ethridge is, in fact, related.

Worden, empathic to these concerns, then contacted James Starrs, a forensic scientist based at George Washington University, about the possibility of obtaining usable DNA from either Chang and Eng's hair or liver. From her handwritten notes in the margins of this printed and archived series of e-mail communications, it appears that she believed in these stories about enslaved children fathered by the twins. Still, Worden emphasized to Starrs the sensitivity of this request: "The general feeling among [the family members] seems to be that they would rather steer clear of any repeat of the Sally Hemings/Jefferson fiasco."[34] Starrs reported back on the feasibility of both sources: DNA testing of the liver would be impossible because the preserving fluids are very destructive to genetic material. However, nuclear DNA would be available in the hair root if any part of it came away from the follicle when it was pulled away by the plaster.[35] There were no messages in the archive following up on this interchange, and I was not able to find any information about whether this testing ever took place or whether descendants are still interested in seeing that it does.

However, someone adopting Martha Hill Moore's ethics of sociality would likely aver that it does not matter if the tools of science can trace Ethridge's hereditary lineage back to Chang and Eng Bunker via Aunt Grace. Although most people would probably concur that having a lab-generated set of data legitimating such a relationship could assuage the anxiety that attends the uncertainty surrounding it—particularly for Aunt Grace's descendants—if one were to follow Moore and treat Ethridge as someone who "could be family," then ideally it matters little whether she is genetically related. If one were to operate under the assumption that "we could be family" with all people at all times, the heightened sense of care one extends to biological kin would have already been extended to Ethridge. Taking Moore's reasoning to its logical conclusion, it would actually be more ethically exemplary if the Bunkers were to develop and maintain kin connections with this descendant of Aunt Grace without any knowledge or even with a willful ignorance of a genetic connection to Chang and Eng. The model of kinship illustrated in Moore's vision of family eventually regards DNA testing as beside the point.

In this case, kinship is less a material fact that needs confirmation before two individuals can begin to build a familial bond and more a metaphor through which the primacy of ethically exemplary relationships with everyone, hereditarily related or not, are valued. Ultimately, the creation, documentation, and nurturing of hereditary links for the Bunker family is not an end in itself—with deviations from these "blood networks" simply regarded as evidence of their flexibility—but a means through which more broad-ranging forms of sociality can be structured. By thinking about kinship in this way, establishing a family tie is not about recognizing a genealogical relation between one person and another but about an ethics of person-to-person contact that extends well beyond hereditary kinship's reach.

Choosing Our Families

The Bunkers' creation of kinship as it dances back and forth between consanguineous and nonconsanguineous relations, natal and non-natal family members—though highly complex—is hardly unique. What the descendants of Chang and Eng Bunker do to generate and sustain a communal identity that is both organized and fluid resembles processes found in many other social networks that have been previously studied. In context after context, ethnographers have noted that kinship—its discursive invention by anthropology notwithstanding—is a dynamic activity. It is a practice performed by participants rather than an inert object. The very malleability of kinship reveals its capacity for adapting to historical and political circumstances that inevitably impact affective ties, domestic arrangements, and extended webs of interpersonal relations.

Barbara Myerhoff's seminal work on the elderly residents of a Jewish neighborhood reveals the structuring and flexibility that kin-like networks of interdependency take on among her informants. Conducted at a community center in the 1970s, the ethnography of immigrants who had fled Eastern Europe during the rise of Nazism shows that "family" needed to be reimagined in the United States in ways that went beyond the natal or biogenetic bond.[36] The triumph of the reconsolidation of family, however, is a measured one. Despite the successes of the community center in facilitating ties that allowed these older adults to maintain a valued sense of self-sufficiency, many of Myerhoff's informants expressed an "ambivalen[ce] about living so closely with others brought into contact with them more by circumstance than by choice."[37] The pressures exerted on the nuclear family by the material and psychic costs of forced migration in Myerhoff's study are echoed in Nazli Kibria's ethnography of Vietnamese refugees. Kibria observes that the effects of the war in Southeast Asia had occasioned a reorganization of family ties upon resettlement in the United States. As a survival mechanism, refugees "shift[ed] and expand[ed] the criteria for inclusion in the family circle. . . . [F]riends and distant relatives who had been marginal members of the family circle in Vietnam became part of the active circle of kin relations in the United States,"[38] even while the ordered rituals of family life continued to define these relationships.[39]

Kath Weston provides what is perhaps the best-known example of how the "chosen family," which foregrounds the primacy of elective affinities, nevertheless refrains from abandoning the symbolic capital of heredity altogether. In her research on gay and lesbian families in the 1980s, Weston finds that as much as the language of volition informs their creation, one cannot uphold them as somehow separate from how heterosexuals structure their kinship units. In fact, she maintains that it is impossible to study them in isolation from the natal families in which her informants were raised.[40] Thus, issues such as biological procreation, parenting, and the distribution of resources—major concerns in heterosexual families—also emerge repeatedly in her informants' experience. Their extended networks of family, composed of hereditary and nonhereditary relations alike, syncretize the socially sanctioned ideas about blood relations that David Schneider observed among Americans with affective ties fashioned through connections with other gays and lesbians.

In effect, all families are chosen ones, biogenetic or not. Despite Myerhoff's informants' perception about a lack of choice through which their nonbiological ties were drawn and Weston's valorization of her informants' agency in this same regard, all kin associations are volitional. The old adage that "you can choose your friends, but you can't choose your family" overlooks how membership in family networks is always an active and elective process. My observations about the Bunker descendants' relationships show that, despite the steadfast and meticulous embrace of genealogical pathways back to Chang and Eng, ongoing connections between one relative and another are not effortlessly maintained. These relationships, any relationships, require work. The ritual of the family reunion—with its advance planning, coordinating, and follow-through—is a major production that requires large amounts of collaboration and commitment. A lot of collective labor is expended to make the Bunker family exist. Of course, along with this process-oriented model of kinship, comes the unavoidable contradictions, paradoxes, and points of dissent. In the end, these characteristics are recognizable to most, if not all, families, regardless of how they are configured.

On my last day at the 2010 Bunker family reunion in Mount Airy, North Carolina, I arrived at Kathy Bryant Proctor's house with a red velvet cake. I had not wanted to visit empty-handed, but I felt sheepish asking Proctor and her mother, Jessie Bunker Bryant, to celebrate my birthday with me, my status as an honorary family member notwithstanding. Having undergone the ceremonial induction into to the Bunker fold and having been hailed by Martha Hill Moore as someone who "could be family," I wondered how my status as a researcher would affect my access to the kinds of activities—like sharing birthday cake—that are associated with one's natal family. As I pulled up the long driveway, I started to wish I had brought something else, but that trepidation disappeared when Bryant and Proctor came outside smiling and warmly greeted me before I got out of the car. With more than a small amount of child-like glee, I announced the occasion of my birthday.

At the time, Bryant was living in an assisted living community in the town of High Point, a short distance from Proctorsville, where Proctor lives. At the ripe age of eighty-three, she was still driving, still energetic, and she visited her daughter on a weekly basis. As we relaxed and talked long into the afternoon about family, friends, and major life milestones, I almost forgot that this was work for me. At one point, Proctor got up and gingerly walked into the kitchen—she had a sprained ankle—while I continued to talk with her mother. After a few minutes, she returned to the living room and announced that it was time for cake. When I went into the kitchen, I saw that there were several candles waiting to be set ablaze atop the thick layer of cream cheese frosting. Bryant and Proctor were the only familiar faces I saw on that day, which would later be spent heading back home on I-77 and checking into a desolate hotel faintly reeking of disinfectant somewhere in West Virginia. Because the reunion is consistently held on the last weekend in July, it was not the first time my birthday had fallen on a date when I was present. I had, in fact, already begun to think about my birthday as an event that sometimes coincided with my fieldwork.

As my visit drew to a close, Proctor pressed several clementines into my hand. "For the long drive ahead," she said. I started to reflect on the circumstances that drew us together for the first time seven years earlier and the paths we had begun even earlier than that. As the daughter of the family genealogist, Proctor holds a special place among the Bunkers, even as all the descendants with whom I spoke expressed their seriousness about their roles in continuing the family tradition. We became acquainted for the first time right before I finished graduate school, and we have continually met up over the years at the family reunion as this manuscript has taken various shapes in its "long drive ahead." Although *Chang and Eng Reconnected* is the reason that my relationship with the Bunkers exists to begin with, it has also seemed at times to be simply the whirr and hum in the background as I have deepened my connections with them over the years. No doubt, these relationships have affected my work in ways more subtle than I can detect. As much as this book documents how Chang and Eng Bunker continue to live in the American imagination, it also is a document that issued and grew from my growing ties and accountability to living people who are related to these twins. The practices of kin making are never as straightforward as the stark lines mapping a family tree would suggest.

Epilogue

Alone or Together?

Eng: I am lonely.
Chang: I am alone.
beat—
Eng: I am *lonely*.
Chang: I am *alone*.
They put their arms around each other's shoulders—
Chang: I reach out—
Grips Eng's neck—
Eng: I reach out—
Grips Chang's neck—
Both: We are together. Forever. Forever—
—Philip Kan Gotanda, *I Dream of Chang and Eng*

Thus, not only does democracy make every man forget his ancestors, but it hides his descendants, and separates his contemporaries from him; it throws him back forever upon himself alone, and threatens in the end to confine him entirely within the solitude of his own heart.
—Alexis de Tocqueville, *Democracy in America*

A great-great grandson of the original conjoined twins was released from jail on Tuesday. He was released for time served after killing his twin brother in June. Brian Neal Bunker of Mount Airy was initially charged with first-degree murder. But he pleaded guilty in Superior Court to the lesser offense of

> involuntary manslaughter. The judge sentenced Bunker to four months active sentence and five years supervised probation. Police say Brian Bunker shot his brother Brad once in the chest at close range. Relatives say they had a fight over a six-pack of beer that Brian had hidden in a barn. When the beer disappeared, Brian accused Brad of taking it.
>
> —Associated Press, "Chang and Eng Relative Released from Jail"

In March 2011, the University of California, Berkeley, held a symposium in conjunction with the world premiere of playwright Philip Kan Gotanda's *I Dream of Chang and Eng.* The play, a fictionalized account of the lives of the Bunkers with elements of magical realism, contained one hundred thirty costume changes for a cast of nineteen, and it ran for more than three hours with two intermissions. Asked why he chose to work with a student theater for this ambitious project, Gotanda emphasized the resources of universities and the openness of young actors to experimentation.[1] The highly polished production at Berkeley's Zellerbach Hall was a far cry from the improvisational street theater scene in Maxine Hong Kingston's *Tripmaster Monkey*, and most (if not all) of the actors in Gotanda's play were not yet born when Kingston's novel was published. What ties them together across a generation is the attention writers continue to pay to these nineteenth-century celebrities whose lives were so complex and whose embodiment was so emblematic of the contradictions of American identity.

The panelists who spoke from multiple disciplinary backgrounds at the symposium confirmed that Chang and Eng Bunker remain an easily recognizable symbol on which to base discussion of a range of concerns about race and the anomalous body in American history. From Ellen Samuels's indictment of medical authority in her analysis of the literature on conjoined sisters Millie and Christine McKoy, to Amma Ghartey-Tagoe Kootin's reclamation of African American spectatorship at the 1901 Buffalo Pan-American Exposition, to Eric Hayot's discussion of nineteenth-century white America's fascination with Chinese bodies in pain, the Bunkers' figural legacies produce multiple—possibly endless—points of inquiry into complex operations of power.

As two people who shared one body, Chang and Eng Bunker taught a staunchly independent America about collaboration and compromise. However, as *Chang and Eng Reconnected* demonstrates, if these acts of reconciliation often resulted in the persistence of inequality, the solution was hardly to return to exalted notions of individualism that were never plausible or possible to begin with. The epigraph—culled from Alexis de Tocqueville's *Democracy in America*—with which I begin this book is often cited out of context as a laudatory passage about how Americans have overcome the limitations of a European aristocratic social order. What Tocqueville means to convey, however, is the belief that the egalitarian spirit behind this commitment to self-actualization produces both a diachronic and synchronic isolation on the part of the self-actualized American: ancestors forgotten, descendants hidden, and peers separated. It may be that the tyranny of the individual, stuck in both time and space, winds up ironically replicating the conditions of immobility that resemble the social stratifications from which Americans had fled. Instead of, as Tocqueville words it, "imagin[ing] that their whole destiny is in their own hands,"[2] Americans find themselves destined toward new forms of remaining in place. Instead of resolving competing interests in ways that enable civic justice, the retreat into individualism maintains the status quo.

As reported in a life-imitating-fiction news release, two Bunker descendants who were twins themselves got into an altercation in 2003 that left one of them dead. According to information drawn from the Bunker family's genealogical research, Bradford and Brian Bunker, the youngest of six children, were born in 1976 to James Bunker (great-grandson of Eng) and Doris Jean Priddy Bunker. Both brothers were graduates of North Surry High School in Mount Airy. Bradford worked in construction, while Brian was a landscaper.[3] A photograph taken of these other Bunker twins, just before their eighteenth birthdays at the 1994 family reunion, is printed in Jessie Bunker Bryant's *The Connected Bunkers*. In it, Brian and Bradford are seated in Chang and Eng's original double chair—thighs and shoulders touching, with an uncle beside them—and smiling at the camera in a way that makes it impossible to anticipate the events nine years later.

The disinterested tone of the Associated Press's article about Brian and Brad Bunker does not hide the abjected stereotypes that are conjured about gun-toting "rednecks" who stash household supplies in barns and are willing to defend cheap beer to the death. All may not be well in Mayberry, and one wonders how Sheriff Andy Taylor would have responded to that call.[4] Far from the respectable whiteness that Leslie Bow assumes in the triangular framework she nicely sets up in *Partly Colored*, the whiteness the popular media simplistically invokes here connotes not Southern middle-class gentility but trash.[5] The minimal sentence of four months for a homicide, however, reminds us that this case is removed from how African Americans are commonly treated by the criminal justice system. The twins' whiteness, albeit a working-class version, grants them a measure of privilege others do not have.

The affected objectivity in the Associated Press's journalese can simply be the anonymous author's way of avoiding the tendency to sensationalize stories like these. More insidiously, it could also be intended (or merely interpreted) as deadpan humor similar to that found in Mark Twain's absurdist portrayal of Chang and Eng's brawl with each other in "Personal Habits of the Siamese Twins." The fight scene in fictionalized conjoined twin narratives, which has become obligatory and second only to the sex scene, is a cliché come true. Hence, the headline proclaiming that these present-day Bunkers trace their line back to the nineteenth century's most famous twins both is and is not an essential piece of information. Even *I Dream of Chang and Eng* begins with a fight—in utero, no less—the twins' gripping of each others' necks turning into choking and punching despite their declarations of loneliness.[6]

It seems as if everyone wants a piece of Chang and Eng. In the present, as with in the past, everyone seems susceptible to their magnetism as they search for their next big idea, their key to professional success, their sense of belonging—or some order and logic in an otherwise chaotic world. It is because of this allure that Chang and Eng Bunker have become much more than who they were as actual people. These twins seductively beckon as we seek to fulfill our desires, whatever they may be. From medical personnel to family members; from museum professionals to artists; from fiction writers to journalists to playwrights to filmmakers; from descendants to scholars: no one is immune to the wonder they generate. The stakeholders I present over the course of *Chang and Eng Reconnected* hold differing investments in the representation of this figure. No doubt, any number of them could take issue with how I engage the topic here. The purpose, however, is not to resolve these tensions but to listen to what their inner workings tell us.

For these reasons, Chang and Eng Bunker anticipate interdisciplinarity. They demand the array of methods and lenses that are required to make them legible in ways that do justice to this deeply textured trail of meaning left in their wake. Nowhere have I felt this more palpably as when I have visited one archive after another, chatted with one descendant after another, or pored over text upon text—be it of paper, plaster, organic tissue, or celluloid. The meandering, sometimes plodding paths of knowledge production about the discursive Chang and Eng leave me only with the belief that there is still more work left to do.

The stories about the Bunkers have not ceased yet. If anything, the Original Siamese Twins persist as an ongoing site of negotiation about the nature of negotiation itself.

Notes

INTRODUCTION

1. Quoted in Irving Wallace and Amy Wallace, *The Two: A Biography: The Story of the Original Siamese Twins* (New York: Simon and Schuster, 1978), 53.

2. Ibid., 59.

3. Kay Hunter, *Duet for a Lifetime: The Story of the Original Siamese Twins* (New York: Coward-McCann, 1964); Wallace and Wallace, *The Two.*

4. See, for instance, Robert W. Rydell, *All the World's a Fair: Visions of Empire at American International Expositions, 1876–1916* (Chicago: University of Chicago Press, 1987); Robert Bogdan, *Freak Show: Presenting Human Oddities for Amusement and Profit* (Chicago: University of Chicago Press, 1988); Rosemarie Garland-Thomson, ed., *Freakery: Cultural Spectacles of the Extraordinary Body* (New York: New York University Press, 1996); Rosemarie Garland-Thomson, *Extraordinary Bodies: Figuring Physical Disability in American Culture and Literature* (New York: Columbia University Press, 1997); Rachel Adams, *Sideshow U.S.A.: Freaks and the American Cultural Imagination* (Chicago: University of Chicago Press, 2001); and Janet M. Davis, *The Circus Age: Culture and Society under the Big Top* (Chapel Hill: University of North Carolina Press, 2002).

5. Multiple anecdotal explanations exist for why the name "Bunker" was chosen, but none of them have been conclusively verified.

6. Material for the Bunkers' personal history is taken from the aforementioned biographies.

7. Leonard Kriegel, "Uncle Tom and Tiny Tim: Some Reflections on the Cripple as Negro," *American Scholar* 38 (1969): 412–430.

8. Leslie Fiedler, *Freaks: Myths and Images of the Secret Self* (New York: Simon and Schuster, 1978), 17.

9. The list of scholars who have contributed to this line of analysis is long and impossible to cite in its entirety, given that it encompasses almost all early disability studies work in the field of literature in English. An example of proto-disability studies scholarship, Peter Hays's *The Limping Hero: Grotesques in Literature* (New York: New York University Press, 1971), links injuries of the foot and/or leg among male protagonists with a failure of masculinity. For texts that place disabled characters within a gendered symbolic economy, see Leonard Kriegel, "The Cripple in Literature," in *Images of the Disabled, Disabling Images*, ed. Alan Gartner and Tom Joe (New York: Praeger, 1986),

31–46; Deborah Kent, "In Search of a Heroine," in *Images of Women with Disabilities: Essays in Psychology, Culture, and Politics*, ed. Michelle Fine and Adrienne Asch (Philadelphia: Temple University Press, 1988), 90–110; and Diane Price Herndl, *Invalid Women: Figuring Feminine Illness in American Fiction and Culture, 1840–1940* (Chapel Hill: University of North Carolina Press, 1993). Garland-Thomson's *Extraordinary Bodies* is best known for establishing an analysis that finds transformative potential in disabled literary characters. Another early work that sees disability beyond irrecuperable negativity is Cindy LaCom, "It Is More than Lame: Female Disability, Sexuality, and the Maternal in the Nineteenth-Century Novel," in *The Body and Physical Difference: Discourses of Disability*, ed. David T. Mitchell and Sharon L. Snyder (Ann Arbor: University of Michigan Press, 1997), 189–201. For a formative study on disabled characters in film, see Martin Norden, *The Cinema of Isolation* (New Brunswick, NJ: Rutgers University Press, 1994).

10. Lennard J. Davis stresses throughout the book that launched this line of thinking that his project is not about disabled characters in literature. Although this maneuver may appear somewhat defensive now, its presence at this point in the trajectory of disability studies speaks to the need to find other approaches that do not fall predictably into an analysis of "representation." See *Enforcing Normalcy: Disability, Deafness, and the Body* (New York: Verso, 1995).

11. This shift within disability studies resembles the one that took place in the transition from gay and lesbian studies to queer theory. As Eve Kosofsky Sedgwick explains, the former conceives of "homo/heterosexual definition . . . as an issue of active importance primarily for a small, distinct, relatively fixed homosexual minority" while the latter regards it "as an issue of continuing, determinative importance in the lives of people across the spectrum of sexualities." *Epistemology of the Closet* (Berkeley: University of California Press, 1990), 1.

12. Lennard J. Davis, *Bending Over Backwards: Dismodernism and Other Difficult Positions* (New York: New York University Press, 2002), chap. 1.

13. Najia Aarim-Heriot claims that nativist fears about Chinese labor stemmed from its proximity to enslaved labor. Both threatened liberal republican ideals of free labor. See *Chinese Immigrants, African Americans, and Racial Anxiety in the United States, 1848–1882* (Champaign: University of Illinois Press, 2006).

14. Alan M. Kraut, *Silent Travelers: Germs, Genes, and the "Immigrant Menace"* (Baltimore: Johns Hopkins University Press, 1994), 81–96.

15. Nayan Shah, *Contagious Divides: Epidemics and Race in San Francisco's Chinatown* (Berkeley: University of California Press, 2001), 85–88; Susan Craddock, *City of Plagues: Disease, Poverty, and Deviance in San Francisco* (Minneapolis: University of Minnesota Press, 2000), 92–95.

16. Tobin Siebers, *Disability Theory* (Ann Arbor: University of Michigan Press, 2008), 6.

17. This germinal scholarship in Asian American studies is too extensive to cite in its entirety. Key texts in this tradition include Gary Y. Okihiro, *Cane Fires: The Anti-Japanese Movement in Hawaii, 1865–1945* (Philadelphia: Temple University Press, 1991); Ronald Takaki, *Pau Hana: Plantation Life and Labor in Hawaii* (Honolulu: University of Hawaii Press, 1983); Alexander Saxton, *The Indispensable Enemy: Labor and the Anti-Chinese Movement in California* (Berkeley: University of California Press, 1971); and Roger Daniels, *The Politics of Prejudice: The Anti-Japanese American Movement in California and the Struggle for Japanese Exclusion* (Berkeley: University of California Press, 1962).

18. Mikhail Bakhtin, *Rabelais and His World*, trans. Hélène Iswolsky (Bloomington: Indiana University Press, 1984).

CHAPTER 1

1. Susan M. Schweik, *The Ugly Laws: Disability in Public* (New York: New York University Press, 2009), 103.

2. Ibid., 109 (emphasis in original).

3. For example, when the woman's novelty started to fade, P. T. Barnum anonymously published an exposé in a newspaper claiming that she was not even human but an automaton. The charges spurred those who had already seen the exhibit to come back for a second look. *Struggles and Triumphs*, ed. Carl Bode (New York: Penguin, 1987), 12–13.

4. Benjamin Reiss, *The Showman and the Slave: Race, Death, and Memory in Barnum's America* (Cambridge, MA: Harvard University Press, 2001), 20, 100–101.

5. Irving Wallace and Amy Wallace, *The Two: A Biography: The Story of the Original Siamese Twins* (New York: Simon and Schuster, 1978), 228–229, 261.

6. Ibid., 228.

7. Ellen Samuels presents the case of Millie and Christine McCoy, African American conjoined sisters, who lived at the time of Chang and Eng Bunker. Samuels argues that people who have attempted to read agency into the McCoy's lives, particularly those who consider the twins' autobiography empirically, underestimate the oppressive conditions of their enslavement and overlook how enslaved people have always been forced to perform in ways mandated by their owners. "Examining Millie and Christine McCoy: Where Enslavement and Enfreakment Meet," *Signs* 37, no. 1 (2011): 53–81.

8. These artifacts are located in the Chang and Eng Bunker papers at the Southern Historical Collection in the Louis Round Wilson Special Collections Library at the University of North Carolina.

9. "Propertied subject" is Grace Kyungwon Hong's term for "an individuated subject formed through the ability to assert will." The propertied subject emerged as an effect of the nation-state to resolve the contradictions under which the United States incorporated racialized labor into the workforce at the same time it denied property rights to the very laborers who provided it. *The Ruptures of American Capital: Women of Color Feminism and the Culture of Immigrant Labor* (Minneapolis: University of Minnesota Press, 2006), 3–4.

10. C. B. Macpherson points out that debates about whether Locke was an individualist or a collectivist are beside the point. Rather, the model of individualism Locke proposes needs to actualize itself collectively. *The Political Theory of Possessive Individualism: Hobbes to Locke* (New York: Oxford University Press, 1962), 255.

11. Barbara Jeanne Fields, "Slavery, Race, and Ideology in the United States of America," *New Left Review* 181 (May/June 1990): 114.

12. Amy Dru Stanley, "'The Right to Possess All the Faculties That God Has Given': Possessive Individualism, Slave Women, and Abolitionist Thought," in *Moral Problems in American Life: New Perspectives on Cultural History*, ed. Karen Halttunen and Lewis Perry (Ithaca, NY: Cornell University Press, 1998), 129. See also Gillian Brown, *Domestic Individualism: Imagining Self in Nineteenth-Century America* (Berkeley: University of California Press, 1990), particularly the chapters on Harriet Beecher Stowe, for how private interiors informed a gendered self-fashioning in abolitionist thought.

13. Wallace and Wallace cite an extensively documented account of these business transactions between Chang and Eng Bunker; Abel Coffin; Coffin's wife, Susan; and the

various other associates managing the Bunkers' career in these early years. See chapters 3 and 4 of *The Two*.

14. Wallace and Wallace, *The Two*, 131.

15. *Face to Face: The Schappell Twins*, directed by Ellen Weissbrod (New York: A&E Home Video, 2000), DVD.

16. J. David Smith, *Psychological Profiles of Conjoined Twins: Heredity, Environment, and Identity* (Santa Barbara, CA: Praeger, 1988).

17. Allison Pingree, "The 'Exceptions That Prove the Rule': Daisy and Violet Hilton, the 'New Woman,' and the Bonds of Marriage," in *Freakery: Cultural Spectacles of the Extraordinary Body*, ed. Rosemarie Garland-Thomson (New York: New York University Press, 1996), 175–177.

18. Ronald Takaki, *Iron Cages: Race and Culture in Nineteenth-Century America* (New York: Oxford University Press, 1979), 217.

19. Najia Aarim-Heriot, *Chinese Immigrants, African Americans, and Racial Anxiety in the United States, 1848–82* (Urbana and Chicago: University of Illinois Press, 2003), 38.

20. Joseph Jeon offers the possibility that perceptions about the insufficient individuation between conjoined twins is another element that links the Bunkers with other Chinese immigrants. This insight comes from a conversation with Jeon about a paper I presented at the Pomona College Department of English conference "As Yet Unnamed: Queer Nineteenth Centuries," March 3, 2012, Claremont, CA.

21. Chris Vials, *Realism for the Masses: Aesthetics, Popular Front Pluralism, and U.S. Culture, 1935–1947* (Jackson: University of Mississippi Press, 2009), 125.

22. Lucy M. Cohen, *Chinese in the Post–Civil War South: A People without a History* (Baton Rouge: Louisiana State University Press, 1984), 1–8.

23. Ibid., 2, 17–18. For an explanation of how Chinese migrants to Cuba functioned in the Spanish colony's slave economy and later in the Cuban revolution, see Lisa Yun, "Chinese Freedom Fighters in Cuba: From Bondage to Liberation, 1847–1898," in *Afro Asia: Revolutionary Political and Cultural Connections between African Americans and Asian Americans*, ed. Fred Ho and Bill V. Mullen (Durham, NC: Duke University Press, 2008): 30–54.

24. Moon-Ho Jung, *Coolies and Cane: Race, Labor, and Sugar in the Age of Emancipation* (Baltimore: Johns Hopkins University Press, 2006), 11–38.

25. See Matthew Pratt Guterl, "After Slavery: Asian Labor, the American South, and the Age of Emancipation," *Journal of World History* 24, no. 2 (2003): 209–241.

26. James W. Loewen, *The Mississippi Chinese: Between Black and White* (Prospect Heights, IL: Waveland Press, 1971), 22–23.

27. Tera W. Hunter, *To 'Joy My Freedom: Southern Black Women's Lives and Labors after the Civil War* (Cambridge, MA: Harvard University Press, 1997), 78.

28. Cohen, *Chinese in the Post–Civil War South*, 167.

29. Loewen, *The Mississippi Chinese*, 61–62.

30. Ibid., 64, 74–75.

31. Leslie Bow, *Partly Colored: Asian Americans and Racial Anomaly in the Segregated South* (New York: New York University Press, 2010), 97.

32. Naturalization papers for Chang and Eng Bunker, 1839, file 916.1, Siamese Twins (1811–1874) Papers, North Carolina State Archives, Raleigh, North Carolina.

33. Marriage documents, April 13, 1843, folder 9, Chang and Eng Bunker Papers 3761, Southern Historical Collection, Wilson Library, University of North Carolina, Chapel Hill.

34. Wallace and Wallace, *The Two*, 176.

35. Bill of sale, November 20, 1855, folder 3, Chang and Eng Bunker Papers 3761, Southern Historical Collection.

36. I am thankful to Jim Stewart for these insights. Property records show that as of 1860, five years after this transfer, Eng owned sixteen slaves and Chang owned twelve. Property records, file 916.1, Siamese Twins (1811–1874) Papers, North Carolina State Archives.

37. In addition, Chang and Eng drew up separate wills, further differentiating them as individuated property owners even as their wills stressed the egalitarian and shared nature of property division among their surviving kin. Copies of these documents are transcribed and displayed in the gallery at the Surry Arts Council in Mount Airy, North Carolina. Special thanks go to Tanya Jones, executive director of the Surry Arts Council and Chang descendant, for a personal tour of the premises.

38. Personal correspondence from two men who had served as the twins' managers during this early period shows that they referred to them as "Cherokee rascals," linking them by dint of their racial difference to indigenous Americans, and the inexplicable orientalist nickname "Qui Hi." Letters between James Hale and Charles Harris, 1831–1844, file 916.1, Siamese Twins (1811–1874) Papers, North Carolina State Archives.

39. A news clipping in the North Carolina State Archives on which the information "Winston-Salem Journal 8/6/77" is penciled announces the Surry County Historical Society's acquisition of Chang and Eng Bunkers' original contract from a descendant of Abel Coffin. The facsimile of the contract is reproduced in the article. Contract between Chang and Eng Bunker and Robert Hunter and Abel Coffin, April 1, 1829, file 916.1, Siamese Twins (1811–1874) Papers, North Carolina State Archives.

40. Chang and Eng to Captain Davison, April 16, 1838, Chang and Eng Bunker file, College of Physicians of Philadelphia Mütter Museum Archives.

41. Eng Bunker and unidentified offspring to the Bunker family, December 10, 1860, folder 3, Chang and Eng Bunker Papers 3761, Southern Historical Collection.

42. Christopher Wren Bunker to Chang Bunker, February 13, 1866, folder 3, Chang and Eng Bunker Papers 3761, Southern Historical Collection.

43. Tera Hunter (*To 'Joy My Freedom*) tells of how recently emancipated women entrepreneurs functioned in the late-nineteenth-century U.S. economy.

44. Antiques dealer to Chang and Eng Bunker, December 10, 1870, folder 3, Chang and Eng Bunker Papers 3761, Southern Historical Collection.

45. P. A. Browne to Chang and Eng Bunker, July 9, 1850, folder 2, Chang and Eng Bunker Papers 3761, Southern Historical Collection.

46. Daryl Maeda provides an account of Asian American and African American coalitional politics that was both antiracist and anti-imperialist. *Chains of Babylon: The Rise of Asian America* (Minneapolis: University of Minnesota Press, 2009).

47. A series of feature journalism articles in the wake of the Watts uprisings cast Asian Americans as paragons of upward mobility by demonizing African Americans, who were portrayed as dangerous and unruly. Among these were William Petersen, "Success Story: Japanese American Style," *New York Times Magazine*, January 9, 1966, 20–21, 33, 36, 38, 40–41, 43; and "Success Story of One Minority Group in U.S.," *U.S. News and World Report*, December 26, 1966, 73–76.

48. Ronald Takaki's work is perhaps the best-known example. See, in particular, the aforementioned *Iron Cages*.

49. Gary Y. Okihiro, *Margins and Mainstreams: Asians in American History and Culture* (Seattle: University of Washington Press, 1994), 34. Okihiro's collection of essays comes from a series of lectures he gave during his residence at Amherst College in spring

1992 when these pressing concerns about black-Asian relations were at the forefront of Asian Americanist thought. See also the special issue of *Amerasia Journal* 19, no. 2 (1993) for another example of the intellectual production that immediately followed the Rodney King verdict.

50. Claire Jean Kim, *Bitter Fruit: The Politics of Black-Korean Conflict in New York City* (New Haven, CT: Yale University Press, 2000); Min Hyoung Song, *Strange Future: Pessimism and the 1992 Los Angeles Riots* (Durham, NC: Duke University Press, 2005); Nadia Y. Kim, *Imperial Citizens: Koreans and Race from Seoul to L.A.* (Stanford, CA: Stanford University Press, 2008).

51. This body of scholarship is too extensive to cite in its entirety. Some key examples are Vijay Prashad, *The Karma of Brown Folk* (Minneapolis: University of Minnesota Press, 2001); Viet Thanh Nguyen, *Race and Resistance: Literature and Politics in Asian America* (New York: Oxford University Press, 2002); a guest-edited special issue by Deborah Wong of the *Journal of Asian American Studies* 5, no. 1 (2002); James Kyung-Jin Lee, *Urban Triage: Race and the Fictions of Multiculturalism* (Minneapolis: University of Minnesota Press, 2004); and Grace Kyungwon Hong, *The Ruptures of American Capital.* In addition, the aforementioned books by Moon-Ho Jung and Leslie Bow would fall into this category.

52. Orlando Patterson, *Slavery and Social Death: A Comparative Study* (Cambridge, MA: Harvard University Press, 1985).

CHAPTER 2

1. Susan Stewart, *On Longing: Narratives of the Miniature, the Gigantic, the Souvenir, the Collection* (Durham, NC: Duke University Press, 1993), 111.

2. Irving Wallace and Amy Wallace, *The Two: A Biography: The Story of the Original Siamese Twins* (New York: Simon and Schuster, 1978).

3. A. Peña Chavarria and P. G. Shipley, "The Siamese Twins of Española," *Annals of Medical History* 6, no. 3 (1924): 302.

4. Fidelio Jimenez, "The First Autopsy in the New World," *Bulletin of the New York Academy of Medicine* 54, no. 6 (1978): 619.

5. See Robert Bogdan, *Freak Show: Presenting Human Oddities for Amusement and Profit* (Chicago: University of Chicago Press, 1988), 62, 106–107.

6. Historian Michael Sappol finds that anatomy demonstrations in the nineteenth century were a form of mass spectacle that existed in close proximity to the sideshow, despite physician-performers' intentions in distancing their craft from that of the carnival barker. See *A Traffic of Dead Bodies: Anatomy and Embodied Social Identity in Nineteenth-Century America* (Princeton, NJ: Princeton University Press, 2002), 208.

7. Bogdan, *Freak Show*, 64.

8. The circumstances of the Bunkers' death are gleaned from "Chang and Eng," *Philadelphia Medical Times*, February 19, 1874, 327–330; and Wallace and Wallace, *The Two.*

9. "Chang and Eng," 328.

10. Chang and Eng were buried in the cellar because of the family's fear that they would be stolen. A letter written by Nancy Bunker, one of Chang's daughters, to her brother Christopher, who was in San Francisco at the time, informing him of their father's and uncle's deaths reveals the urgency with which the Bunker family felt they needed to guard the body. Nancy Bunker to Christopher Wren Bunker, January 19, 1974, file 916.1, Siamese Twins (1811–1874) Papers, North Carolina State Archives, Raleigh, North Carolina.

11. William H. Pancoast, "Report on the Surgical Considerations in Regard to the Propriety of an Operation for the Separation of Eng and Chang Bunker," *Transactions of the College of Physicians of Philadelphia* 1 (1875): 150–151.

12. The pursuing of Robert Wadlow, who stood eight feet eleven inches, by doctor Charles D. Humberd in 1936 illustrates an extreme example of this entitlement. The physician hounded the young man about examining him, even arriving unannounced at his home. When Robert and the Wadlow family ushered him out, Humberd published his unsubstantiated findings about Robert in the *Journal of the American Medical Association*. See Bogdan, *Freak Show*, 275.

13. A. J. Thomas, *Practical Guide for Making Post-Mortem Examinations and for the Study of Morbid Anatomy with Directions for Embalming the Dead, and for the Preservation of Specimens of Morbid Anatomy* (New York: Boericke and Tafel, 1873), 20.

14. William H. Pancoast and Harrison Allen, "Phonographic Report: The Siamese Twins at the College of Physicians," *Philadelphia Medical Times*, February 19, 1874, 321.

15. "Chang and Eng," 328.

16. The family's resistance to disturbing the twins' body was so great that a newspaper initially reported on its front page: "There has been no post mortem examination of the bodies of Chang and Eng nor will there be." "The Siamese Twins: Objection of Their Families to a Post Mortem Examination," *Morning Star* (Wilmington, NC), January 24, 1874, 1.

17. Lester S. King and Marjorie C. Meehan, "A History of the Autopsy: A Review," *American Journal of Pathology* 73, no. 2 (1973): 532.

18. The autopsy of the Ballestero twins is a key example. In this case, the autopsy *was* performed on religious/spiritual grounds.

19. Michel Foucault, *The Birth of the Clinic: An Archaeology of Medical Perception*, trans. A. M. Sheridan Smith (New York: Random House, 1973), 135–136.

20. Ruth Richardson, *Death, Dissection, and the Destitute* (Chicago: University of Chicago Press, 2001), 41; Sappol, *A Traffic of Dead Bodies*, 117.

21. Sappol, *A Traffic of Dead Bodies*, 85.

22. Tanya Telfair Sharpe, "Grandison Harris: The Medical College of Georgia's Resurrection Man," in *Bones in the Basement: Postmortem Racism in Nineteenth-Century Medical Training*, ed. Robert L. Blakely and Judith M. Harrington (Washington, DC: Smithsonian Institution Press, 1997), 206–244.

23. For an exposition of how these sympathizers repatriated Baartman's remains, see *The Return of Sara Baartman*, directed by Zola Maseko (New York: First Run Icarus Films, 2003), DVD.

24. Benjamin Reiss, *The Showman and the Slave: Race, Death, and Memory in Barnum's America* (Cambridge, MA: Harvard University Press, 2001), 135–139.

25. Harrison Allen, "Report of an Autopsy on the Bodies of Chang and Eng Bunker, Commonly Known as the Siamese Twins," *Transactions of the College of Physicians of Philadelphia* 3, no. 1 (1875): 9.

26. Ibid., 9–10.

27. The failure of language to accommodate embodied experiences of conjoinment is shown by medical ethicist David Wasserman. About the highly publicized legal case in 2000 that pitted British surgeons against the parents of conjoined twins who were then known by the pseudonyms "Mary" and "Jodie," Wasserman finds that Lord Justice Ward's decision to rule in favor of allowing the surgeons to perform the separation surgery was laced with metaphoric language suggesting that Mary was a parasite of Jodie. Wasserman argues convincingly that this ruling rested on the assumption that the two

sets of organs in the singular body could be parceled out as belonging to either Mary or Jodie but not to both collectively. See "Killing Mary to Save Jodie: Conjoined Twins and Individual Rights," *Philosophy and Public Policy Quarterly* 21, no. 1 (2001): 9–14.

28. This is Sappol's central claim in *A Traffic in Dead Bodies*. The primacy of anatomy in medical discourse eventually diminished as anatomy gave way to bacteriology at the beginning of the twentieth century. Judith Walzer Leavitt traces the rise of bacteriology through the circumstances surrounding Mary Mallon, the Irish American domestic cook who was branded "Typhoid Mary." See *Typhoid Mary: Captive to the Public's Health* (Boston: Beacon Press, 1997).

29. Sappol provides an analysis of the racialized, classed, and gendered dynamics between physicians and cadavers in the nineteenth century. See *A Traffic of Dead Bodies*, chap. 3.

30. Foucault, *The Birth of the Clinic*, 130–131.

31. Ibid., 165.

32. Pancoast and Allen, "Phonographic Report," 323.

33. Francis Delafield, *A Handbook of Postmortem Examinations and Morbid Anatomy* (New York: William Wood, 1872).

34. Pancoast and Allen, "Phonographic Report," 321.

35. Special thanks to Christine Guzaitis for pointing out the awkward and cumbersome positioning that would occur if only one physician had been involved at this moment. This insight comes from Guzaitis's formal panel comments at the Pomona College Department of English conference "As Yet Unnamed: Queer Nineteenth Centuries," March 3, 2012, Claremont, CA.

36. Sappol, *A Traffic of Dead Bodies*, 81. Allan C. Braddock makes a similar claim about Thomas Eakins and doctor William Smith Forbes at Jefferson Medical College, noting that "although the anatomical body was not always female, like [Eve Kosofsky] Sedgwick's go-between, it tended historically to become a binding object of epistemological, even romantic, desire among men in nineteenth-century dissection rooms." "'Jeff College Boys': Thomas Eakins, Dr. Forbes, and Anatomical Fraternity in Postbellum Philadelphia," *American Quarterly* 57, no. 2 (2005): 360.

37. Ibid., 87.

38. Alice Domurat Dreger, "The Limits of Individuality: Ritual and Sacrifice in the Lives and Medical Treatment of Conjoined Twins," *Studies in the History and Philosophy of Biology and Biomedical Sciences* 29, no. 1 (1998): 24.

39. Pancoast, "Report on the Surgical Considerations," 154.

40. Ibid., 156.

41. Ibid., 157.

42. Ibid.

43. Ibid., 166–167.

44. Allen, "Report of an Autopsy on the Bodies of Chang and Eng Bunker," 38.

45. Ibid., 40 (emphasis added).

46. Worth B. Daniels, "The Siamese Twins: Some Observations on their Life, Last Illness, and Autopsy," *Transactions of the American Clinical and Climatological Association* 73 (1961): lxiv.

47. Leslie Fiedler, *Freaks: Myths and Images of the Secret Self* (New York: Simon and Schuster, 1978), 218.

48. Irving Wallace and Amy Wallace report that even before Pancoast and Allen conducted the autopsy, William Hollingsworth, the Bunker family physician, postulated that Eng had died from an acute sense of fright. If this is the case, then Pancoast and

Allen could have stacked the deck in favor of this outcome, and their conclusion may have been inductive rather than deductive. See *The Two*, 312.

49. Allen, "Autopsy on the Bodies of Chang and Eng Bunker," 39.

50. Kay Hunter, *Duet for a Lifetime: The Story of the Original Siamese Twins* (New York: Coward-McCann, 1964), 121.

51. Wallace and Wallace, *The Two*, 326 (emphasis in original).

52. Ibid.

53. Hunter, *Duet for a Lifetime*, 121.

54. C. W. and S. D. Bunker to Harrison Allen, April 1, 1874, folder 8, Chang and Eng Bunker Papers 3761, Southern Historical Collection, Wilson Library, University of North Carolina, Chapel Hill.

55. Ella N. Wade, "A Tin Coffin for the Siamese Twins," *Transactions and Studies of the College of Physicians of Philadelphia* 30, no. 1 (1962): 40.

CHAPTER 3

1. These two photographs are available in the Southern Historical Collection at the University of North Carolina. I have provided this information should readers be inclined to seek it out. However, I have made a deliberate choice not to reproduce the photographs given that I do not perform a close reading of them, and merely including them without a pressing analytical rationale would risk sensationalizing them.

2. Duncan F. Cameron, "The Museum: A Temple or the Forum?" *Curator* 14 (1971): 17.

3. Whitfield J. Bell Jr., *The College of Physicians of Philadelphia: A Bicentennial History* (Canton, MA: Science History Publications, 1987), 14–15 (emphasis in original).

4. Nora Jones, "The Mütter Museum: The Body as Spectacle, Specimen, and Art" (Ph.D. diss. Temple University, 2002), 18.

5. Paul Starr, *The Social Transformation of American Medicine: The Rise of a Sovereign Profession and the Making of a Vast Industry* (New York: Basic Books, 1984), 112–123.

6. Robert Bogdan, *Freak Show: Presenting Human Oddities for Amusement and Profit* (Chicago: University of Chicago Press, 1988), 66.

7. Jones, "The Mütter Museum," 22.

8. Ibid., 25–27.

9. Stephen E. Weil, *Making Museums Matter* (Washington, DC: Smithsonian Institution Press, 2002), 28–29.

10. Martin R. Lipp's description of the College of Physicians of Philadelphia building, which houses the Mütter is markedly reverent, describing it as "elegant," "impressive," and "baronial." However, he is not above invoking the museum's ability to entertain, calling one artifact a "real crowd pleaser." *Medical Landmarks U.S.A.: A Travel Guide* (New York: McGraw-Hill, 1991), 182.

11. Saul Rubin does not indicate what qualifies a museum as "offbeat" and therefore worthy of inclusion. He simply uses nondescript words, such as "fun" and "outside the mainstream," to describe museums that "amaze," "inspire," and "enlighten." A quick glance through the guide shows that it features, by and large, social history museums—exhibit spaces that tell the stories of everyday life and objects rather than the master narratives of U.S. history. *Offbeat Museums: The Collections and Curators of America's Most Unusual Museums* (Santa Monica, CA: Santa Monica Press, 1997), 6.

12. The very language authors Doug Kirby, Ken Smith, and Mike Watkins use to describe their book summons monstrous birth and the conjoined body: "*The New Roadside*

America is our baby, a two-headed psychoactive monster baby. One is the benevolent head of hearty appreciation and fair play. The other is the wrathful head of judgment, brought down on those who bulldoze our favorite attractions, turn old Stuckeys into notions boutiques, and charge $17.99 to watch glass get blown." *The New Roadside America: The Modern Traveler's Guide to the Wild and Wonderful World of America's Tourist Attractions* (New York: Simon and Schuster, 1992), 10.

13. For a discussion about ableist standards of architectural integrity that obscure wheelchair ramps or direct those who use them to side or rear entrances, see Tobin Siebers, *Disability Aesthetics* (Ann Arbor: University of Michigan Press, 2010), 75.

14. When I first visited the Mütter in 1999, the gift shop consisted only of a modest glass cabinet at the front desk that displayed a few items directly related to the museum exhibits. Since then, the retail area has expanded and moved across the foyer so that it is inside the temporary gallery entrance.

15. Hyrtl was a contemporary of Samuel Morton (also based in Philadelphia), the scientist infamous for experiments in which he measured the cranial volume of skulls. Using dubious methods, he determined that European-descended skulls were the largest in a lineup that put African-descended skulls at the bottom, thus deeming them intellectually inferior. Morton has since been debunked by evolutionary biologist Stephen Jay Gould in *The Mismeasure of Man* (New York: Norton, 1981), chap. 2.

16. Bogdan, *Freak Show*, 10.

17. Néstor Garcia Canclini, *Transforming Modernity: Popular Culture in Mexico*, trans. Lidia Lozano (Austin: University of Texas Press, 1993), 80. Stephen Greenblatt makes a similar observation about the display of possessions removed from Jewish homes by the Nazi regime during the Holocaust in "Resonance and Wonder," in *Exhibiting Cultures: The Poetics and Politics of Museum Display*, ed. Ivan Karp and Steven D. Lavine (Washington, DC: Smithsonian Institute Press, 1991), 46–48. Barbara Kirshenblatt-Gimblett describes this process of decontextualization succinctly: "Ethnographic objects are objects of ethnography." She goes on to clarify this tautology by stating, "They are artifacts created by ethnographers. Objects become ethnographic by virtue of being defined, segmented, and carried away by ethnographers." "Objects of Ethnography," in *Exhibiting Cultures*, 387.

18. Petra Kuppers argues similarly about Gunther von Hagens's *Body Worlds*, a popular exhibit of plastinated human and other animal bodies that has traveled internationally. Although the sanitized plastinated bodies are inarguably beautiful, some even referencing iconic works of art, what haunts Kuppers is how they are removed and isolated from human lived experience. *The Scar of Visibility: Medical Performances and Contemporary Art* (Minneapolis: University of Minnesota Press, 2007), 44.

19. Jones, "The Mütter Museum," 25, 161. The use of Mütter specimens as models for studying drawing technique is most likely a regular occurrence. During my first visit, I saw a large group of young people with sketchpads and pencils in the permanent collection, making it slightly difficult for me to navigate the exhibits.

20. I thank Martin Pernick for pushing my thinking further in this direction.

21. Barbara Maria Stafford, *Body Criticism: Imaging the Unseen in Enlightenment Art and Medicine* (Cambridge: Massachusetts Institute of Technology Press, 1991), 2.

22. Many of these calendar images were later reproduced in book form in Gretchen Worden, ed. *Mütter Museum of the College of Physicians of Philadelphia* (New York: Blast Books, 2002).

23. Jones, "The Mütter Museum," 176–177, 181–185.

24. This is where my treatment of the fine art world's entrance into the Mütter differs from Jones's.

25. There is something so arresting about Chang and Eng Bunker's body cast that Mütter visitors sometimes sense the presence of the twins while viewing it. In a letter dated October 9, 1962, and addressed to Worth Daniels, a prominent physician and researcher, former curator Ella Wade shares stories about museum guests who inquire about the twins: "You spoke about foolish questions being asked about them, such as 'were they brothers?' I have been asked if their bodies were inside of the casts here, since a few hairs [embedded from the plaster process] show in the armpits." Folder 7, Chang and Eng Bunker Papers 3761, Southern Historical Collection, Wilson Library, University of North Carolina, Chapel Hill.

26. Rosamond Wolff Purcell and Stephen Jay Gould, *Illuminations: A Bestiary* (New York: Norton, 1987), 11.

27. Ibid., 116.

28. Tobin Siebers argues that it is the very manipulation of human remains that engenders the aesthetic. See "The New Art," in *The Body Aesthetic: From Fine Art to Body Modification*, ed. Tobin Siebers (Ann Arbor: University of Michigan Press, 2000), 239.

29. For a critique of Haraway's text that calls attention to its elision of disability, see David T. Mitchell and Sharon L. Snyder, eds., introduction to *The Body and Physical Difference: Discourses of Disability* (Ann Arbor: University of Michigan, 1997), 8. Elena Tajima Creef takes "A Cyborg Manifesto" to task for its ahistorical figuration of the Asian transnational woman factory worker. See *Imaging Japanese America: The Visual Construction of Citizenship, Nation, and the Body* (New York: New York University Press, 2004), 188.

30. Martin Kemp, "A Perfect and Faithful Record," in *Beauty of Another Order: Photography in Science*, ed. Ann Thomas (New Haven, CT: Yale University Press, 1997), 122–123.

31. David Hevey makes a similar claim in *The Creatures Time Forgot: Photography and Disability Imagery* (New York: Routledge, 1992). Most well known for his coinage of the term "enfreakment," Hevey argues that it is the processes of visualization, rather than the materiality of physical bodies, through which people with disabilities are rendered strange and troubling.

32. *The Siamese Connection*, directed by Josh Gibson (Durham, NC: Hard Light, 2008), DVD.

33. Sadiah Qureshi, "Displaying Sara Baartman, the 'Hottentot Venus,'" *History of Science* 42 (2004): 246.

34. *The Life and Times of Sara Baartman*, directed by Zola Maseko (New York: First Run/Icarus Films, 1998), DVD.

35. The most well known of these revisionist accounts is Suzan-Lori Parks, *Venus* (New York: Theatre Communications Group, 1997). See also Deborah Willis, ed., *Black Venus 2010: They Called Her "Hottentot"* (Philadelphia: Temple University Press, 2010).

36. Qureshi provides an extensive account of these historical records in "Displaying Sara Baartman."

37. Margaret Carney to Gretchen Worden, e-mail, May 11, 2004, Chang and Eng Bunker file, College of Physicians of Philadelphia Mütter Museum Archives.

38. James Starr to Gretchen Worden, e-mail, August 26, 2003, Chang and Eng Bunker file, Mütter Museum Archives. Chapter 7 discusses this family debate in greater detail.

39. At one point, Margaret Carney had extended a friendly invitation to Gretchen Worden to speak at the upcoming family reunion, a request that Worden regretted having to decline because of a scheduling conflict. Gretchen Worden to Margaret Carney, e-mail, May 7, 2002, Chang and Eng Bunker file, Mütter Museum Archives.

40. As of 2012, the space known as the "wall" had been redesigned by Facebook. Users can choose either the "wall" or the "timeline" format.

41. James W. Cook, *The Arts of Deception: Playing with Fraud in the Age of Barnum* (Cambridge, MA: Harvard University Press, 2001), 125.

42. Steven Conn, *Do Museums Still Need Objects?* (Philadelphia: University of Pennsylvania Press, 2009), 23.

43. Ibid., 47–48.

44. A recent anthology initiates dialogue about disability between museum professionals and scholars in museum studies. See Richard Sandell, Jocelyn Dodd, and Rosemarie Garland-Thomson, eds., *Re-Presenting Disability: Activism and Agency in the Museum* (New York: Routledge, 2010).

CHAPTER 4

1. Robert Bogdan, *Freak Show: Presenting Human Oddities for Amusement and Profit* (Chicago: University of Chicago Press, 1988), 62–66.

2. This is Rachel Adams's main premise in *Sideshow U.S.A.: Freaks and the American Cultural Imagination* (Chicago: University of Chicago Press, 2001).

3. Allison Pingree, "America's 'United Siamese Brothers': Chang and Eng and Nineteenth-Century Ideologies of Democracy and Domesticity," in *Monster Theory: Reading Culture*, ed. Jeffrey Jerome Cohen (Minneapolis: University of Minnesota Press, 1996), 92–114.

4. See Alexander Saxton, *The Indispensable Enemy: Labor and the Anti-Chinese Movement in California* (Berkeley: University of California Press, 1971), 5–6; Ronald Takaki, *Strangers from a Different Shore: A History of Asian Americans* (New York: Penguin, 1989), 25; and Tera W. Hunter, *To 'Joy My Freedom: Southern Black Women's Lives and Labors after the Civil War* (Cambridge: Harvard University Press, 1997), 78–79.

5. Wanni W. Anderson and Robert G. Lee report that "one of the first economic imperatives of the newly independent United States was to secure a foothold in the lucrative China market." *Displacements and Diasporas: Asians in the Americas* (New Brunswick, NJ: Rutgers University Press, 2005), 4.

6. See James S. Moy, *Marginal Sights: Staging the Chinese in America* (Iowa City: University of Iowa Press, 1993), 12; John Kuo Wei Tchen, *New York Before Chinatown* (Baltimore: Johns Hopkins University Press, 1999), 108; Robert G. Lee, *Orientals: Asian Americans in Popular Culture* (Philadelphia: Temple University Press, 1999), 32; Gary Y. Okihiro, *Common Ground: Reimagining American History* (Princeton, NJ: Princeton University Press, 2001), 75; and Krystyn R. Moon, *Yellowface: Creating the Chinese in American Popular Music and Performance, 1850s–1920s* (New Brunswick, NJ: Rutgers University Press, 2005), 59.

7. Tchen, *New York Before Chinatown*, 105.

8. Rosemarie Garland-Thomson, *Extraordinary Bodies: Figuring Physical Disability in American Culture and Literature* (New York: Columbia University Press, 1997), 65.

9. See Lucy Cohen, *Chinese in the Post–Civil War South: A People without a History* (Baton Rouge: Louisiana State University Press, 1984), 1–21.

10. Herman Melville, *The Confidence-Man: His Masquerade*, ed. Stephen Matterson (New York: Penguin, 1990), 131.

11. Herman Melville, "Billy Budd, Sailor," in *Great Short Works of Herman Melville*, ed. Warner Berthoff (New York: Harper and Row, 1969), 459.

12. Chang had a stroke later in life, which limited his mobility.

13. Herman Melville, *Moby-Dick; or, The Whale*, ed. Alfred Kazin (Boston: Houghton Mifflin, 1956), 253.

14. Paul Fatout, ed., *Mark Twain Speaking* (Iowa City: University of Iowa Press, 1976), 238, 541.

15. Literary critics have commonly regarded the twinning motif in these two novels and in Twain's work more broadly as a device for discussing black-white racial binaries. Susan Gillman has produced the most extensive work on the theme of the double in Twain. See *Dark Twins: Imposture and Identity in Mark Twain's America* (Chicago: University of Chicago Press, 1989). See also Susan Gillman and Forrest G. Robinson, eds., *Mark Twain's "Pudd'nhead Wilson": Race, Conflict, and Culture* (Durham, NC: Duke University Press, 1990).

16. Mark Twain, *"The Tragedy of Pudd'nhead Wilson" and the Comedy "Those Extraordinary Twins,"* ed. Shelley Fisher Fishkin (New York: Oxford University Press, 1996), 311. At the time of *Pudd'nhead Wilson*'s publication, images of Italians were undergoing a shift similar to that of Chinese people following 1849. Previously linked with high culture, Italians become increasingly associated with dirt, disease, and hard labor with the entrance of working-class Italian immigrants into the U.S. workforce. See Alan M. Kraut, *Silent Travelers: Germs, Genes, and the "Immigrant Menace"* (Baltimore: Johns Hopkins University Press, 1994), 103–135.

17. As mentioned previously, the real-life Bunkers were slaveholders and Confederate sympathizers, and two of their sons fought for the Confederate Army.

18. For a reading of literary texts about sectional reunion after the Civil War, see David W. Blight, *Race and Reunion: The Civil War in American Memory* (Cambridge, MA: Harvard University Press, 2001), 211–254.

19. In actuality, it was Chang who had been the alcoholic and Eng the teetotaler.

20. According to anecdotal evidence, even when Chang was drunk, Eng remained sober. Physicians' examinations—on the living twins and during their autopsy—indicated that the degree of connectedness between the circulatory system of Chang and the circulatory system of Eng was minimal. For an observation made about the vascular connection between the twins, see George Buckley Bolton, *On the United Siamese Twins* (London: Red Lion Court, 1830), 182.

21. Mark Twain, "The Siamese Twins," in *Sketches New and Old* (New York: Harper and Brothers, 1875), 253.

22. Ibid.

23. Ibid.

24. See Ronald Bailey, "'Those Valuable People, the Africans': The Economic Impact of the Slave(ry) Trade on Textile Industrialization in New England," in *The Meaning of Slavery in the North*, ed. David Roediger and Martin H. Blatt (New York: Routledge, 1998), 3–32; and Myron O. Stachiw, "'For the Sake of Commerce': Slavery, Antislavery, and Northern Industry," in *The Meaning of Slavery in the North*, 33–44.

25. It is widely known that black as well as white soldiers fought in the Civil War, but little attention has been paid to Civil War soldiers of Asian descent. Historical documents show that soldiers of Chinese descent were in the ranks on both the Union and Confederate sides. Civil War hobbyist Gordon Kwok maintains a website documenting them at http://sites.google.com/site/accsacw.

26. In *Race and Reunion*, Blight argues that the cultural productions emerging in the postbellum period celebrating sectional reunion between Northern and Southern whites came at the cost of ignoring the divide between black and white Americans. Elizabeth Young claims that by casting resolutions of sectional conflict in the guise

of domesticity, the negotiations of power among white women, white men, and black workers (regardless of gender) inside the home became acts of nation building in the postbellum period. See *Disarming the Nation: Women's Writing and the American Civil War* (Chicago: University of Chicago Press, 1999).

27. Mark Twain, "The Siamese Twins," 248.

28. Ibid., 253.

29. Irving Wallace and Amy Wallace, *The Two: A Biography: The Story of the Original Siamese Twins* (New York: Simon and Schuster, 1978), 176.

30. As I discuss in Chapter 1, images of Chang and Eng Bunker from early in their career picture them as childlike and with coded Asian features, while images created when they were older men and had become fathers fall more in line with the illustrations in Twain's *Sketches New and Old*.

31. Mark Twain, *Roughing It*, ed. Shelley Fisher Fishkin (New York: Oxford University Press, 1997), 297.

32. See James Moy, *Marginal Sights*, 23–34.

33. The illustration of Chang and Eng that accompanies Twain's essay, however, clearly depicts their unusual anatomy.

34. On the other hand, class and regional conflict were often interrelated. See Eric Foner, *A Short History of Reconstruction, 1863–1877* (New York: Harper and Row, 1990), 129; and Kenneth M. Stampp, *The Era of Reconstruction, 1865–1877* (New York: Knopf, 1965), 159–160.

35. Thomas Nast, "The American Twins," *Harper's Weekly*, February 7, 1874, 136.

36. On the same page as Nast's cartoon in *Harper's Weekly* is an image from another illustrator that is blatantly, rather than subtly, anti-Irish.

37. For a discussion of how the interests of the white working classes were framed in a way that excluded participation from Chinese workers, see Tomas Almaguer, *Racial Fault Lines: The Historical Origins of White Supremacy in California* (Berkeley: University of California Press, 1994), 153–182; and Nayan Shah, *Contagious Divides: Epidemics and Race in San Francisco's Chinatown* (Berkeley: University of California Press, 2001), 158–178.

38. James W. Cook argues that the freak show and related forms of entertainment provided a forum for spectators to debate the authenticity of the exhibits and that this opportunity for discussion was often more of an attraction than the exhibits themselves. See *The Arts of Deception: Playing with Fraud in the Age of Barnum* (Cambridge, MA: Harvard University Press, 2001).

39. Ibid., 65.

40. Kandice Chuh, *Imagine Otherwise: On Asian Americanist Critique* (Durham, NC: Duke University Press, 2003), 59.

CHAPTER 5

1. One of Wong's stated goals is to provide the conditions of possibility for the formation of such a literary canon—what she calls a "textual coalition." *Reading Asian American Literature: From Necessity to Extravagance* (Princeton, NJ: Princeton University Press, 1993), 9.

2. Ibid., 77.

3. The two texts in question are Frank Chin, "This Is Not an Autobiography," *Genre* 18 (1985): 109–130; and Frank Chin, "Come All Ye Asian American Writers of the Real and the Fake," in *The Big Aiiieeeee! An Anthology of Chinese American and Japanese*

American Literature, eds. Jeffery Paul Chan, Frank Chin, Lawson Fusao Inada, and Shawn Wong (New York: Meridian, 1991).

4. Elliot H. Shapiro does an extensive job of tracking many of Kingston's references in *Tripmaster Monkey.* "Authentic Watermelon: Maxine Hong Kingston's American Novel," *MELUS* 26, no. 1 (2001): 5–28.

5. Walt Whitman's influence in U.S. multiethnic literatures has been documented in Werner Sollors, *Beyond Ethnicity: Consent and Descent in American Culture* (New York: Oxford University Press, 1986), 256–258.

6. Maxine Hong Kingston, *Tripmaster Monkey: His Fake Book* (New York: Vintage, 1987), 290.

7. Ibid., 293.

8. There are moments in *Tripmaster Monkey* that poke fun at Wittman's normative masculinity and homophobia, but although the novel can be read as a challenge to Chin's disdain about the license Kingston takes in her refashioning of Chinese folklore, it does not as easily lend itself to a reading that responds to his charge that her feminism is at odds with an Asian American antiracist politics. These two points of contention, of course, are linked within the logic of cultural nationalism. For two feminist readings that debunk Chin's charges, see King-Kok Cheung, "The Woman Warrior versus the Chinaman Pacific: Must a Chinese American Critique Choose Between Feminism and Heroism?" in *Conflicts in Feminism*, ed. Marianne Hirsch and Evelyn Fox Keller (New York: Routledge, 1990); and Sau-ling Cynthia Wong, "Autobiography as Guided Chinatown Tour? Maxine Hong Kingston's *The Woman Warrior* and the Chinese American Autobiographical Controversy," in *Multicultural Autobiography, American Lives*, ed. James Robert Payne (Knoxville: University of Tennessee Press, 1992), 248–279. For a discussion of Chin's homophobia, see Daniel Y. Kim, "The Strange Love of Frank Chin," in *Q&A: Queer in Asian America*, ed. David L. Eng and Alice Y. Hom (Philadelphia: Temple University Press, 1998), 270–303; and David L. Eng, *Racial Castration: Managing Masculinity in Asian America* (Durham, NC: Duke University Press, 2001), chap. 1.

9. David Palumbo-Liu, *Asian/American: Historical Crossings of a Racial Frontier* (Stanford, CA: Stanford University Press, 1999), 1. For another way in which the hyphen is problematized—specifically by bringing the Asian diaspora in Canada into consideration—see Eleanor Ty and Donald C. Goellnicht, eds., introduction to *Beyond the Hyphen: Asian North American Identities* (Bloomington: Indiana University Press, 2004), 1–14.

10. Doris Sommer pays attention to moments where writers with minoritarian subjectivities make their opacity visible to their intended audience. See *Proceed with Caution, When Engaged by Minority Writing in the Americas* (Cambridge, MA: Harvard University Press, 1999).

11. Ibid., ix.

12. Traise Yamamoto, *Masking Selves, Making Subjects: Japanese American Women, Identity, and the Body* (Berkeley: University of California Press, 1999), 122–126.

13. Ibid., 126.

14. Monica Sone, *Nisei Daughter* (Seattle: University of Washington Press, 1979), 5.

15. Ibid., 4.

16. Ibid., 19.

17. Ibid., 4.

18. Ibid., 158–159.

19. Ibid., 236.

20. Ibid., 238.

21. Sau-ling Cynthia Wong, *Reading Asian American Literature*, 113.

22. Stephen H. Sumida, "Protest and Accommodation, Self-Satire and Self-Effacement, and Monica Sone's *Nisei Daughter*," in *Multicultural Autobiography, American Lives*, ed. James Robert Payne (Knoxville: University of Tennessee Press, 1992), 235.

23. Elaine Kim, *Asian American Literature: An Introduction to the Writings and Their Social Context* (Philadelphia: Temple University Press, 1982), 80.

24. Shirley Goek-lin Lim, "Japanese American Women's Life Stories: Maternality in Monica Sone's *Nisei Daughter* and Joy Kogawa's *Obasan*," *Feminist Studies* 16, no. 2 (1990), 300.

25. Sone, *Nisei Daughter*, 137.

26. Susan Sontag, *Illness as Metaphor and AIDS and Its Metaphors* (New York: Anchor, 1988), 35.

27. Sone, *Nisei Daughter*, 141.

28. Ibid., 142.

29. For instance, "craniopagus" refers to twins joined at the head and "omphalopagus" to twins joined at the chest.

30. Greta Aiyu Niu, "People of the Pagus: Orientalized Bodies and Migration in an Asian Pacific Rim" (Ph.D. diss., Duke University, 1998), 38.

31. The most extensive treatments of *Mulberry and Peach* are Sau-ling Cynthia Wong, "The Stakes of Textual Border-Crossing: Hualing Nieh's *Mulberry and Peach* in Sinocentric, Asian American, and Feminist Critical Practices," in *Orientations: Mapping Studies in the Asian Diaspora*, ed. Kandice Chuh and Karen Shimakawa (Durham, NC: Duke University Press, 2001): 130–152; Yu-Fang Cho, "Rewriting Exile, Remapping Empire, Re-Membering Home: Hualing Nieh's *Mulberry and Peach*," *Meridians* 5, no. 1 (2004): 157–200; and Tina Chen, *Double Agency: Acts of Impersonation in Asian American Literature and Culture* (Stanford, CA: Stanford University Press, 2005), chap. 4.

32. This timeline on the novel's publication history is taken from Wong, "The Stakes of Textual Border-Crossing," 132–133.

33. Wong notes that the English version, "intended for non-Chinese audiences, was politically safe" within the context of its circulation in the People's Republic of China. Ibid., 132.

34. Hualing Nieh, *Mulberry and Peach: Two Women of China*, trans. Jane Parish Yang with Linda Lappin (New York: Feminist Press, 1998), 116.

35. Immigration Act of 1882, 22 Stat. 214 (1882).

36. Alan M. Kraut, *Silent Travelers: Germs, Genes, and the "Immigrant Menace"* (Baltimore: Johns Hopkins University Press, 1994), 70–71.

37. Sander L. Gilman, *Seeing the Insane* (Lincoln: University of Nebraska Press, 1996), 2.

38. Kraut, *Silent Travelers*, 75, 71.

39. Nieh, *Mulberry and Peach*, 3.

40. Anna Pegler-Gordon, *In Sight of America: Photography and the Development of U.S. Immigration Policy* (Berkeley: University of California Press, 2009).

41. Nieh, *Mulberry and Peach*, 7.

42. Susan Craddock, *City of Plagues: Disease, Poverty, and Deviance in San Francisco* (Minneapolis: University of Minnesota Press, 2000), 89–94; Nayah Shah, *Contagious Divides: Epidemics and Race in San Francisco's Chinatown* (Berkeley: University of California Press, 2001), 85–87.

43. George Anthony Peffer notes that the Page Law was so aggressively enforced that even those women married to men already living in the United States faced difficulty

when their husbands sent for them. See *If They Don't Bring Their Women Here* (Urbana: University of Illinois Press, 1999), 57–72.

44. Eithne Luibhéid, *Entry Denied: Controlling Sexuality at the Border* (Minneapolis: University of Minnesota Press, 2002), 38–41.

45. Nieh, *Mulberry and Peach*, 182.

46. According to Lisa Lowe, "The concept of the immigrant in American sociology and public policy has historically signified 'European immigrants,' seeking to universalize the temporality of assimilation attributed to Irish Americans and Italian Americans to ethnic minority groups from the 'Third World.'" *Immigrant Acts: On Asian American Cultural Politics* (Durham, NC: Duke University Press, 1996), 177. Like Lowe, I maintain that this tendency erases the historical differences between European immigrant groups and others. Mae M. Ngai reminds us that although the Immigration Act of 1924 affected immigration from a variety of Asian and European countries, "the Chinese have the dubious distinction of being the only group to be excluded from immigration into the United States explicitly by name." *Impossible Subjects: Illegal Aliens and the Making of Modern America* (Princeton, NJ: Princeton University Press, 2004), 202.

47. Nieh, *Mulberry and Peach*, 183.

48. Ibid., 204.

49. Cathy Park Hong, "Ontology of Chang and Eng, the Original Siamese Twins," in *Translating Mo'um* (New York: Hanging Loose Press, 2002), 15.

50. Hong, *Translating Mo'um*, 9.

51. I express in the Introduction my reservations about how Mikhail Bakhtin co-opts the physical body to promote a utopian vision of liberation.

52. Amy Ling, ed., introduction to *Yellow Light: The Flowering of Asian American Arts* (Philadelphia: Temple University Press, 1999), 5.

53. Karen Tei Yamashita, "Siamese Twins and Mongoloids: Cultural Appropriation and the Deconstruction of Stereotype via the Absurdity of Metaphor," in *Yellow Light*, 134–135.

54. The most often-cited example of this work is probably Aihwa Ong, *Flexible Citizenship: The Cultural Logic of Transnationality* (Durham, NC: Duke University Press, 1999). Additionally, a transnational analysis creates room for discussing class privilege in the Asian diaspora that could intervene in the working class–centered scholarship, which attended the focus on immigration in the field's earliest days.

55. Jee Yoon Lee, "Toward a Queer Korean American Diasporic History," in *Q&A: Queer in Asian America*.

CHAPTER 6

1. Terri Kapsalis, *Public Privates: Performing Gynecology from Both Ends of the Speculum* (Durham, NC: Duke University Press, 1997), chap. 1.

2. Elizabeth Siegel Watkins, *On the Pill: A Social History of Oral Contraceptives, 1950–1970* (Baltimore: Johns Hopkins University Press, 1998), 31; Lara V. Marks, *Sexual Chemistry: A History of the Contraceptive Pill* (New Haven, CT: Yale University Press, 2001), 101–110.

3. Annette B. Ramirez de Arellano and Conrad Seipp, *Colonialism, Catholicism, and Contraception: A History of Birth Control in Puerto Rico* (Chapel Hill: University of North Carolina Press, 1983).

4. Women of color and women of the global South continue to make up a disproportionate number of subjects who participate in birth control trials. Terri Kapsalis

unpacks the inversion of nineteenth-century logic in the role that African American women played in developing Norplant in the late twentieth century. The development of subdermal contraceptives went together with population control projects in poor urban neighborhoods that had high concentrations of African Americans. See *Public Privates*, 50–56.

5. The pathologizing of white middle-class men's heterosexual excesses took place a century earlier. Jonathan Ned Katz points out that late-nineteenth-century sexologist Richard von Krafft-Ebing's attention to heterosexual aberrancy focused on male non-procreative desire for women. See *The Invention of Heterosexuality* (Chicago: University of Chicago Press, 1995), 21–23.

6. In Chapter 4, I address the hermeneutic effects of visual representations of a whitened Chang and Eng consorting with white women in drawings accompanying Mark Twain's fictional take on the twins.

7. Conjoined twins appear extensively in contemporary culture. They can be found in works of literary fiction, such as John Barth's "Petition," from his short story collection *Lost in the Funhouse*; Katherine Dunn's *Geek Love*; Shelley Jackson's *Half Life*; Andrew Beierle's *First Person Plural*; Cary Holladay's "Heaven," from *The Quick-Change Artist*; and Joanne Martell's *Millie-Christine*. Conjoined twins appear as well in theater and film, as in playwright Burton Cohen's *The Wedding of the Siamese Twins*, Keith Fulton's film *Brothers of the Head*, and Bill Russell's musical-theatrical play *Side Show*.

8. Archie Robertson, "Chang-Eng's American Heritage," *Life*, August 11, 1952, 70.

9. Rosemarie Garland-Thomson, *Staring: How We Look* (New York: Oxford University Press, 2009), 179–180. Alice Domurat Dreger also nods approvingly at the normalizing function *Life* effects for Abigail and Brittany Hensel. See *One of Us: Conjoined Twins and the Future of Normal* (Cambridge, MA: Harvard University Press, 2004), 37. This favorable assessment of the Hensels in *Life* seems to be Garland-Thomson's measured rethinking of her earlier work that reclaims the institution of the freak show as a liberatory space where social minorities could resist the demands of standardization during the industrial era. See *Extraordinary Bodies: Figuring Physical Disability in American Culture and Literature* (New York: Columbia University Press, 1997), 65–69. In the case of the Hensels, who live in the present day with different social and political circumstances, such a means for engaging with the public would be out of place.

10. Judith Rossner, *Attachments* (New York: Simon and Schuster, 1977), 20.

11. Ibid.

12. Ibid., 230.

13. Ibid., 392.

14. An extensive account of this case can be found in popular nonfiction writer Ron Rosenbaum's *The Secret Parts of Fortune: Three Decades of Intense Investigations and Edgy Enthusiasms* (New York: Harper Perennial, 2001), 97–117.

15. Barbara Creed links male hysteria to castration anxiety in the film. See "Phallic Panic: Male Hysteria and *Dead Ringers*," *Screen* 31, no. 2 (1990): 133.

16. The most well-known articulations of these fears come from the popular press right after the bombing of Pearl Harbor: "How to Tell Japs from the Chinese," *Life*, December 22, 1941, 81–82; and "How to Tell Your Friends from the Japs," *Time*, December 22, 1941, 33. More recently, Jasbir Puar highlights a piece of post-9/11 conceptual art in which nine male Brown University students of Arab or South Asian descent participated. These students deliberately mismatched photographs and names on their university identification cards so that each student was left with a photograph that was not his own, suggesting the anxiety-laden interchangeability of brown faces during a

time of national security paranoia. *Terrorist Assemblages: Homonationalism in Queer Times* (Durham, NC: Duke University Press, 2007), 161.

17. David Henry Hwang, afterword to *M. Butterfly* (New York: Plume, 1988), 95.

18. Mary Russo, *The Female Grotesque: Risk, Excess, and Modernity* (New York: Routledge, 1995), 125.

19. Hwang, *M. Butterfly*, 17.

20. Thomas Laqueur, *Making Sex: Body and Gender from the Greeks to Freud* (Cambridge, MA: Harvard University Press, 1990), 79–83.

21. Kapsalis, *Public Privates*, 143–146.

22. See David L. Clark and Catherine Myser, "Being Humaned: Medical Documentaries and the Hyperealization of Conjoined Twins," in *Freakery: Cultural Spectacles of the Extraordinary Body*, ed. Rosemarie Garland-Thomson (New York: New York University Press, 1996): 338–355.

23. Robert Bogdan, *Freak Show: Presenting Human Oddities for Amusement and Profit* (Chicago: University of Chicago Press, 1988), 81–83.

24. David A. Gerber, "The 'Careers' of People Exhibited in Freak Shows: The Problem of Volition and Valorization," in *Freakery*, 38–54.

25. Darin Strauss, *Chang and Eng: A Novel* (New York: Dutton, 2000), 11.

26. Mark Slouka, *God's Fool* (New York: Knopf, 2002), 24.

27. For a discussion of disability in the Farrelly brothers' films, see Kathleen LeBesco, "There's Something about Disabled People: The Contradictions of Freakery in the Films of the Farrelly Brothers," *Disability Studies Quarterly* 24, no. 4 (2004). Available at http://dsq-sds.org/article/view/895/1070.

28. C. Thomas Couser observes that this unassuming and low-budget music video in *Face to Face* mocks the conventions of its commercial counterparts and "takes the twins decisively out of the freak show and into the celebrity culture of their time. . . . In this final sequence, they display themselves on their own terms for their own purposes." *Signifying Bodies: Disability in Contemporary Life Writing* (Ann Arbor: University of Michigan Press, 2009), 64.

29. The awkwardness created by the costume the Polishes wear is reminiscent of Gaylyn Studlar's discussion of early-twentieth-century film actor Lon Cheney. Even as Cheney became known as a performer who relished playing showy roles that foregrounded some form of physical difference, the costuming he wore for these films often was debilitating to the actor himself. *This Mad Masquerade: Stardom and Masculinity in the Jazz Age* (New York: Columbia University Press, 1996), chap. 4.

CHAPTER 7

1. Jessie Bunker Bryant, *The Connected Bunkers* (Winston-Salem, NC: Jostens Graphics, 2001), xi.

2. David Schneider, *American Kinship: A Cultural Account* (Englewood Cliffs, NJ: Prentice Hall, 1968), v–vi.

3. Ibid., 15–16. Although Schneider's reasoning follows a logical progression, he does not challenge the American exceptionalist underpinnings in his claims. For example, he writes, "Kinship and family practices [in the United States] have not stood in the way of economic development as they have in other countries" (15).

4. David M. Schneider, *A Critique of the Study of Kinship* (Ann Arbor: University of Michigan Press, 1984), 198–199.

5. Jessie Bunker Bryant, personal conversation, August 1, 2010.

6. Jessie Bunker Bryant, letter to author, June 17, 2003.

7. Jessie Bunker Bryant, personal conversation, August 1, 2010.

8. Program of the 21st Annual Reunion of the Descendants of the Original Siamese Twins, July 31, 2010.

9. As expected, Sink received the Democratic Party's nomination on August 24, 2010. However, she narrowly lost the election the following November to Republican Rick Scott.

10. For instance, in 2008, documentarian Josh Gibson screened his recently completed *The Siamese Connection*, and in 2011, I gave a presentation containing material from Chapters 4, 5, and 6 of *Chang and Eng Reconnected*.

11. Laurence A. Basirico, *The Family Reunion Survival Guide: How to Avoid Problems with Your Family without Avoiding Your Family* (Burlington, NC: Identity, 2003), 20.

12. Ibid., 4–5.

13. Specific figures can be found in Pauli Murray, ed., *States' Laws on Race and Color* (Athens: University of Georgia Press, 1997).

14. David A. Hollinger, "Amalgamation and Hypodescent: The Question of Ethnoracial Mixture in the History of the United States," *American Historical Review* 108, no. 5 (2003): 1368.

15. Lucy M. Cohen, *Chinese in the Post–Civil War South: A People without a History* (Baton Rouge: Louisiana State University Press, 1984), 167.

16. Irving Wallace and Amy Wallace, *The Two: The Story of the Original Siamese Twins* (New York: Simon and Schuster, 1978), 176.

17. Anonymous, personal conversation, July 26, 2003.

18. Daryl Maeda, *Chains of Babylon: The Rise of Asian America* (Minneapolis: University of Minnesota Press, 2009); William Wei, *The Asian American Movement* (Philadelphia: Temple University Press, 1993).

19. Aihwa Ong, *Flexible Citizenship: The Cultural Logics of Transnationality* (Durham, NC: Duke University Press, 1999); Vicente L. Rafael, *White Love and Other Events in Filipino History* (Durham, NC: Duke University Press, 2000).

20. Interview by author with Margaret Kansa, July 28, 2007.

21. There is some evidence that George Ashby's colleagues knew about his Asian ancestry and judged him accordingly. See Maury Klein, *Union Pacific, Volume II, 1894–1969* (Minneapolis: University of Minnesota Press, 2006), 437.

22. Interview by author with Margaret Kansa, July 28, 2007.

23. Ibid.

24. The Supreme Court cases of *Ozawa v. United States* (1922) and *United States v. Thind* (1923) show this complex and contradictory relationship between national culture and racial categorization. In the former, Japanese immigrant Takao Ozawa claimed that he should be eligible for U.S. citizenship naturalization because of his wholehearted acculturation to Anglo-American values and practices. This logic was rejected because he was determined not to be of the Caucasoid race. In the latter, Indian immigrant Bhagat Singh Thind successfully convinced the court that the contemporaneous scientific literature classified him as Aryan and, therefore, white. However, his case was struck down on the basis that the common layperson understood Indians not to be white. For an analysis of these cases, see Ian F. Haney López, *White by Law: The Legal Construction of Race* (New York: New York University Press, 1996), chap. 4.

25. This observation is corroborated by Adolph L. Dial and David K. Eliades, *The Only Land I Know: A History of the Lumbee Indians* (San Francisco: Indian Historian Press, 1975). Three-way segregation also existed in several Mississippi towns where there

were separate white, black, and Chinese schools. See James W. Loewen, *The Mississippi Chinese: Between Black and White*, 2nd ed. (Prospect Heights, IL: Waveland Press, 1988), 2.

26. Another informant, however, stresses the role of television in connecting her to larger national and global events while she was, as she puts it, "stuck in Mount Airy, couldn't get out" during the Vietnam War. Interview by author with Martha Hill Moore, July 31, 2010.

27. Interview by author with Tanya Jones, July 29, 2010.

28. Sherry Blackmon, personal conversation with author, July 31, 2010.

29. Schneider, *American Kinship*, 23.

30. Ibid., 24.

31. Interview by author with Martha Hill Moore, July 31, 2010.

32. Ibid.

33. Bunker descendant to Gretchen Worden, e-mail, August 22, 2003, Chang and Eng Bunker file, College of Physicians of Philadelphia Mütter Museum Archives.

34. Gretchen Worden to James Starr, e-mail, August 26, 2003, Chang and Eng Bunker file, Mütter Museum Archives.

35. James Starr to Gretchen Worden, e-mail, August 26, 2003, Chang and Eng Bunker file, Mütter Museum Archives.

36. Barbara Myerhoff, *Number Our Days* (New York: Simon and Schuster, 1978), 109–110.

37. Ibid., 7.

38. Nazli Kibria, *Family Tightrope: The Changing Lives of Vietnamese Americans* (Princeton, NJ: Princeton University Press, 1993), 8.

39. These are simplified synopses of Myerhoff's and Kibria's respective findings. Sylvia Yanagisako cautions that in examining kinship networks among immigrant groups, ethnographers should not make recourse to a "static baseline" of familial structures premigration that are imagined as untouched by social change in countries of origin. *Transforming the Past: Tradition and Kinship among Japanese Americans* (Stanford, CA: Stanford University Press, 1985), 17.

40. Kath Weston, *Families We Choose: Lesbians, Gays, Kinship* (New York: Columbia University Press, 1991), 3.

EPILOGUE

1. Philip Kan Gotanda, "Joining Histories in Performance: The Process of Creating *I Dream of Chang and Eng*" (lecture from the symposium Conjoined Histories: Race, Disability, and Popular Performance in the Nineteenth Century, University of California, Berkeley, CA, March 11, 2011).

2. Alexis de Tocqueville, *Democracy in America, Volume II* (New York: Alfred A. Knopf, 1945), 99.

3. Jessie Bunker Bryant, *The Connected Bunkers* (Winston-Salem, NC: Jostens Graphics, 2001), 7.

4. A refurbished classic car resembling the patrol vehicle on *The Andy Griffith Show* can be seen around Mount Airy as a whimsical attraction for the locals. Taped to the inside of the window is a cardboard image of Griffith's character from the neck up. I was willing to believe that actual law enforcement officers used that car until I made a wrong turn into the police station on my way to the Surry Arts Council and was somewhat disappointed to see, parked in the lot, a fleet of Ford Crown Victorias, which are standard-issue police cruisers.

5. The paradigms in ethnic studies and postcolonial studies merge when we examine the place of Asian Americans alongside that of working-class whites in the United States. Theodore Allen asserts that racism relies on class-subjugated whites to carry out its forces, whereas colonialism similarly relies on the subject population's elite members. Although useful, Allen's assertion is muddled when we take into account the United States' neocolonial investments in Asia and elsewhere. See *The Invention of the White Race*, vol. 1 (New York: Verso, 1994). What I am suggesting—modifying Leslie Bow's model slightly—is that Asian Americans may actually exist in greater proximity with working-class whites than with either sanctioned forms of whiteness or disavowed blackness because of their structural placement as a buffer between affluent whites and African Americans. In this formulation of U.S. empire, which blurs the distinctions between colony and metropole, racial and colonial subjugation merge with each other.

6. The fight does not appear in Philip Gotanda's stage directions for *I Dream of Chang and Eng*. As such, it appears to be director Peter Glazer's interpretation. However, Gotanda himself worked closely with Glazer on this production.

Index

Italic page numbers indicate material in figures.

Cynthia Wu is Assistant Professor of American Studies at the University at Buffalo.